NICHOLAS MEYER'S
THE SEVEN-PER-CENT SOLUTION

THE ASTOUNDING JOINT ADVENTURE OF
SHERLOCK HOLMES AND SIGMUND FREUD

Facebook **facebook.com/idwpublishing**
Twitter **@idwpublishing**
YouTube **youtube.com/idwpublishing**
Tumblr **tumblr.idwpublishing.com**
Instagram **instagram.com/idwpublishing**

COVER ART BY
KELLEY JONES

COVER COLORS BY
JAY FOTOS

SERIES EDITS BY
DAVID HEDGECOCK

COLLECTION EDITS BY
JUSTIN EISINGER
& ALONZO SIMON

PUBLISHER
TED ADAMS

COLLECTION DESIGN BY
SHAWN LEE

978-1-63140-557-0   19 18 17 16   1 2 3 4

SHERLOCK HOLMES: THE SEVEN-PER-CENT SOLUTION. MARCH
2016. FIRST PRINTING. The Seven-Per-Cent Solution copyright © 2016
Nicholas Meyer. All rights reserved. © 2016 Idea and Design Works,
LLC. The IDW logo is registered in the U.S. Patent and Trademark
Office. IDW Publishing, a division of Idea and Design Works, LLC.
Editorial offices: 2765 Truxtun Road, San Diego, CA 92106. Any similari-
ties to persons living or dead are purely coincidental. With the
exception of artwork used for review purposes, none of the contents of
this publication may be reprinted without the permission of Idea and
Design Works, LLC. Printed in Korea. IDW Publishing does not read or
accept unsolicited submissions of ideas, stories, or artwork.

Originally published as THE SEVEN-PER-CENT SOLUTION issues #1–5.

Ted Adams, CEO & Publisher
Greg Goldstein, President & COO
Robbie Robbins, EVP/Sr. Graphic Artist
Chris Ryall, Chief Creative Officer/Editor-in-Chief
Matthew Ruzicka, CPA, Chief Financial Officer
Dirk Wood, VP of Marketing
Lorelei Bunjes, VP of Digital Services
Jeff Webber, VP of Digital Publishing & Business Development
Jerry Bennington, VP of New Product Development

For international rights, please contact licensing@idwpublishing.com

ADAPTED BY
DAVID TIPTON & SCOTT TIPTON
ART BY
RON JOSEPH
COLORS BY
JORDI ESCUIN
LETTERS BY
DERON BENNETT
ANDWORLD DESIGN
& NEIL UYETAKE

ART BY
KELLEY JONES

COLORS BY
JAY FOTOS

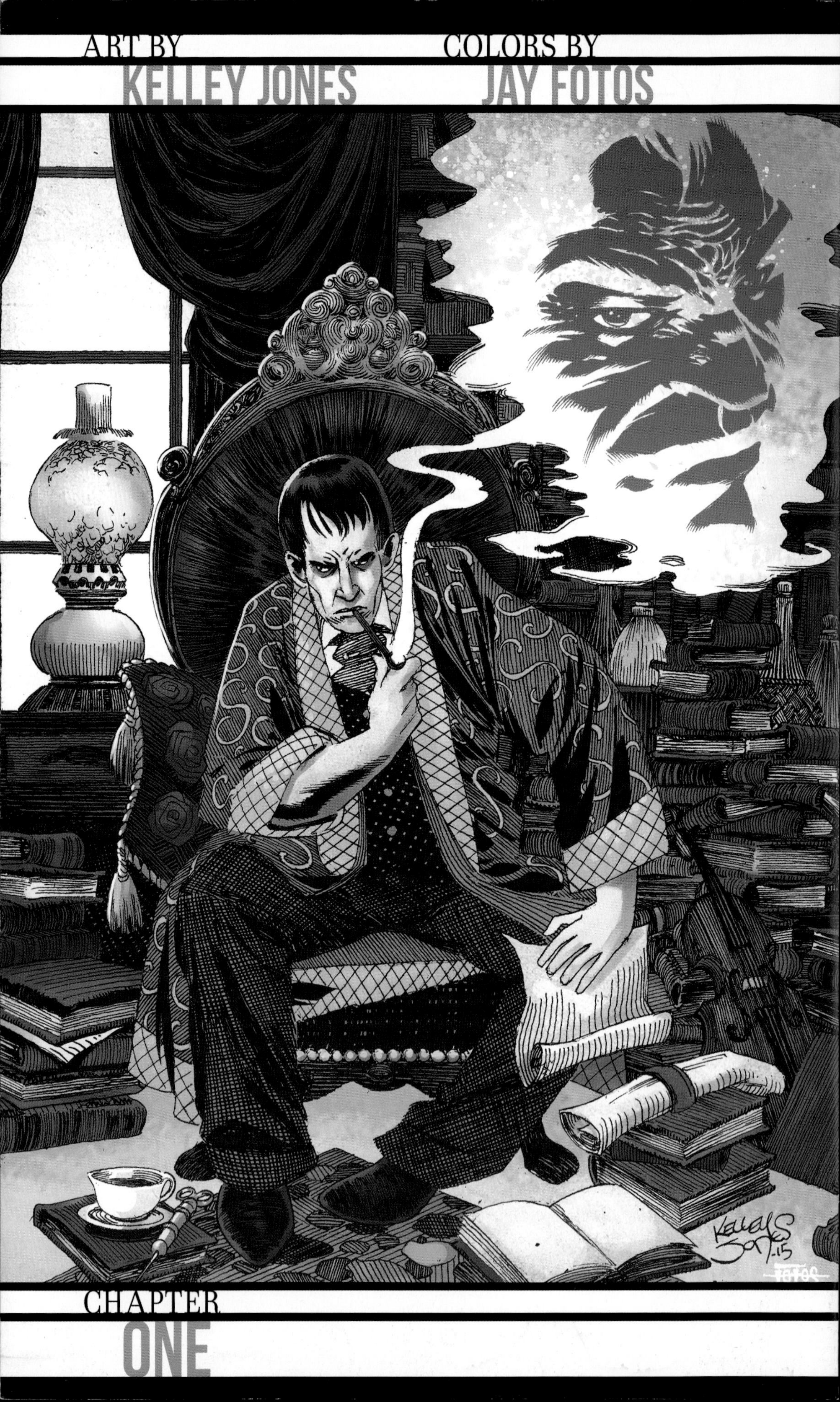
KELLEY JONES '15
FOTOS

CHAPTER
ONE

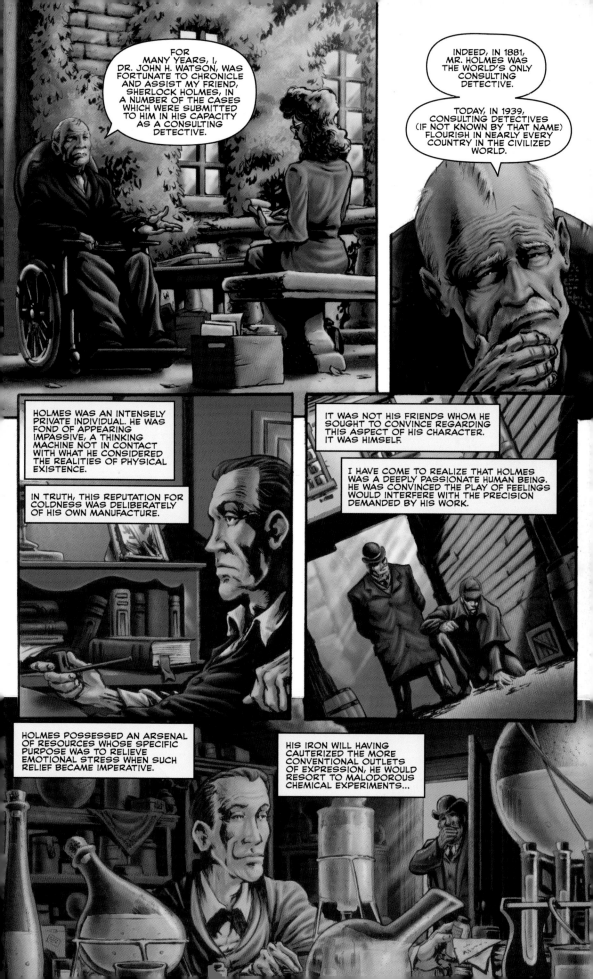

FOR MANY YEARS, I, DR. JOHN H. WATSON, WAS FORTUNATE TO CHRONICLE AND ASSIST MY FRIEND, SHERLOCK HOLMES, IN A NUMBER OF THE CASES WHICH WERE SUBMITTED TO HIM IN HIS CAPACITY AS A CONSULTING DETECTIVE.

INDEED, IN 1881, MR. HOLMES WAS THE WORLD'S ONLY CONSULTING DETECTIVE.

TODAY, IN 1939, CONSULTING DETECTIVES (IF NOT KNOWN BY THAT NAME) FLOURISH IN NEARLY EVERY COUNTRY IN THE CIVILIZED WORLD.

HOLMES WAS AN INTENSELY PRIVATE INDIVIDUAL. HE WAS FOND OF APPEARING IMPASSIVE, A THINKING MACHINE NOT IN CONTACT WITH WHAT HE CONSIDERED THE REALITIES OF PHYSICAL EXISTENCE.

IN TRUTH, THIS REPUTATION FOR COLDNESS WAS DELIBERATELY OF HIS OWN MANUFACTURE.

IT WAS NOT HIS FRIENDS WHOM HE SOUGHT TO CONVINCE REGARDING THIS ASPECT OF HIS CHARACTER. IT WAS HIMSELF.

I HAVE COME TO REALIZE THAT HOLMES WAS A DEEPLY PASSIONATE HUMAN BEING. HE WAS CONVINCED THE PLAY OF FEELINGS WOULD INTERFERE WITH THE PRECISION DEMANDED BY HIS WORK.

HOLMES POSSESSED AN ARSENAL OF RESOURCES WHOSE SPECIFIC PURPOSE WAS TO RELIEVE EMOTIONAL STRESS WHEN SUCH RELIEF BECAME IMPERATIVE.

HIS IRON WILL HAVING CAUTERIZED THE MORE CONVENTIONAL OUTLETS OF EXPRESSION, HE WOULD RESORT TO MALODOROUS CHEMICAL EXPERIMENTS...

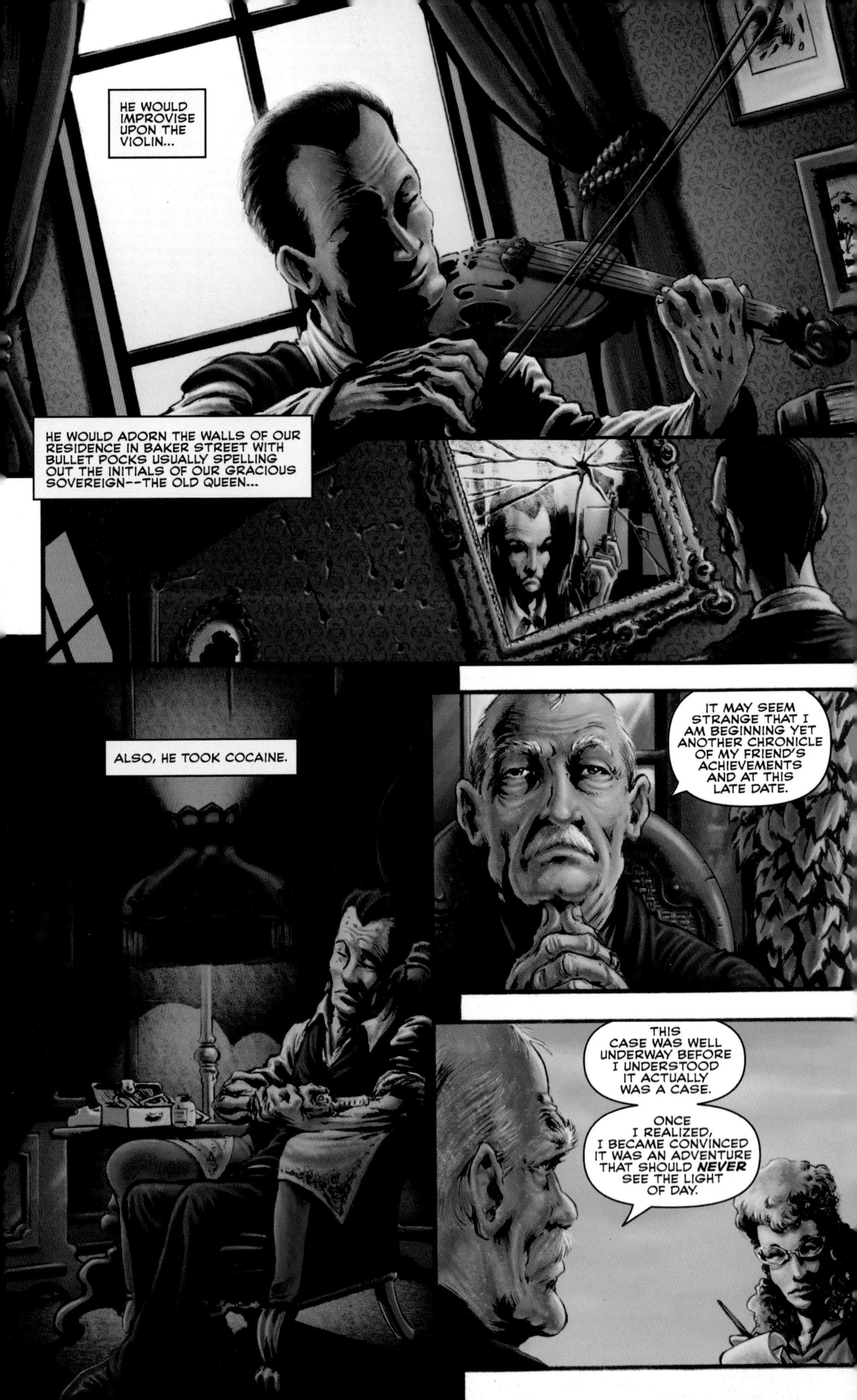
HE WOULD IMPROVISE UPON THE VIOLIN...
HE WOULD ADORN THE WALLS OF OUR RESIDENCE IN BAKER STREET WITH BULLET POCKS USUALLY SPELLING OUT THE INITIALS OF OUR GRACIOUS SOVEREIGN--THE OLD QUEEN...
ALSO, HE TOOK COCAINE.
IT MAY SEEM STRANGE THAT I AM BEGINNING YET ANOTHER CHRONICLE OF MY FRIEND'S ACHIEVEMENTS AND AT THIS LATE DATE.
THIS CASE WAS WELL UNDERWAY BEFORE I UNDERSTOOD IT ACTUALLY WAS A CASE.
ONCE I REALIZED, I BECAME CONVINCED IT WAS AN ADVENTURE THAT SHOULD *NEVER* SEE THE LIGHT OF DAY.

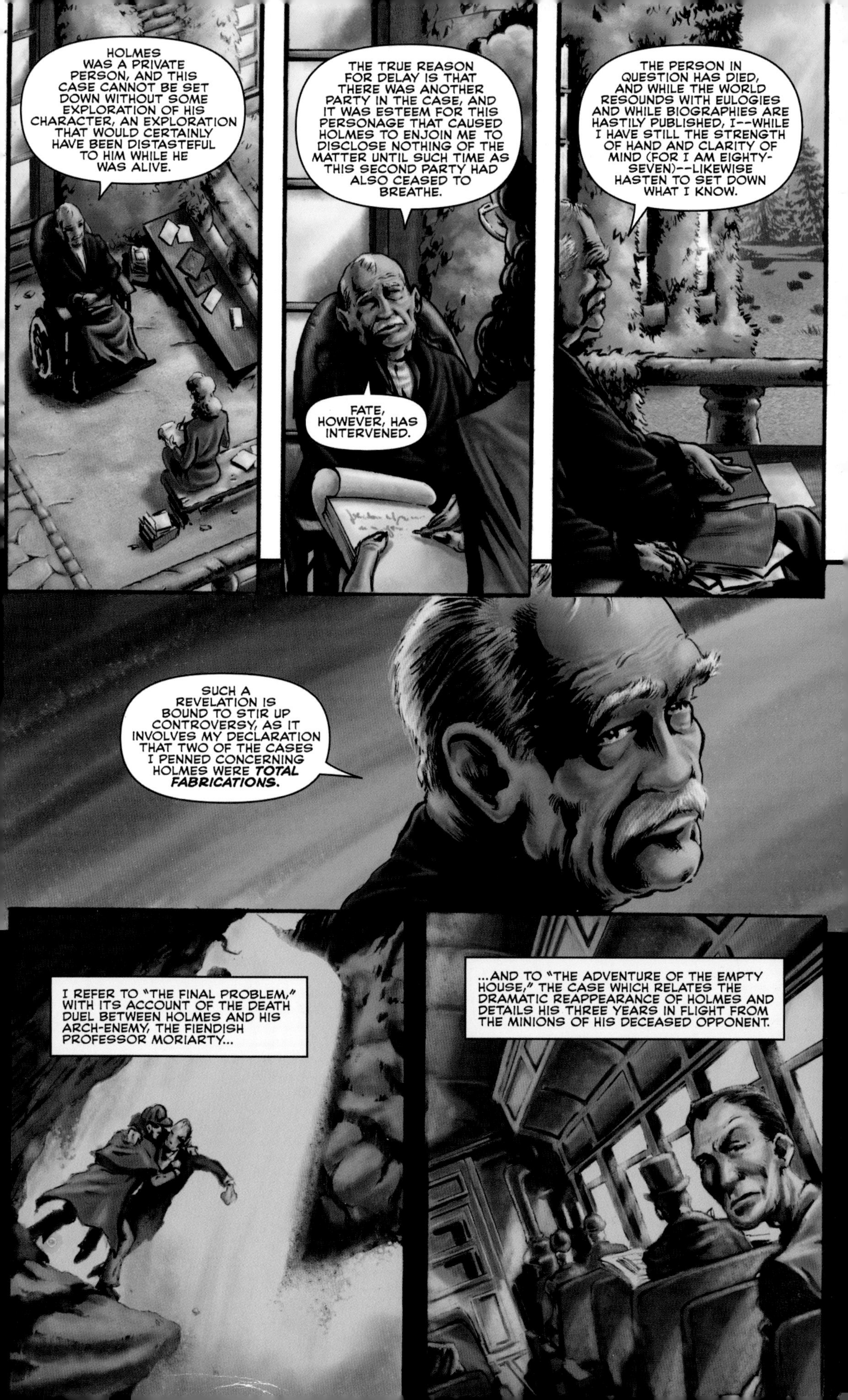
HOLMES WAS A PRIVATE PERSON, AND THIS CASE CANNOT BE SET DOWN WITHOUT SOME EXPLORATION OF HIS CHARACTER, AN EXPLORATION THAT WOULD CERTAINLY HAVE BEEN DISTASTEFUL TO HIM WHILE HE WAS ALIVE.
THE TRUE REASON FOR DELAY IS THAT THERE WAS ANOTHER PARTY IN THE CASE, AND IT WAS ESTEEM FOR THIS PERSONAGE THAT CAUSED HOLMES TO ENJOIN ME TO DISCLOSE NOTHING OF THE MATTER UNTIL SUCH TIME AS THIS SECOND PARTY HAD ALSO CEASED TO BREATHE.
FATE, HOWEVER, HAS INTERVENED.
THE PERSON IN QUESTION HAS DIED, AND WHILE THE WORLD RESOUNDS WITH EULOGIES AND WHILE BIOGRAPHIES ARE HASTILY PUBLISHED, I--WHILE I HAVE STILL THE STRENGTH OF HAND AND CLARITY OF MIND (FOR I AM EIGHTY-SEVEN)--LIKEWISE HASTEN TO SET DOWN WHAT I KNOW.
SUCH A REVELATION IS BOUND TO STIR UP CONTROVERSY, AS IT INVOLVES MY DECLARATION THAT TWO OF THE CASES I PENNED CONCERNING HOLMES WERE ***TOTAL FABRICATIONS***.
I REFER TO "THE FINAL PROBLEM," WITH ITS ACCOUNT OF THE DEATH DUEL BETWEEN HOLMES AND HIS ARCH-ENEMY, THE FIENDISH PROFESSOR MORIARTY...
...AND TO "THE ADVENTURE OF THE EMPTY HOUSE," THE CASE WHICH RELATES THE DRAMATIC REAPPEARANCE OF HOLMES AND DETAILS HIS THREE YEARS IN FLIGHT FROM THE MINIONS OF HIS DECEASED OPPONENT.

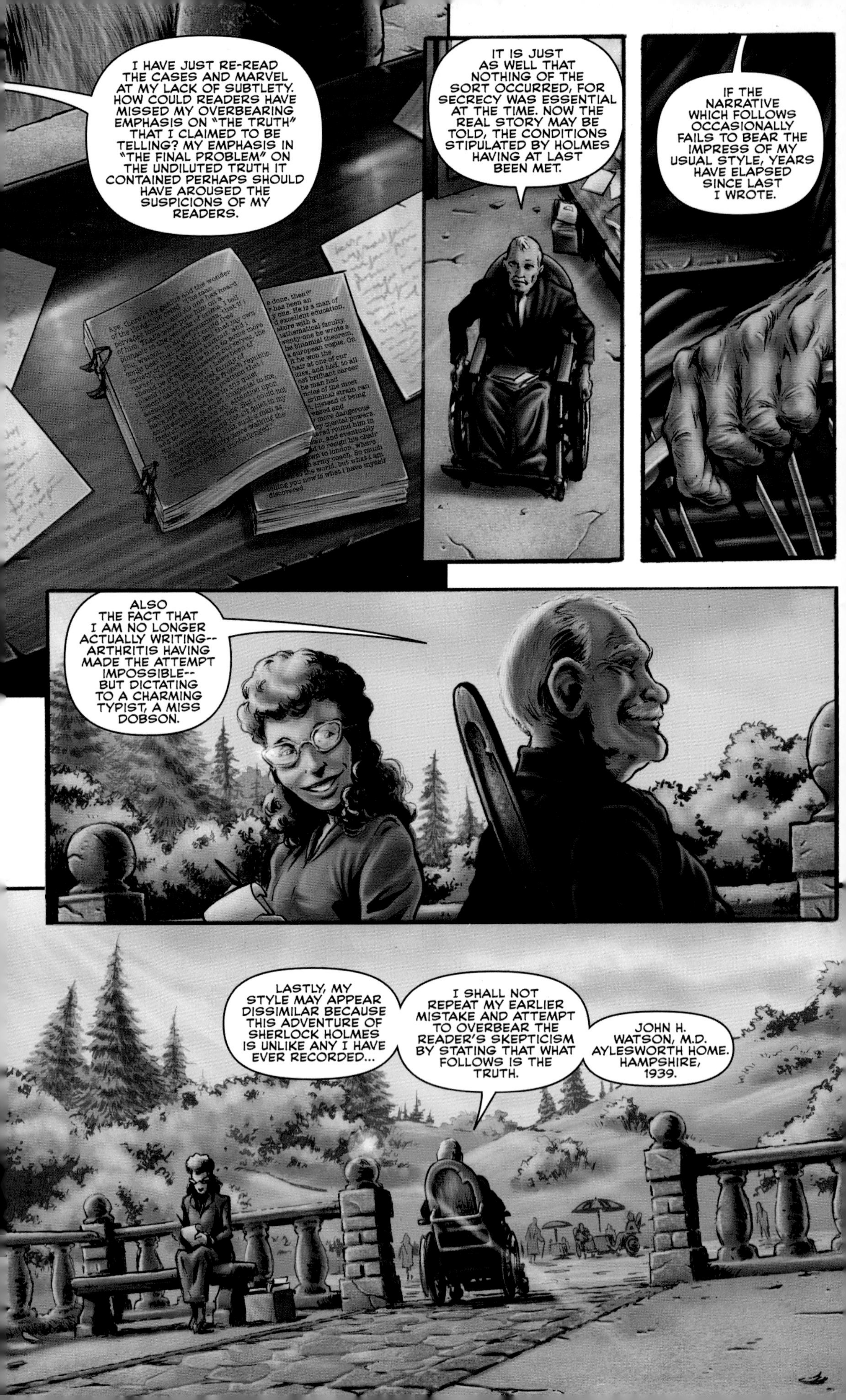
I HAVE JUST RE-READ THE CASES AND MARVEL AT MY LACK OF SUBTLETY. HOW COULD READERS HAVE MISSED MY OVERBEARING EMPHASIS ON "THE TRUTH" THAT I CLAIMED TO BE TELLING? MY EMPHASIS IN "THE FINAL PROBLEM" ON THE UNDILUTED TRUTH IT CONTAINED PERHAPS SHOULD HAVE AROUSED THE SUSPICIONS OF MY READERS.
IT IS JUST AS WELL THAT NOTHING OF THE SORT OCCURRED, FOR SECRECY WAS ESSENTIAL AT THE TIME. NOW THE REAL STORY MAY BE TOLD, THE CONDITIONS STIPULATED BY HOLMES HAVING AT LAST BEEN MET.
IF THE NARRATIVE WHICH FOLLOWS OCCASIONALLY FAILS TO BEAR THE IMPRESS OF MY USUAL STYLE, YEARS HAVE ELAPSED SINCE LAST I WROTE.
ALSO THE FACT THAT I AM NO LONGER ACTUALLY WRITING-- ARTHRITIS HAVING MADE THE ATTEMPT IMPOSSIBLE-- BUT DICTATING TO A CHARMING TYPIST, A MISS DOBSON.
LASTLY, MY STYLE MAY APPEAR DISSIMILAR BECAUSE THIS ADVENTURE OF SHERLOCK HOLMES IS UNLIKE ANY I HAVE EVER RECORDED...
I SHALL NOT REPEAT MY EARLIER MISTAKE AND ATTEMPT TO OVERBEAR THE READER'S SKEPTICISM BY STATING THAT WHAT FOLLOWS IS THE TRUTH.
JOHN H. WATSON, M.D. AYLESWORTH HOME. HAMPSHIRE, 1939.

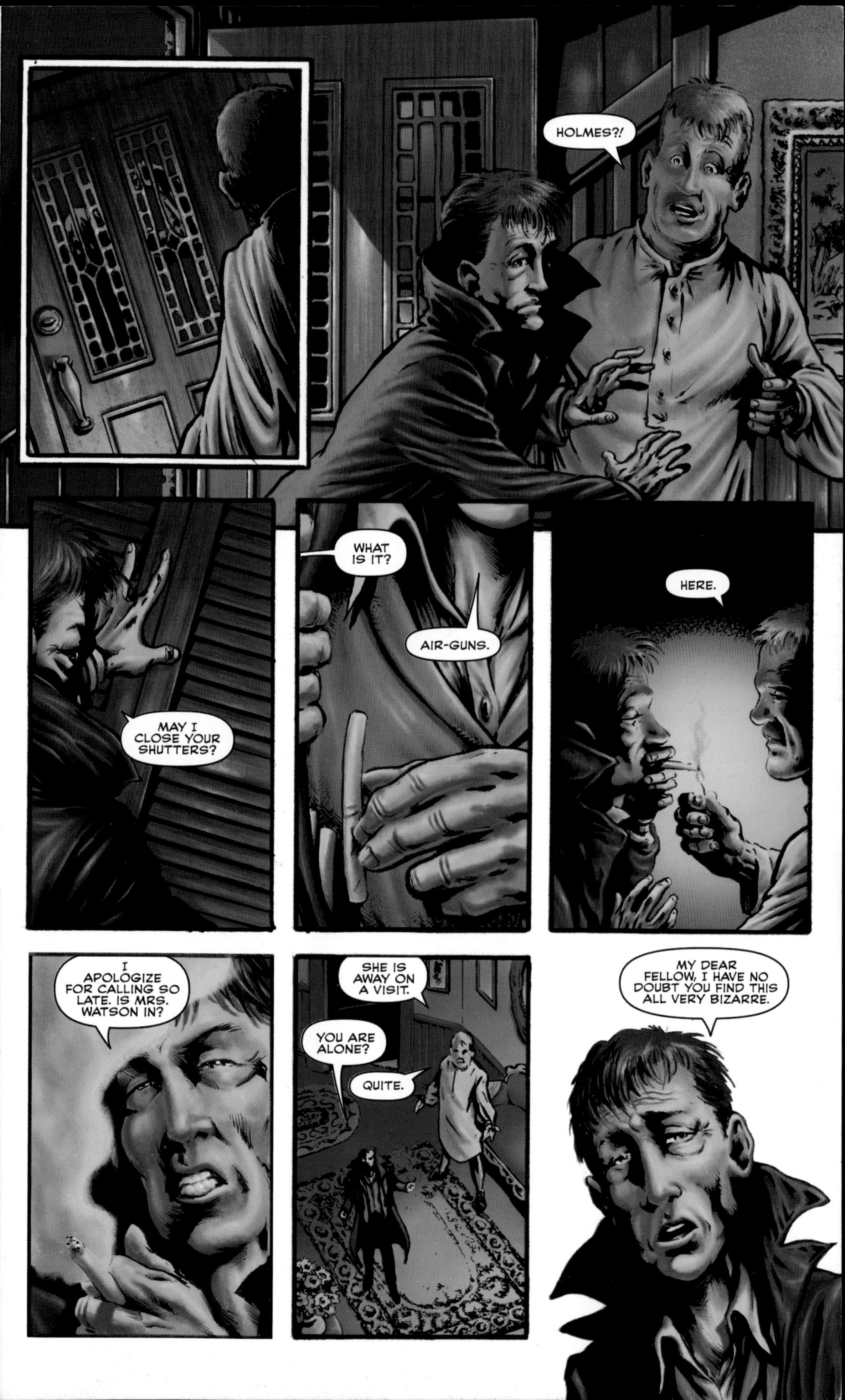
HOLMES?!
MAY I CLOSE YOUR SHUTTERS?
WHAT IS IT?
AIR-GUNS.
HERE.
I APOLOGIZE FOR CALLING SO LATE. IS MRS. WATSON IN?
SHE IS AWAY ON A VISIT.
YOU ARE ALONE?
QUITE.
MY DEAR FELLOW, I HAVE NO DOUBT YOU FIND THIS ALL VERY BIZARRE.

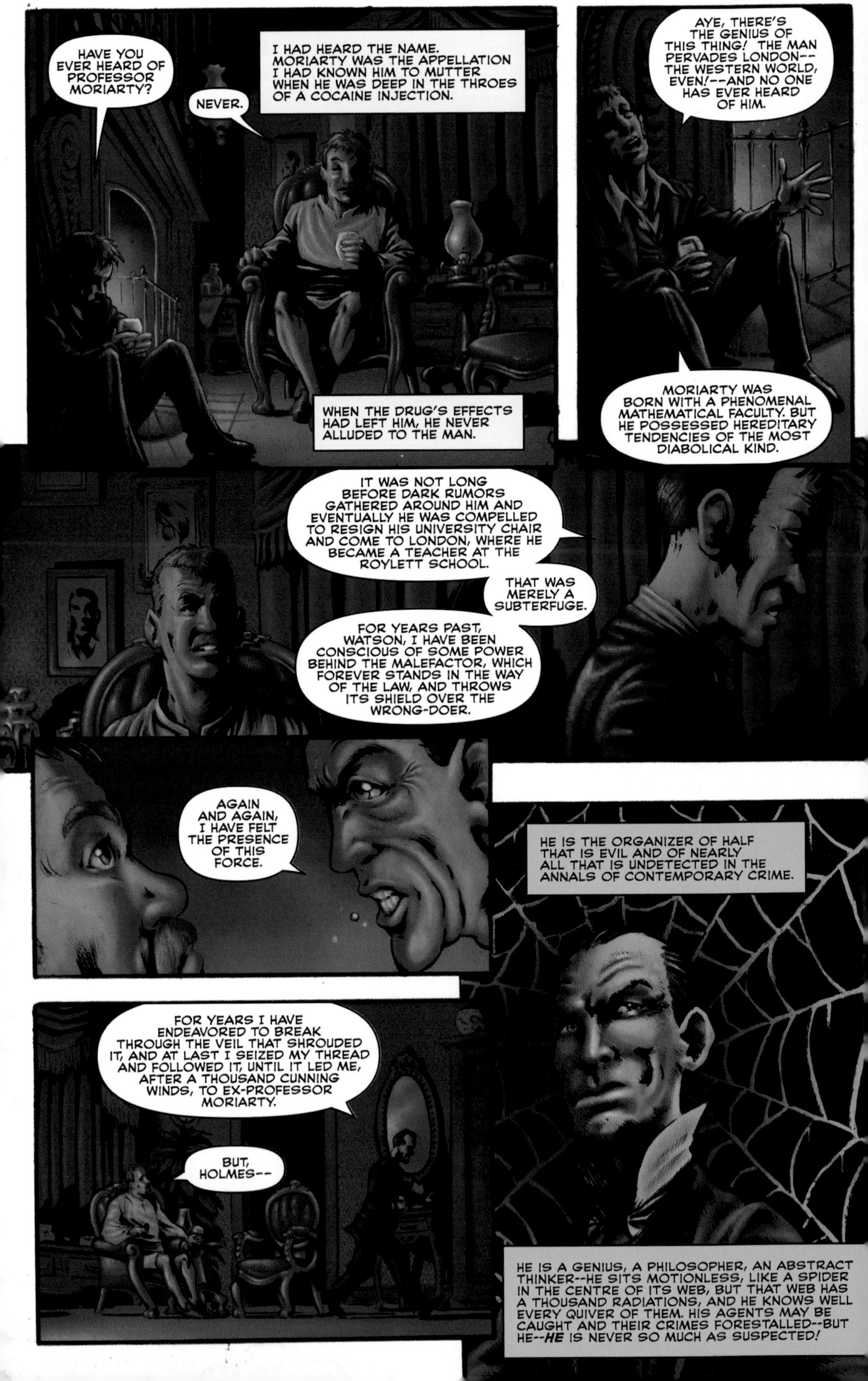
HAVE YOU EVER HEARD OF PROFESSOR MORIARTY?
I HAD HEARD THE NAME. MORIARTY WAS THE APPELLATION I HAD KNOWN HIM TO MUTTER WHEN HE WAS DEEP IN THE THROES OF A COCAINE INJECTION.
NEVER.
WHEN THE DRUG'S EFFECTS HAD LEFT HIM, HE NEVER ALLUDED TO THE MAN.
AYE, THERE'S THE GENIUS OF THIS THING! THE MAN PERVADES LONDON--THE WESTERN WORLD, EVEN!--AND NO ONE HAS EVER HEARD OF HIM.
MORIARTY WAS BORN WITH A PHENOMENAL MATHEMATICAL FACULTY. BUT HE POSSESSED HEREDITARY TENDENCIES OF THE MOST DIABOLICAL KIND.
IT WAS NOT LONG BEFORE DARK RUMORS GATHERED AROUND HIM AND EVENTUALLY HE WAS COMPELLED TO RESIGN HIS UNIVERSITY CHAIR AND COME TO LONDON, WHERE HE BECAME A TEACHER AT THE ROYLETT SCHOOL.
THAT WAS MERELY A SUBTERFUGE.
FOR YEARS PAST, WATSON, I HAVE BEEN CONSCIOUS OF SOME POWER BEHIND THE MALEFACTOR, WHICH FOREVER STANDS IN THE WAY OF THE LAW, AND THROWS ITS SHIELD OVER THE WRONG-DOER.
AGAIN AND AGAIN, I HAVE FELT THE PRESENCE OF THIS FORCE.
HE IS THE ORGANIZER OF HALF THAT IS EVIL AND OF NEARLY ALL THAT IS UNDETECTED IN THE ANNALS OF CONTEMPORARY CRIME.
FOR YEARS I HAVE ENDEAVORED TO BREAK THROUGH THE VEIL THAT SHROUDED IT, AND AT LAST I SEIZED MY THREAD AND FOLLOWED IT, UNTIL IT LED ME, AFTER A THOUSAND CUNNING WINDS, TO EX-PROFESSOR MORIARTY.
BUT, HOLMES--
HE IS A GENIUS, A PHILOSOPHER, AN ABSTRACT THINKER--HE SITS MOTIONLESS, LIKE A SPIDER IN THE CENTRE OF ITS WEB, BUT THAT WEB HAS A THOUSAND RADIATIONS, AND HE KNOWS WELL EVERY QUIVER OF THEM. HIS AGENTS MAY BE CAUGHT AND THEIR CRIMES FORESTALLED--BUT HE--*HE* IS NEVER SO MUCH AS SUSPECTED!

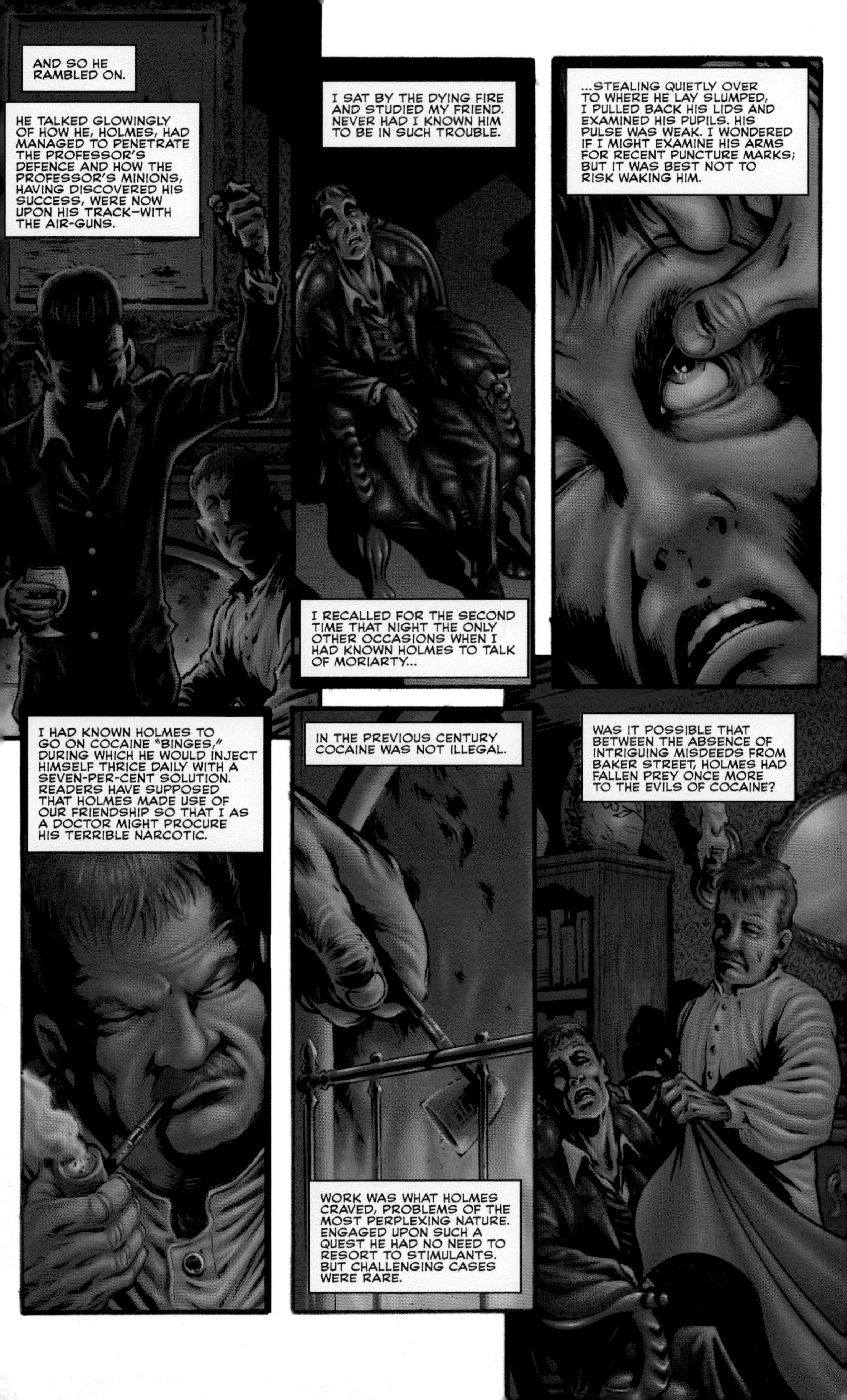
AND SO HE RAMBLED ON.
HE TALKED GLOWINGLY OF HOW HE, HOLMES, HAD MANAGED TO PENETRATE THE PROFESSOR'S DEFENCE AND HOW THE PROFESSOR'S MINIONS, HAVING DISCOVERED HIS SUCCESS, WERE NOW UPON HIS TRACK—WITH THE AIR-GUNS.
I SAT BY THE DYING FIRE AND STUDIED MY FRIEND. NEVER HAD I KNOWN HIM TO BE IN SUCH TROUBLE.
I RECALLED FOR THE SECOND TIME THAT NIGHT THE ONLY OTHER OCCASIONS WHEN I HAD KNOWN HOLMES TO TALK OF MORIARTY...
...STEALING QUIETLY OVER TO WHERE HE LAY SLUMPED, I PULLED BACK HIS LIDS AND EXAMINED HIS PUPILS. HIS PULSE WAS WEAK. I WONDERED IF I MIGHT EXAMINE HIS ARMS FOR RECENT PUNCTURE MARKS; BUT IT WAS BEST NOT TO RISK WAKING HIM.
I HAD KNOWN HOLMES TO GO ON COCAINE "BINGES," DURING WHICH HE WOULD INJECT HIMSELF THRICE DAILY WITH A SEVEN-PER-CENT SOLUTION. READERS HAVE SUPPOSED THAT HOLMES MADE USE OF OUR FRIENDSHIP SO THAT I AS A DOCTOR MIGHT PROCURE HIS TERRIBLE NARCOTIC.
IN THE PREVIOUS CENTURY COCAINE WAS NOT ILLEGAL.
WORK WAS WHAT HOLMES CRAVED, PROBLEMS OF THE MOST PERPLEXING NATURE. ENGAGED UPON SUCH A QUEST HE HAD NO NEED TO RESORT TO STIMULANTS. BUT CHALLENGING CASES WERE RARE.
WAS IT POSSIBLE THAT BETWEEN THE ABSENCE OF INTRIGUING MISDEEDS FROM BAKER STREET, HOLMES HAD FALLEN PREY ONCE MORE TO THE EVILS OF COCAINE?

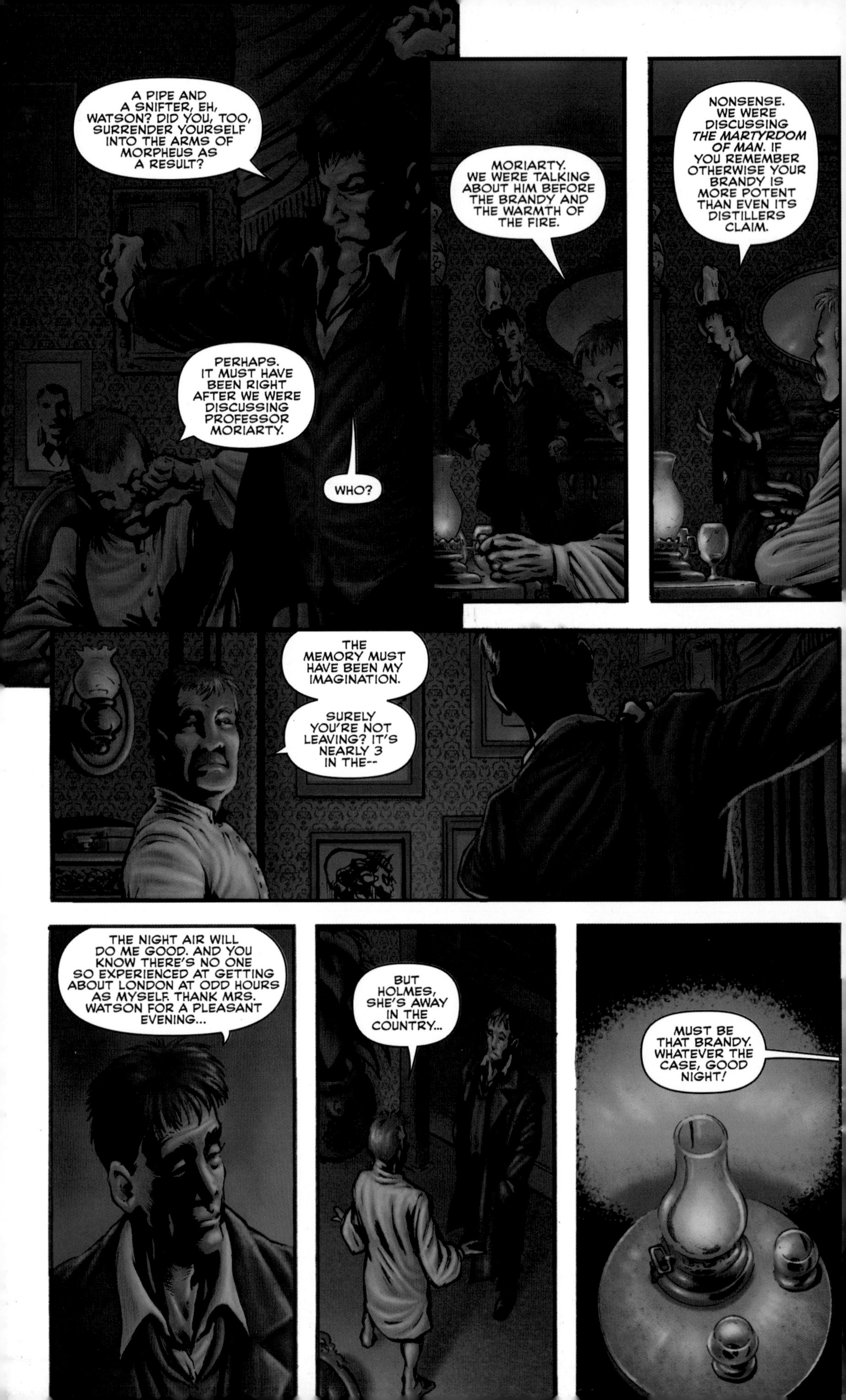
A PIPE AND A SNIFTER, EH, WATSON? DID YOU, TOO, SURRENDER YOURSELF INTO THE ARMS OF MORPHEUS AS A RESULT?
PERHAPS. IT MUST HAVE BEEN RIGHT AFTER WE WERE DISCUSSING PROFESSOR MORIARTY.
WHO?
MORIARTY. WE WERE TALKING ABOUT HIM BEFORE THE BRANDY AND THE WARMTH OF THE FIRE.
NONSENSE. WE WERE DISCUSSING *THE MARTYRDOM OF MAN*. IF YOU REMEMBER OTHERWISE YOUR BRANDY IS MORE POTENT THAN EVEN ITS DISTILLERS CLAIM.
THE MEMORY MUST HAVE BEEN MY IMAGINATION.
SURELY YOU'RE NOT LEAVING? IT'S NEARLY 3 IN THE--
THE NIGHT AIR WILL DO ME GOOD. AND YOU KNOW THERE'S NO ONE SO EXPERIENCED AT GETTING ABOUT LONDON AT ODD HOURS AS MYSELF. THANK MRS. WATSON FOR A PLEASANT EVENING...
BUT HOLMES, SHE'S AWAY IN THE COUNTRY...
MUST BE THAT BRANDY. WHATEVER THE CASE, GOOD NIGHT!

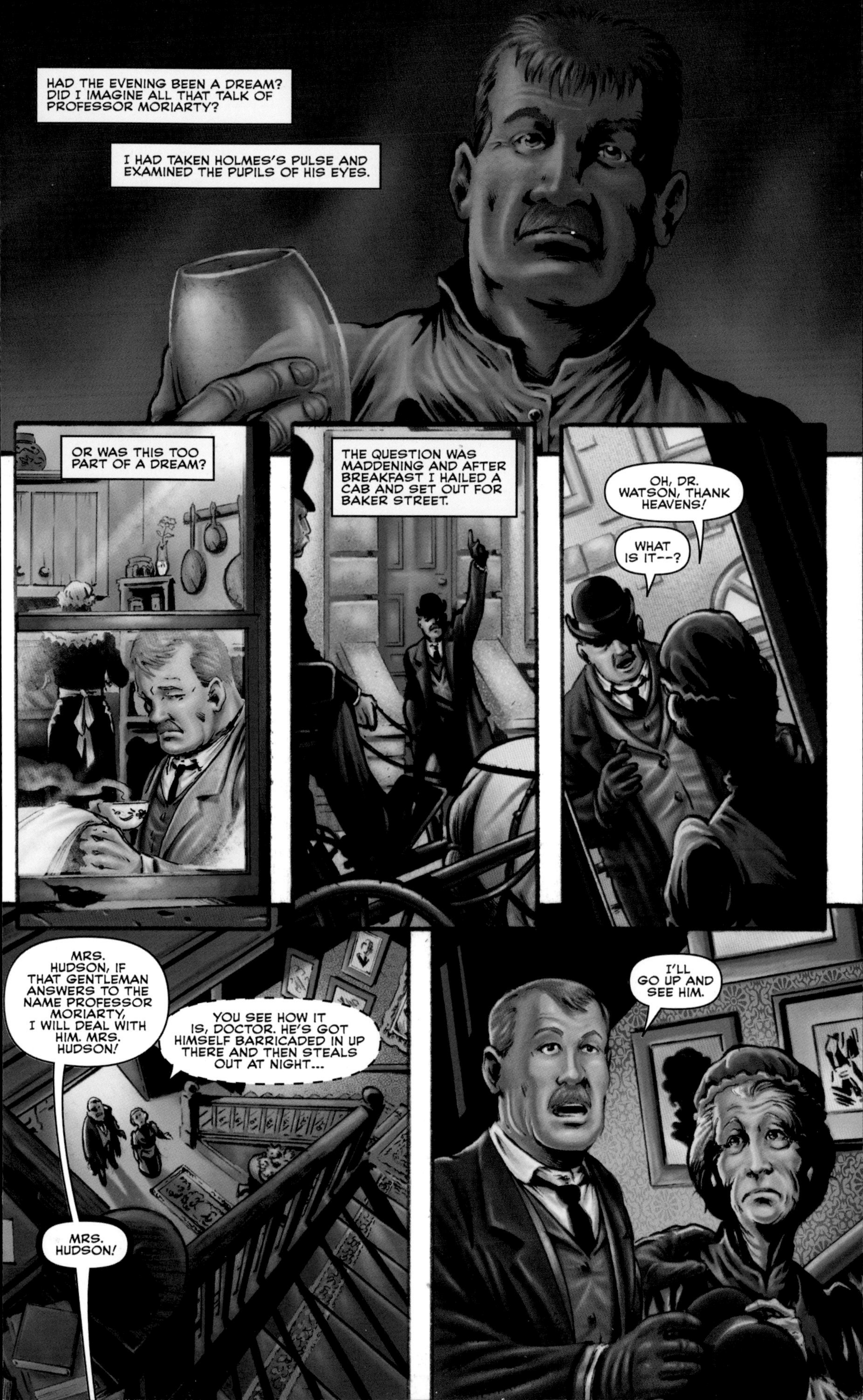
HAD THE EVENING BEEN A DREAM? DID I IMAGINE ALL THAT TALK OF PROFESSOR MORIARTY?
I HAD TAKEN HOLMES'S PULSE AND EXAMINED THE PUPILS OF HIS EYES.
OR WAS THIS TOO PART OF A DREAM?
THE QUESTION WAS MADDENING AND AFTER BREAKFAST I HAILED A CAB AND SET OUT FOR BAKER STREET.
OH, DR. WATSON, THANK HEAVENS!
WHAT IS IT--?
MRS. HUDSON, IF THAT GENTLEMAN ANSWERS TO THE NAME PROFESSOR MORIARTY, I WILL DEAL WITH HIM. MRS. HUDSON!
YOU SEE HOW IT IS, DOCTOR. HE'S GOT HIMSELF BARRICADED IN UP THERE AND THEN STEALS OUT AT NIGHT...
MRS. HUDSON!
I'LL GO UP AND SEE HIM.

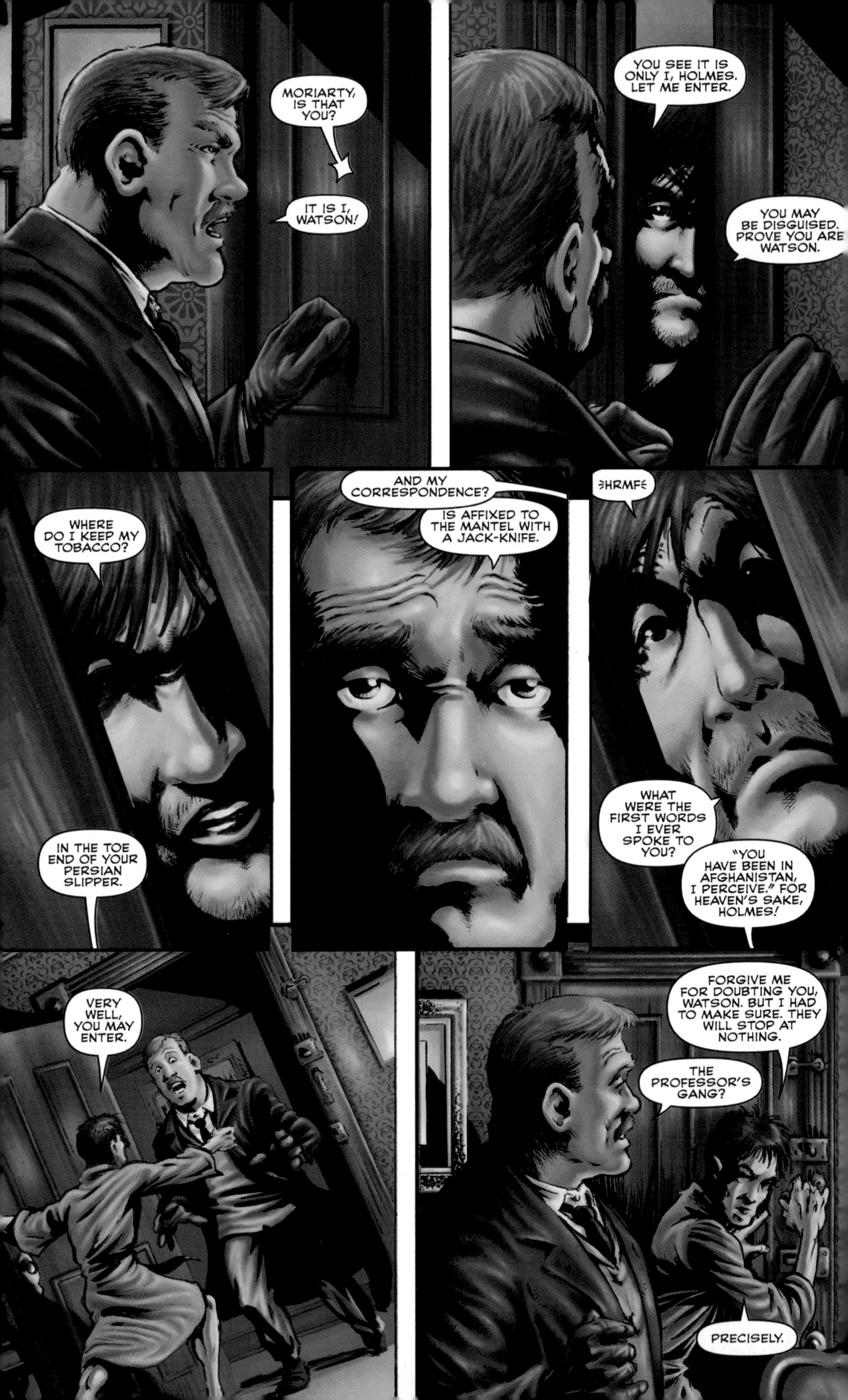
MORIARTY, IS THAT YOU?
IT IS I, WATSON!
YOU SEE IT IS ONLY I, HOLMES. LET ME ENTER.
YOU MAY BE DISGUISED. PROVE YOU ARE WATSON.
WHERE DO I KEEP MY TOBACCO?
IN THE TOE END OF YOUR PERSIAN SLIPPER.
AND MY CORRESPONDENCE?
IS AFFIXED TO THE MANTEL WITH A JACK-KNIFE.
HRMF
WHAT WERE THE FIRST WORDS I EVER SPOKE TO YOU?
"YOU HAVE BEEN IN AFGHANISTAN, I PERCEIVE." FOR HEAVEN'S SAKE, HOLMES!
VERY WELL, YOU MAY ENTER.
FORGIVE ME FOR DOUBTING YOU, WATSON. BUT I HAD TO MAKE SURE. THEY WILL STOP AT NOTHING.
THE PROFESSOR'S GANG?
PRECISELY.

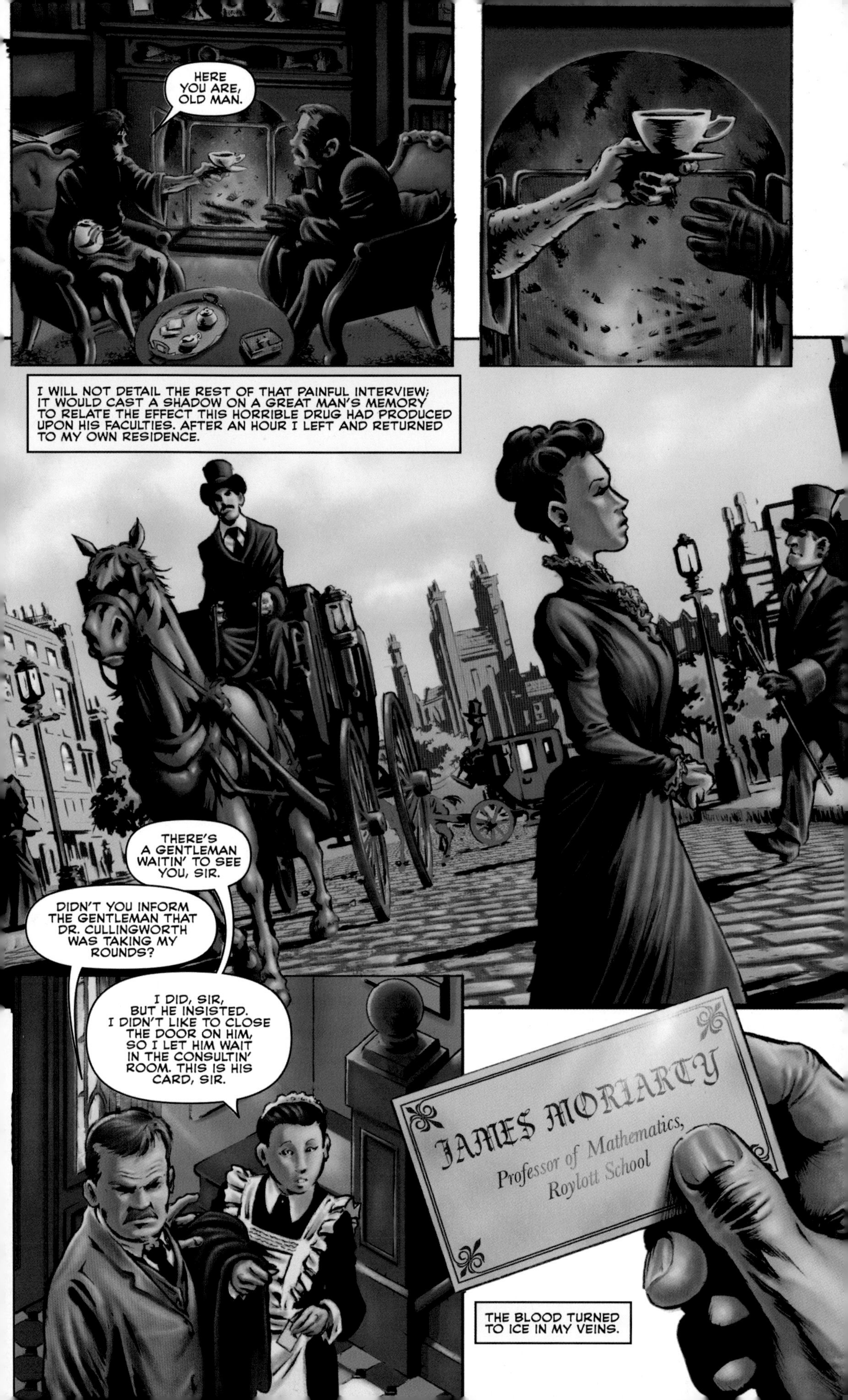
HERE YOU ARE, OLD MAN.
I WILL NOT DETAIL THE REST OF THAT PAINFUL INTERVIEW; IT WOULD CAST A SHADOW ON A GREAT MAN'S MEMORY TO RELATE THE EFFECT THIS HORRIBLE DRUG HAD PRODUCED UPON HIS FACULTIES. AFTER AN HOUR I LEFT AND RETURNED TO MY OWN RESIDENCE.
THERE'S A GENTLEMAN WAITIN' TO SEE YOU, SIR.
DIDN'T YOU INFORM THE GENTLEMAN THAT DR. CULLINGWORTH WAS TAKING MY ROUNDS?
I DID, SIR, BUT HE INSISTED. I DIDN'T LIKE TO CLOSE THE DOOR ON HIM, SO I LET HIM WAIT IN THE CONSULTIN' ROOM. THIS IS HIS CARD, SIR.
JAMES MORIARTY
Professor of Mathematics, Roylott School
THE BLOOD TURNED TO ICE IN MY VEINS.

I DID NOT DARE THINK. LET THIS—THIS "GENTLEMAN," EXPLAIN MATTERS TO ME IF HE COULD. I HAD, FOR THE MOMENT, NO INTENTION OF SPECULATING FURTHER.

PROFESSOR MORIARTY? I AM DR. WATSON.

I HOPE I HAVE NOT INCONVENIENCED YOU, BUT IT WAS YOU, NOT DOCTOR CULLINGWORTH, THAT I WISHED TO—

PRAY TELL ME WHAT IS THE MATTER.

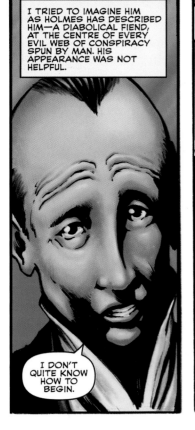

I TRIED TO IMAGINE HIM AS HOLMES HAS DESCRIBED HIM—A DIABOLICAL FIEND, AT THE CENTRE OF EVERY EVIL WEB OF CONSPIRACY SPUN BY MAN. HIS APPEARANCE WAS NOT HELPFUL.

I DON'T QUITE KNOW HOW TO BEGIN.

I KNOW FROM READING YOUR ACCOUNTS THAT YOU ARE MR. SHERLOCK HOLMES'S MOST INTIMATE ACQUAINTANCE.

I HAVE THAT HONOUR.

I AM NOT SURE HOW TO SAY THIS, BUT MR. HOLMES IS—WELL, I SUPPOSE PERSECUTING ME...

PERSECUTING *YOU*?

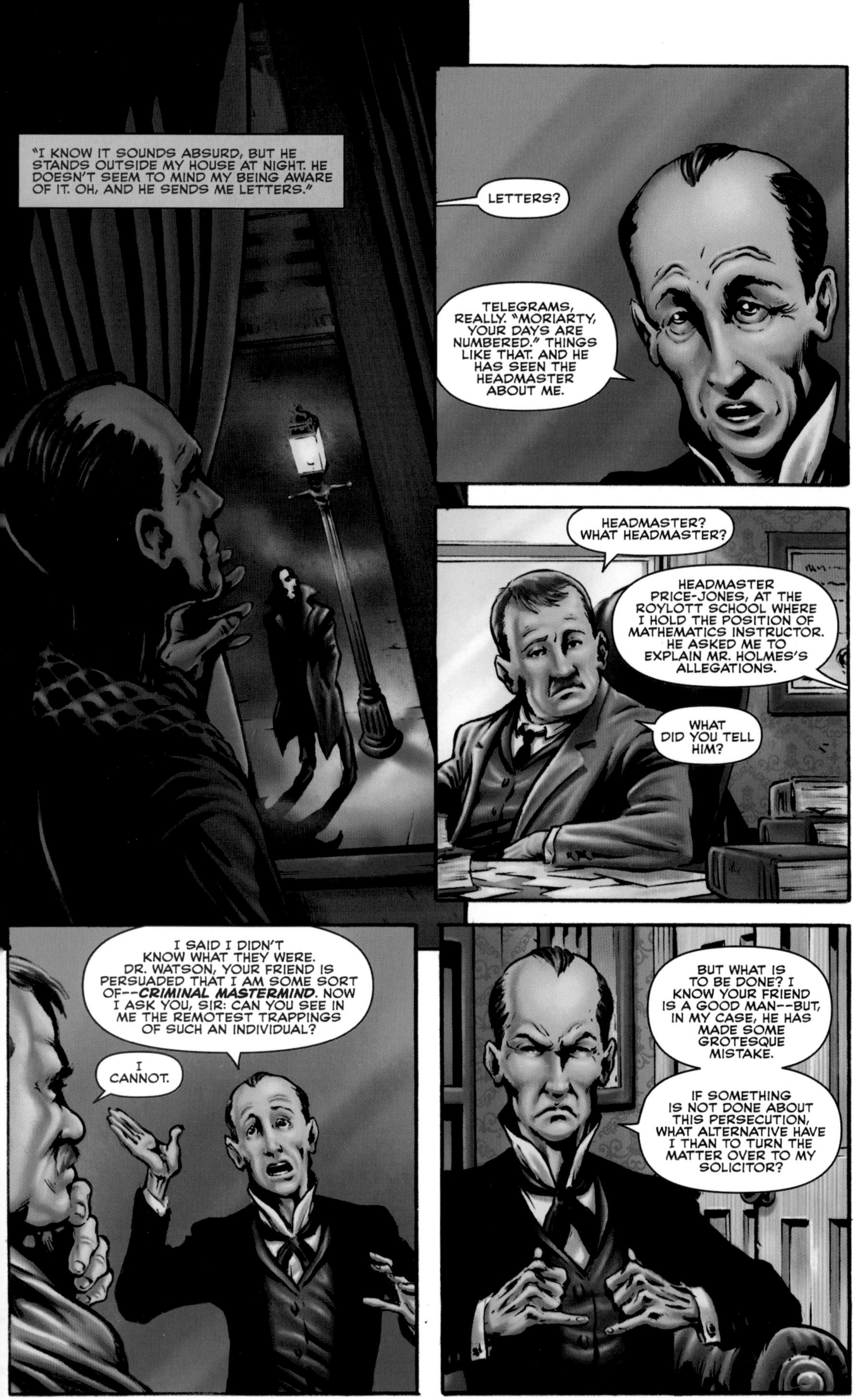
"I KNOW IT SOUNDS ABSURD, BUT HE STANDS OUTSIDE MY HOUSE AT NIGHT. HE DOESN'T SEEM TO MIND MY BEING AWARE OF IT. OH, AND HE SENDS ME LETTERS."
LETTERS?
TELEGRAMS, REALLY. "MORIARTY, YOUR DAYS ARE NUMBERED." THINGS LIKE THAT. AND HE HAS SEEN THE HEADMASTER ABOUT ME.
HEADMASTER? WHAT HEADMASTER?
HEADMASTER PRICE-JONES, AT THE ROYLOTT SCHOOL WHERE I HOLD THE POSITION OF MATHEMATICS INSTRUCTOR. HE ASKED ME TO EXPLAIN MR. HOLMES'S ALLEGATIONS.
WHAT DID YOU TELL HIM?
I SAID I DIDN'T KNOW WHAT THEY WERE. DR. WATSON, YOUR FRIEND IS PERSUADED THAT I AM SOME SORT OF--**CRIMINAL MASTERMIND**. NOW I ASK YOU, SIR: CAN YOU SEE IN ME THE REMOTEST TRAPPINGS OF SUCH AN INDIVIDUAL?
I CANNOT.
BUT WHAT IS TO BE DONE? I KNOW YOUR FRIEND IS A GOOD MAN--BUT, IN MY CASE, HE HAS MADE SOME GROTESQUE MISTAKE.
IF SOMETHING IS NOT DONE ABOUT THIS PERSECUTION, WHAT ALTERNATIVE HAVE I THAN TO TURN THE MATTER OVER TO MY SOLICITOR?

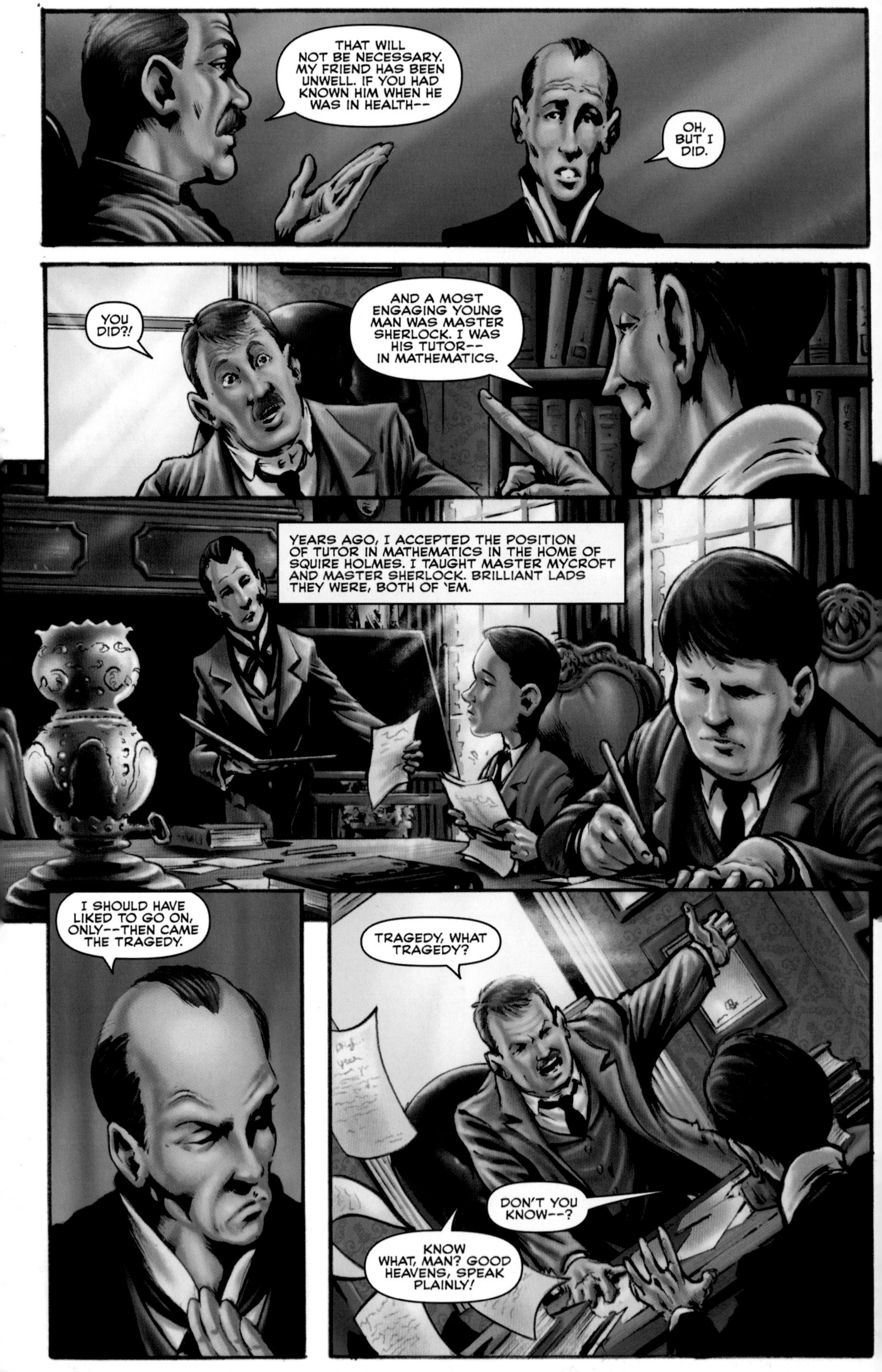
THAT WILL NOT BE NECESSARY. MY FRIEND HAS BEEN UNWELL. IF YOU HAD KNOWN HIM WHEN HE WAS IN HEALTH--
OH, BUT I DID.
YOU DID?!
AND A MOST ENGAGING YOUNG MAN WAS MASTER SHERLOCK. I WAS HIS TUTOR-- IN MATHEMATICS.
YEARS AGO, I ACCEPTED THE POSITION OF TUTOR IN MATHEMATICS IN THE HOME OF SQUIRE HOLMES. I TAUGHT MASTER MYCROFT AND MASTER SHERLOCK. BRILLIANT LADS THEY WERE, BOTH OF 'EM.
I SHOULD HAVE LIKED TO GO ON, ONLY--THEN CAME THE TRAGEDY.
TRAGEDY, WHAT TRAGEDY?
DON'T YOU KNOW--?
KNOW WHAT, MAN? GOOD HEAVENS, SPEAK PLAINLY!

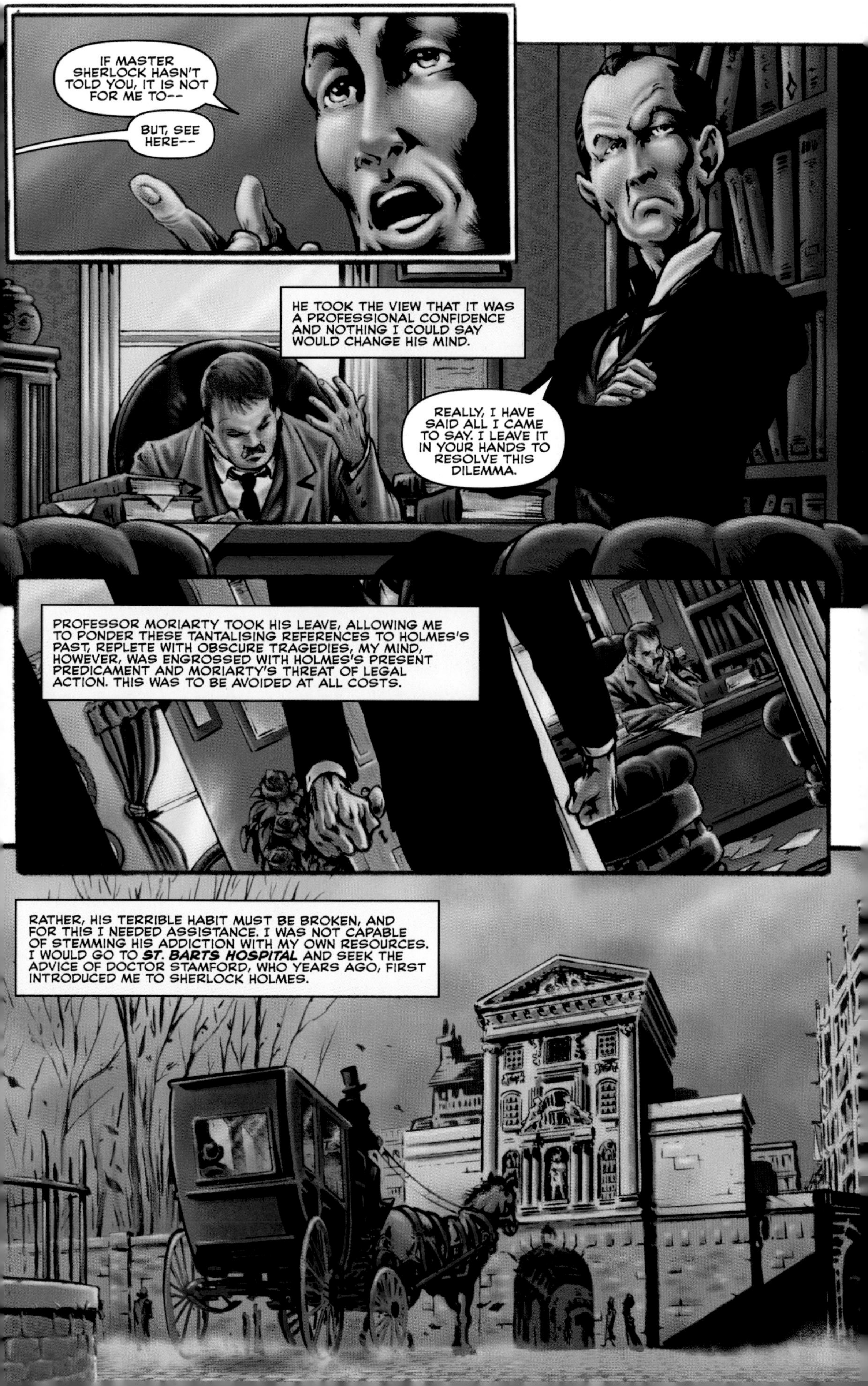
IF MASTER SHERLOCK HASN'T TOLD YOU, IT IS NOT FOR ME TO--
BUT, SEE HERE--
HE TOOK THE VIEW THAT IT WAS A PROFESSIONAL CONFIDENCE AND NOTHING I COULD SAY WOULD CHANGE HIS MIND.
REALLY, I HAVE SAID ALL I CAME TO SAY. I LEAVE IT IN YOUR HANDS TO RESOLVE THIS DILEMMA.
PROFESSOR MORIARTY TOOK HIS LEAVE, ALLOWING ME TO PONDER THESE TANTALISING REFERENCES TO HOLMES'S PAST, REPLETE WITH OBSCURE TRAGEDIES, MY MIND, HOWEVER, WAS ENGROSSED WITH HOLMES'S PRESENT PREDICAMENT AND MORIARTY'S THREAT OF LEGAL ACTION. THIS WAS TO BE AVOIDED AT ALL COSTS.
RATHER, HIS TERRIBLE HABIT MUST BE BROKEN, AND FOR THIS I NEEDED ASSISTANCE. I WAS NOT CAPABLE OF STEMMING HIS ADDICTION WITH MY OWN RESOURCES. I WOULD GO TO ***ST. BARTS HOSPITAL*** AND SEEK THE ADVICE OF DOCTOR STAMFORD, WHO YEARS AGO, FIRST INTRODUCED ME TO SHERLOCK HOLMES.

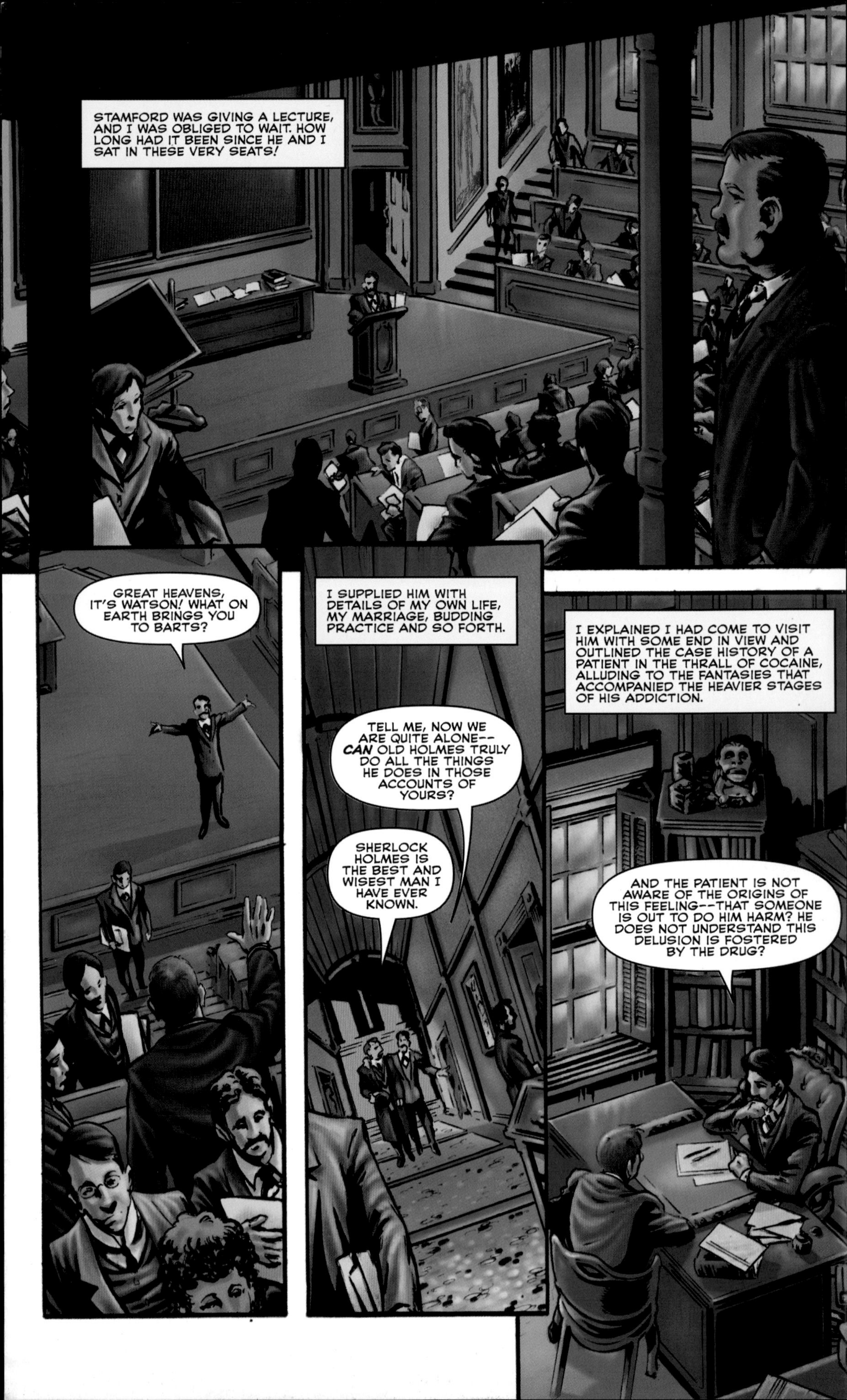
STAMFORD WAS GIVING A LECTURE, AND I WAS OBLIGED TO WAIT. HOW LONG HAD IT BEEN SINCE HE AND I SAT IN THESE VERY SEATS!
GREAT HEAVENS, IT'S WATSON! WHAT ON EARTH BRINGS YOU TO BARTS?
I SUPPLIED HIM WITH DETAILS OF MY OWN LIFE, MY MARRIAGE, BUDDING PRACTICE AND SO FORTH.
TELL ME, NOW WE ARE QUITE ALONE-- CAN OLD HOLMES TRULY DO ALL THE THINGS HE DOES IN THOSE ACCOUNTS OF YOURS?
SHERLOCK HOLMES IS THE BEST AND WISEST MAN I HAVE EVER KNOWN.
I EXPLAINED I HAD COME TO VISIT HIM WITH SOME END IN VIEW AND OUTLINED THE CASE HISTORY OF A PATIENT IN THE THRALL OF COCAINE, ALLUDING TO THE FANTASIES THAT ACCOMPANIED THE HEAVIER STAGES OF HIS ADDICTION.
AND THE PATIENT IS NOT AWARE OF THE ORIGINS OF THIS FEELING--THAT SOMEONE IS OUT TO DO HIM HARM? HE DOES NOT UNDERSTAND THIS DELUSION IS FOSTERED BY THE DRUG?

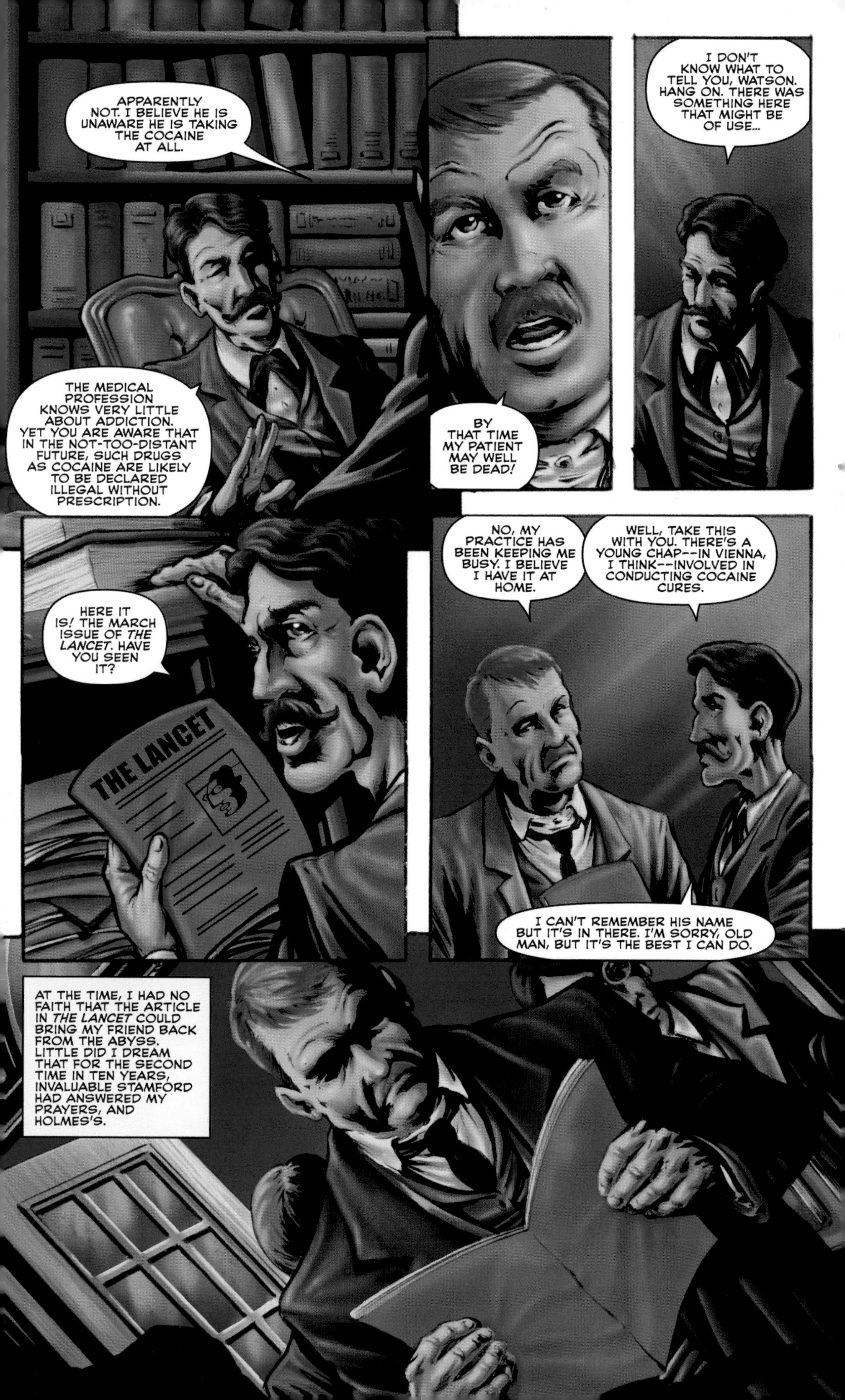
APPARENTLY NOT. I BELIEVE HE IS UNAWARE HE IS TAKING THE COCAINE AT ALL.
THE MEDICAL PROFESSION KNOWS VERY LITTLE ABOUT ADDICTION. YET YOU ARE AWARE THAT IN THE NOT-TOO-DISTANT FUTURE, SUCH DRUGS AS COCAINE ARE LIKELY TO BE DECLARED ILLEGAL WITHOUT PRESCRIPTION.
BY THAT TIME MY PATIENT MAY WELL BE DEAD!
I DON'T KNOW WHAT TO TELL YOU, WATSON. HANG ON. THERE WAS SOMETHING HERE THAT MIGHT BE OF USE...
HERE IT IS! THE MARCH ISSUE OF *THE LANCET*. HAVE YOU SEEN IT?
THE LANCET
NO, MY PRACTICE HAS BEEN KEEPING ME BUSY. I BELIEVE I HAVE IT AT HOME.
WELL, TAKE THIS WITH YOU. THERE'S A YOUNG CHAP--IN VIENNA, I THINK--INVOLVED IN CONDUCTING COCAINE CURES.
I CAN'T REMEMBER HIS NAME BUT IT'S IN THERE. I'M SORRY, OLD MAN, BUT IT'S THE BEST I CAN DO.
AT THE TIME, I HAD NO FAITH THAT THE ARTICLE IN *THE LANCET* COULD BRING MY FRIEND BACK FROM THE ABYSS. LITTLE DID I DREAM THAT FOR THE SECOND TIME IN TEN YEARS, INVALUABLE STAMFORD HAD ANSWERED MY PRAYERS, AND HOLMES'S.

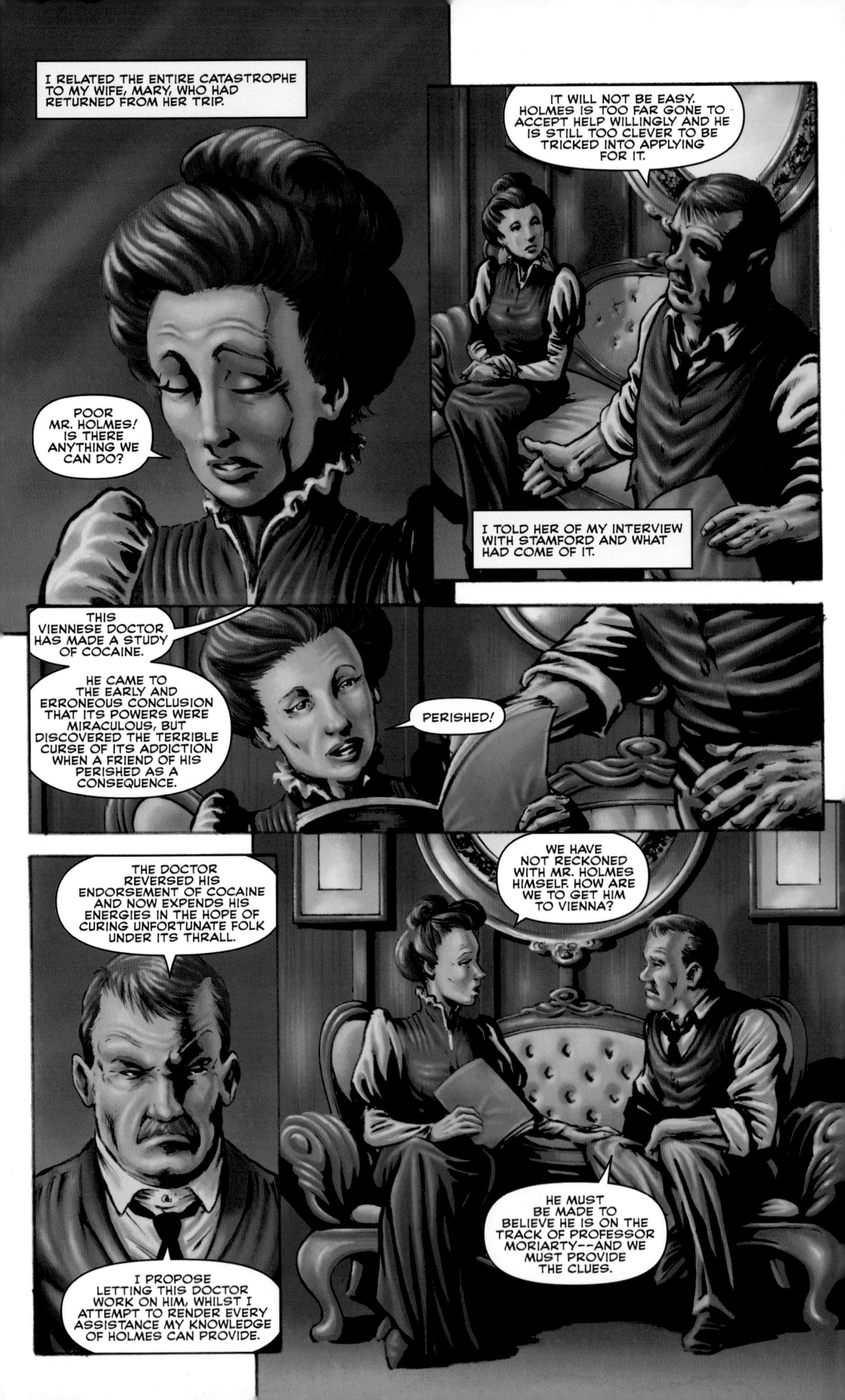
I RELATED THE ENTIRE CATASTROPHE TO MY WIFE, MARY, WHO HAD RETURNED FROM HER TRIP.
POOR MR. HOLMES! IS THERE ANYTHING WE CAN DO?
IT WILL NOT BE EASY. HOLMES IS TOO FAR GONE TO ACCEPT HELP WILLINGLY AND HE IS STILL TOO CLEVER TO BE TRICKED INTO APPLYING FOR IT.
I TOLD HER OF MY INTERVIEW WITH STAMFORD AND WHAT HAD COME OF IT.
THIS VIENNESE DOCTOR HAS MADE A STUDY OF COCAINE.
HE CAME TO THE EARLY AND ERRONEOUS CONCLUSION THAT ITS POWERS WERE MIRACULOUS, BUT DISCOVERED THE TERRIBLE CURSE OF ITS ADDICTION WHEN A FRIEND OF HIS PERISHED AS A CONSEQUENCE.
PERISHED!
THE DOCTOR REVERSED HIS ENDORSEMENT OF COCAINE AND NOW EXPENDS HIS ENERGIES IN THE HOPE OF CURING UNFORTUNATE FOLK UNDER ITS THRALL.
I PROPOSE LETTING THIS DOCTOR WORK ON HIM, WHILST I ATTEMPT TO RENDER EVERY ASSISTANCE MY KNOWLEDGE OF HOLMES CAN PROVIDE.
WE HAVE NOT RECKONED WITH MR. HOLMES HIMSELF. HOW ARE WE TO GET HIM TO VIENNA?
HE MUST BE MADE TO BELIEVE HE IS ON THE TRACK OF PROFESSOR MORIARTY--AND WE MUST PROVIDE THE CLUES.

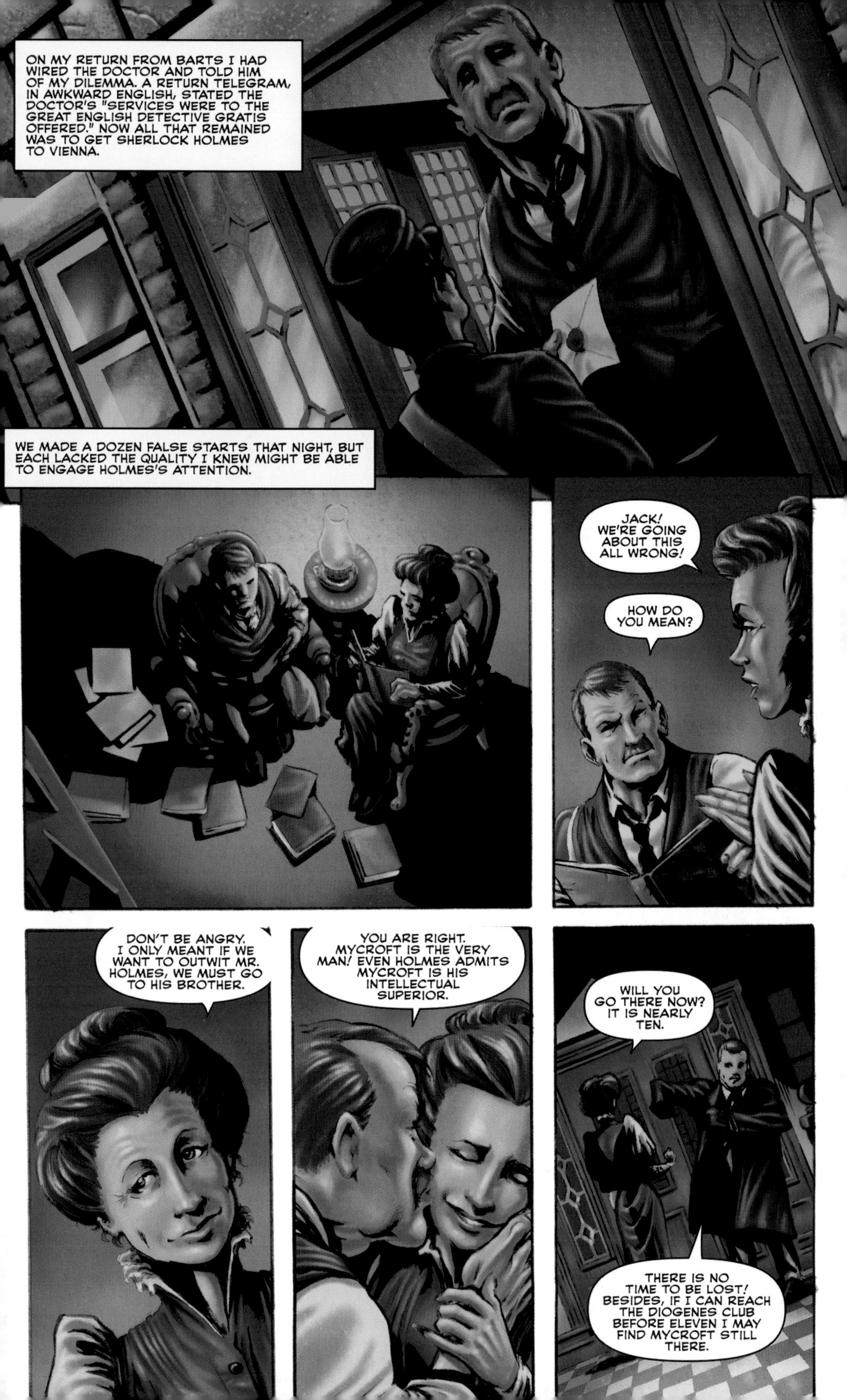
ON MY RETURN FROM BARTS I HAD WIRED THE DOCTOR AND TOLD HIM OF MY DILEMMA. A RETURN TELEGRAM, IN AWKWARD ENGLISH, STATED THE DOCTOR'S "SERVICES WERE TO THE GREAT ENGLISH DETECTIVE GRATIS OFFERED." NOW ALL THAT REMAINED WAS TO GET SHERLOCK HOLMES TO VIENNA.
WE MADE A DOZEN FALSE STARTS THAT NIGHT, BUT EACH LACKED THE QUALITY I KNEW MIGHT BE ABLE TO ENGAGE HOLMES'S ATTENTION.
JACK! WE'RE GOING ABOUT THIS ALL WRONG!
HOW DO YOU MEAN?
DON'T BE ANGRY. I ONLY MEANT IF WE WANT TO OUTWIT MR. HOLMES, WE MUST GO TO HIS BROTHER.
YOU ARE RIGHT. MYCROFT IS THE VERY MAN! EVEN HOLMES ADMITS MYCROFT IS HIS INTELLECTUAL SUPERIOR.
WILL YOU GO THERE NOW? IT IS NEARLY TEN.
THERE IS NO TIME TO BE LOST! BESIDES, IF I CAN REACH THE DIOGENES CLUB BEFORE ELEVEN I MAY FIND MYCROFT STILL THERE.

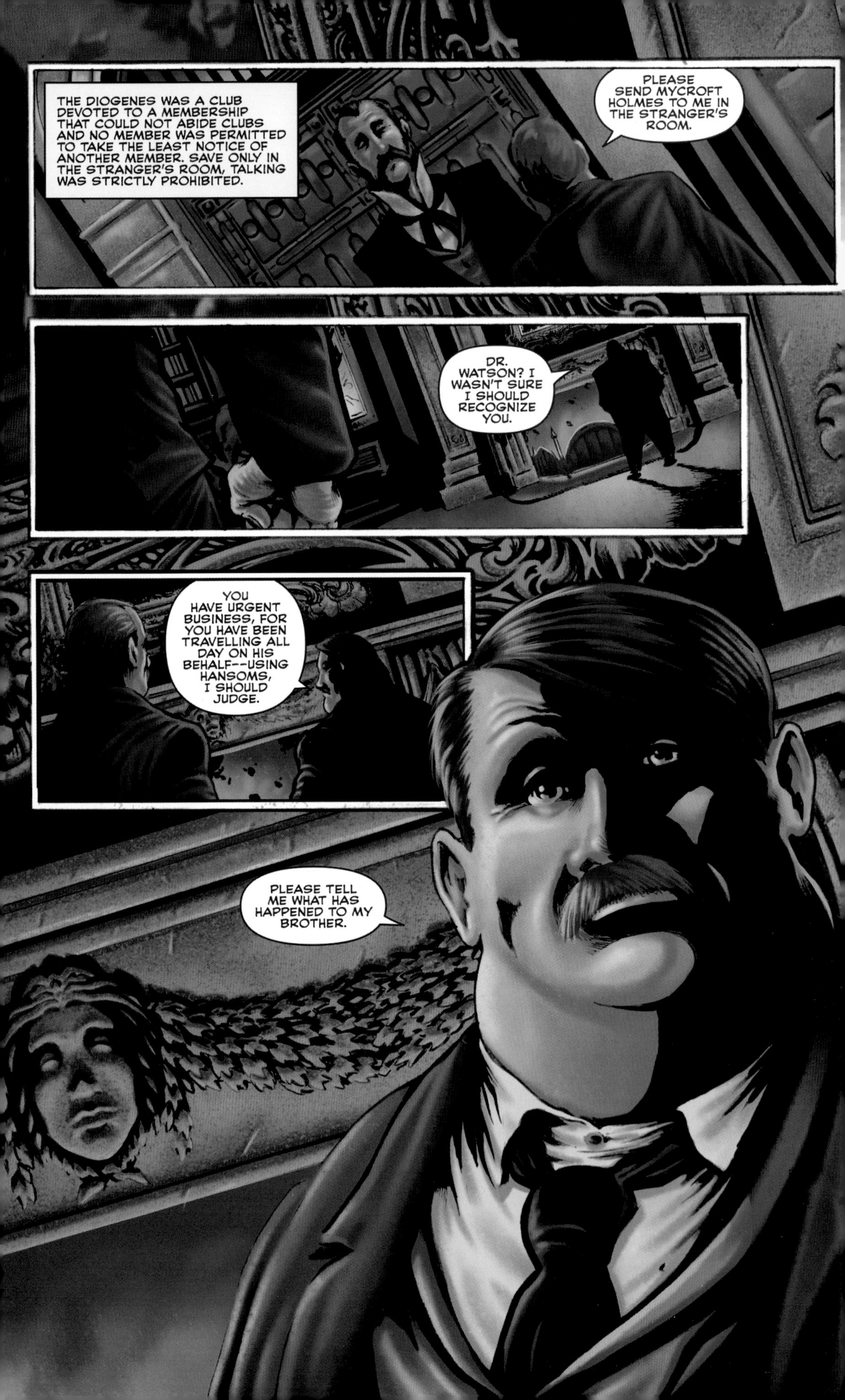
THE DIOGENES WAS A CLUB DEVOTED TO A MEMBERSHIP THAT COULD NOT ABIDE CLUBS AND NO MEMBER WAS PERMITTED TO TAKE THE LEAST NOTICE OF ANOTHER MEMBER. SAVE ONLY IN THE STRANGER'S ROOM, TALKING WAS STRICTLY PROHIBITED.
PLEASE SEND MYCROFT HOLMES TO ME IN THE STRANGER'S ROOM.
DR. WATSON? I WASN'T SURE I SHOULD RECOGNIZE YOU.
YOU HAVE URGENT BUSINESS, FOR YOU HAVE BEEN TRAVELLING ALL DAY ON HIS BEHALF--USING HANSOMS, I SHOULD JUDGE.
PLEASE TELL ME WHAT HAS HAPPENED TO MY BROTHER.

ART BY
KELLEY JONES

COLORS BY
JAY FOTOS

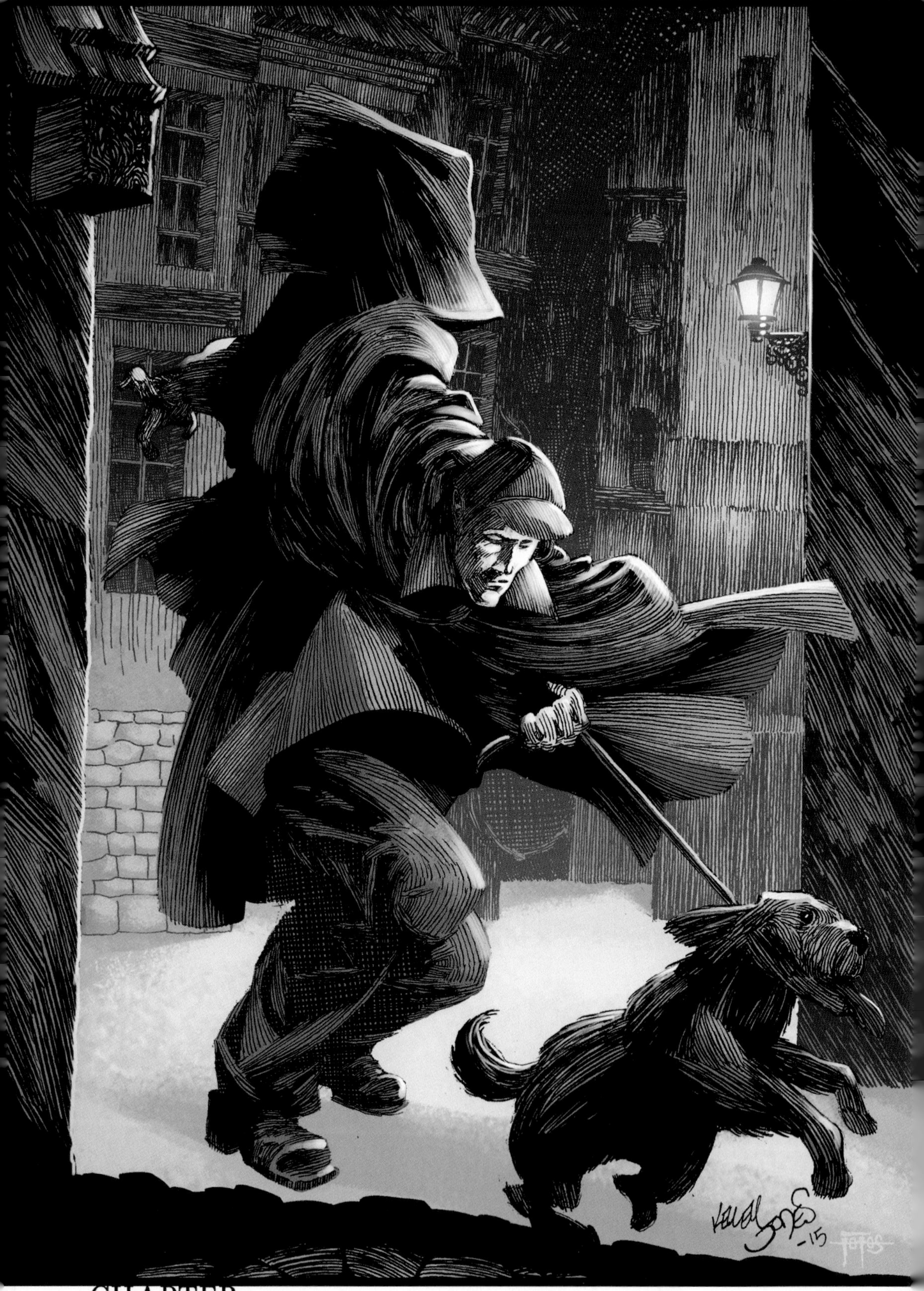

CHAPTER TWO

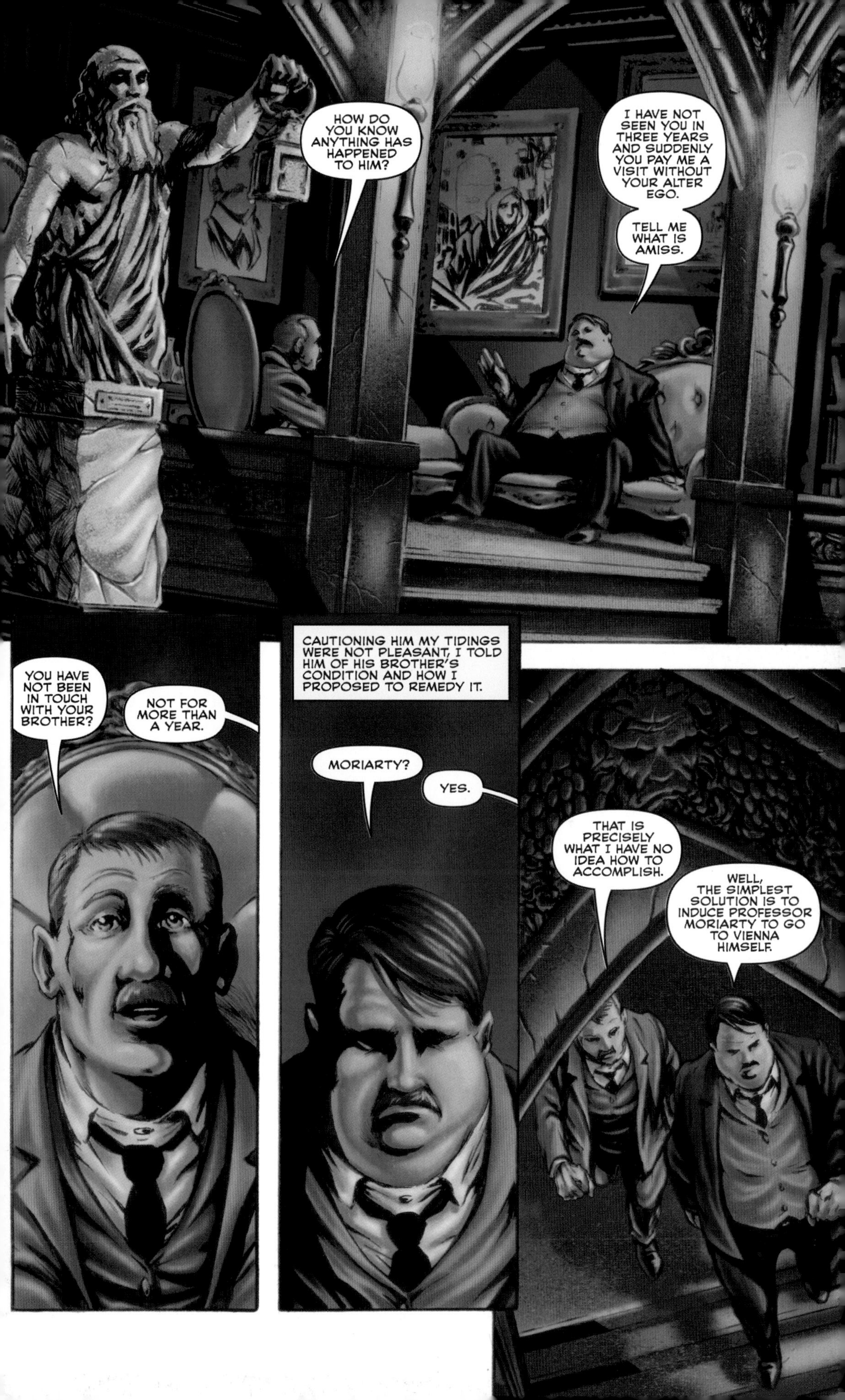
HOW DO YOU KNOW ANYTHING HAS HAPPENED TO HIM?
I HAVE NOT SEEN YOU IN THREE YEARS AND SUDDENLY YOU PAY ME A VISIT WITHOUT YOUR ALTER EGO.
TELL ME WHAT IS AMISS.
YOU HAVE NOT BEEN IN TOUCH WITH YOUR BROTHER?
NOT FOR MORE THAN A YEAR.
CAUTIONING HIM MY TIDINGS WERE NOT PLEASANT, I TOLD HIM OF HIS BROTHER'S CONDITION AND HOW I PROPOSED TO REMEDY IT.
MORIARTY?
YES.
THAT IS PRECISELY WHAT I HAVE NO IDEA HOW TO ACCOMPLISH.
WELL, THE SIMPLEST SOLUTION IS TO INDUCE PROFESSOR MORIARTY TO GO TO VIENNA HIMSELF.

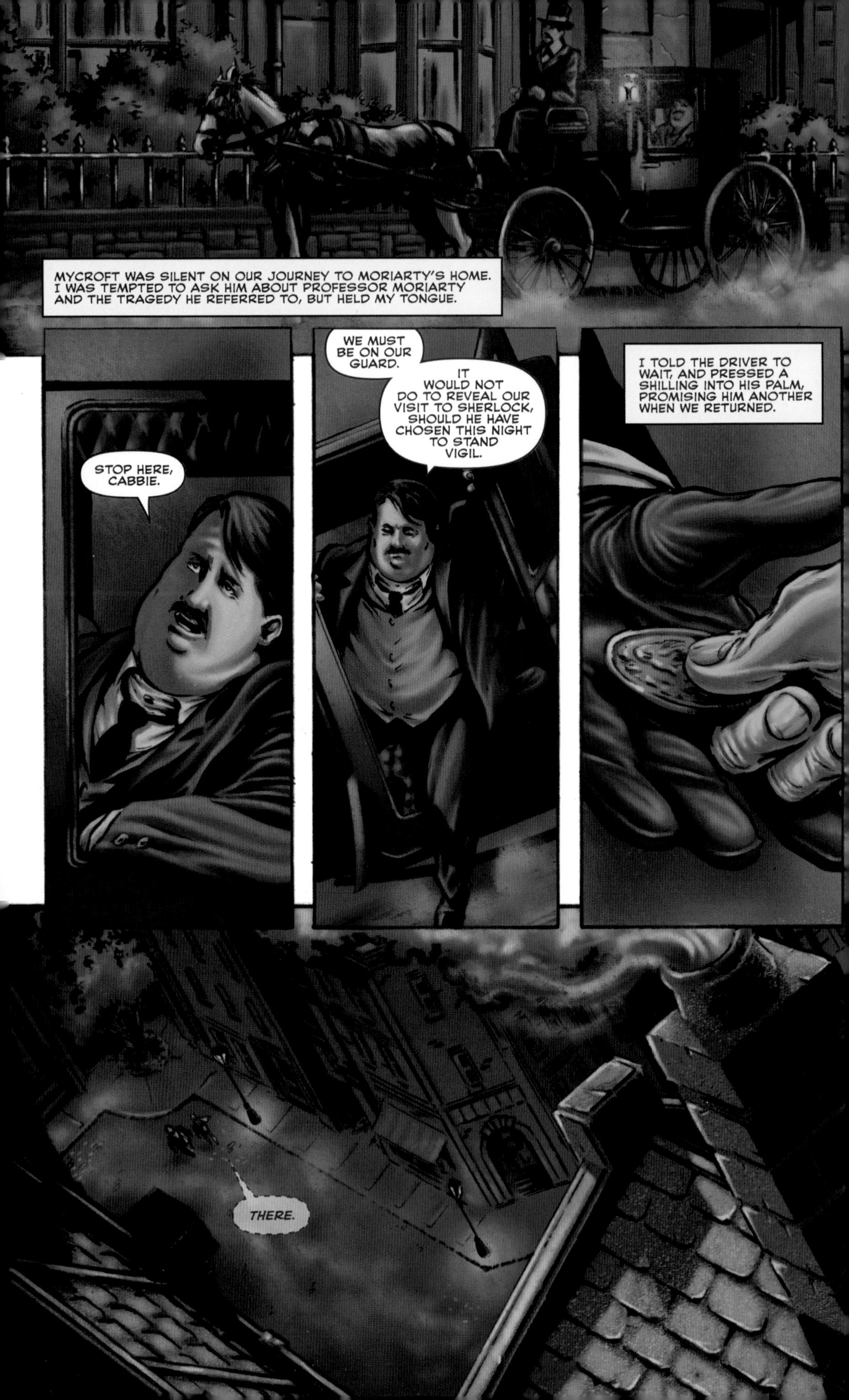
MYCROFT WAS SILENT ON OUR JOURNEY TO MORIARTY'S HOME. I WAS TEMPTED TO ASK HIM ABOUT PROFESSOR MORIARTY AND THE TRAGEDY HE REFERRED TO, BUT HELD MY TONGUE.
STOP HERE, CABBIE.
WE MUST BE ON OUR GUARD.
IT WOULD NOT DO TO REVEAL OUR VISIT TO SHERLOCK, SHOULD HE HAVE CHOSEN THIS NIGHT TO STAND VIGIL.
I TOLD THE DRIVER TO WAIT, AND PRESSED A SHILLING INTO HIS PALM, PROMISING HIM ANOTHER WHEN WE RETURNED.
THERE.

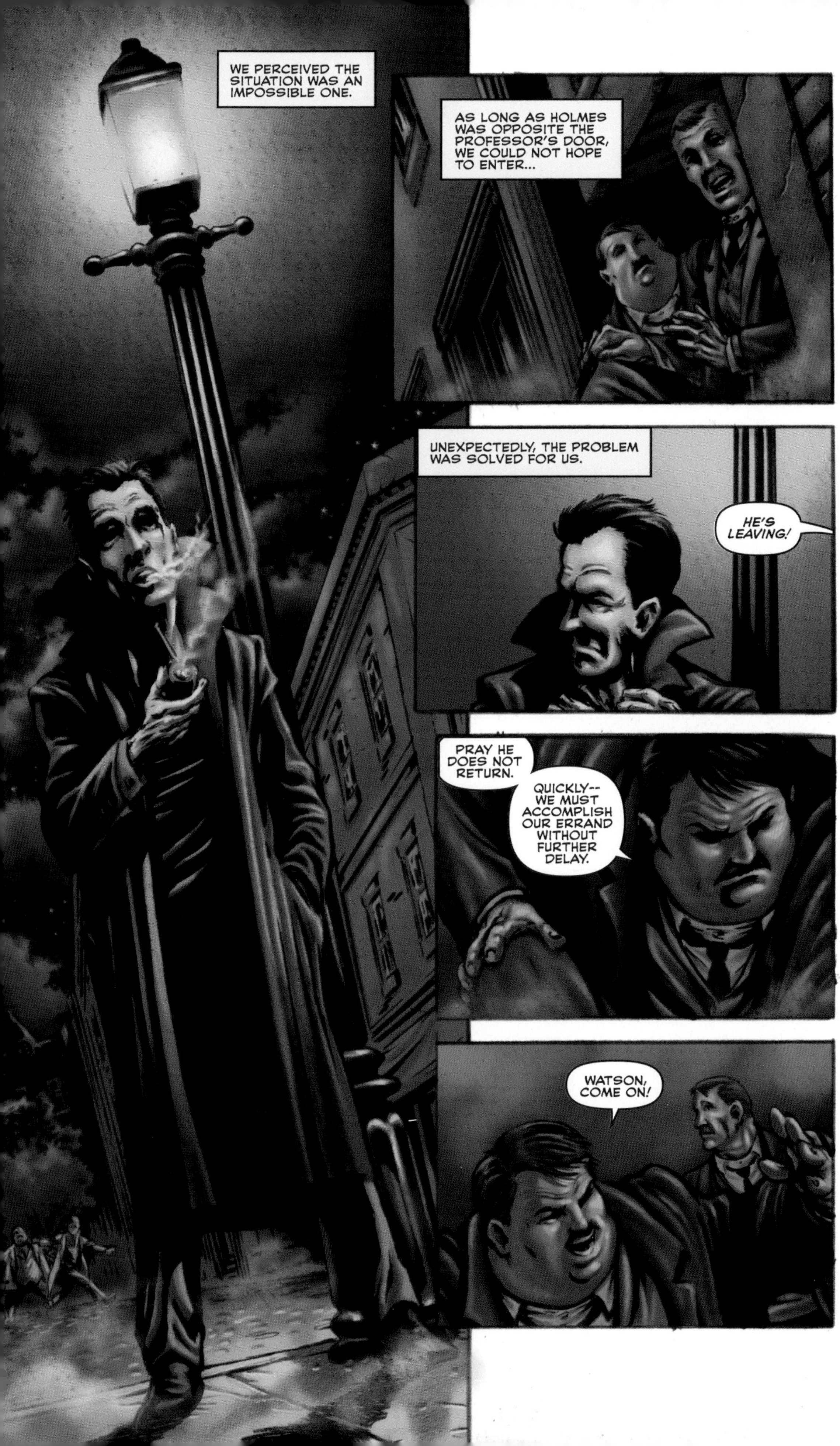
WE PERCEIVED THE SITUATION WAS AN IMPOSSIBLE ONE.
AS LONG AS HOLMES WAS OPPOSITE THE PROFESSOR'S DOOR, WE COULD NOT HOPE TO ENTER...
UNEXPECTEDLY, THE PROBLEM WAS SOLVED FOR US.
HE'S LEAVING!
PRAY HE DOES NOT RETURN.
QUICKLY-- WE MUST ACCOMPLISH OUR ERRAND WITHOUT FURTHER DELAY.
WATSON, COME ON!

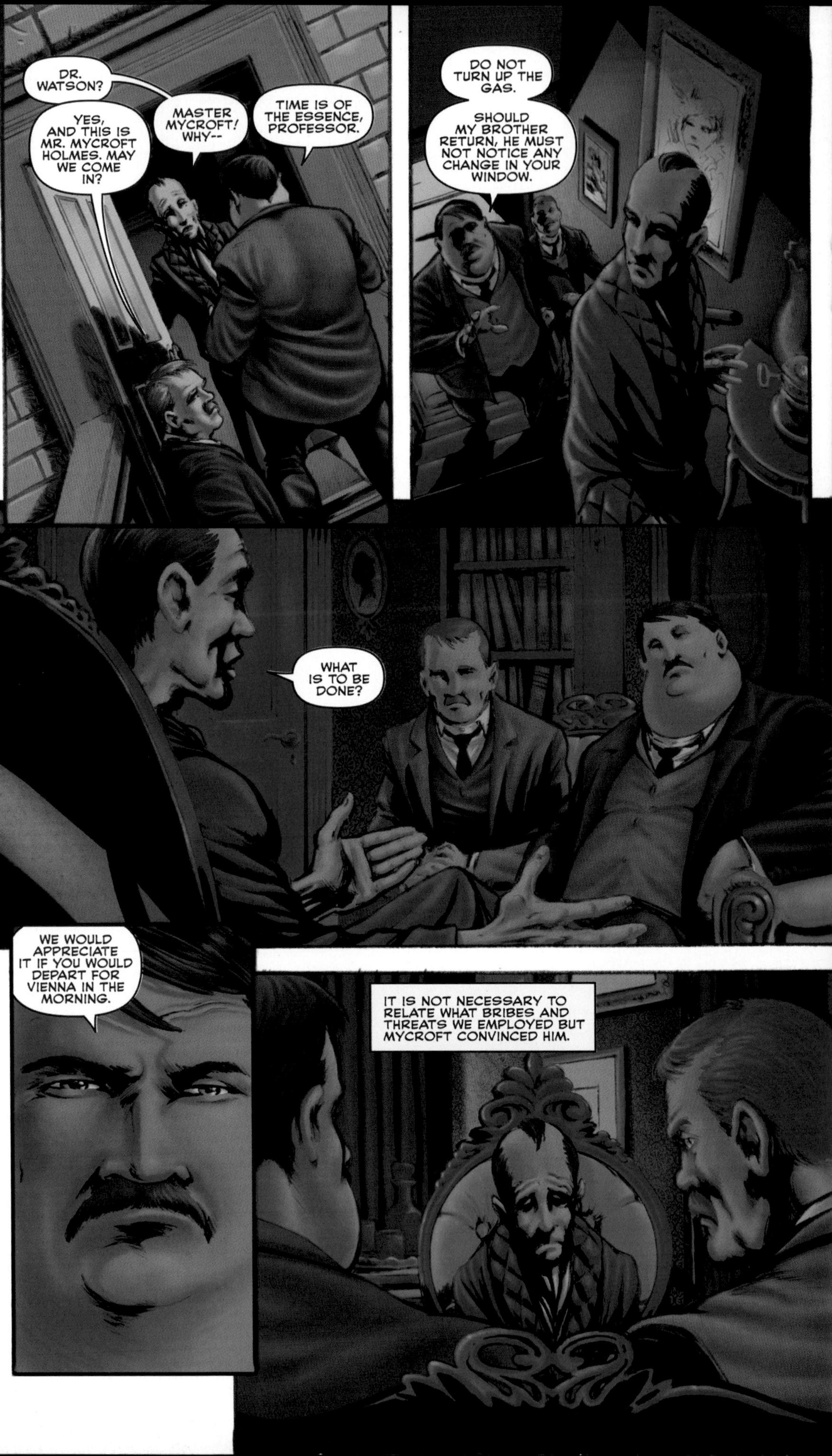

DR. WATSON?
YES, AND THIS IS MR. MYCROFT HOLMES. MAY WE COME IN?
MASTER MYCROFT! WHY--
TIME IS OF THE ESSENCE, PROFESSOR.
DO NOT TURN UP THE GAS.
SHOULD MY BROTHER RETURN, HE MUST NOT NOTICE ANY CHANGE IN YOUR WINDOW.
WHAT IS TO BE DONE?
WE WOULD APPRECIATE IT IF YOU WOULD DEPART FOR VIENNA IN THE MORNING.
IT IS NOT NECESSARY TO RELATE WHAT BRIBES AND THREATS WE EMPLOYED BUT MYCROFT CONVINCED HIM.

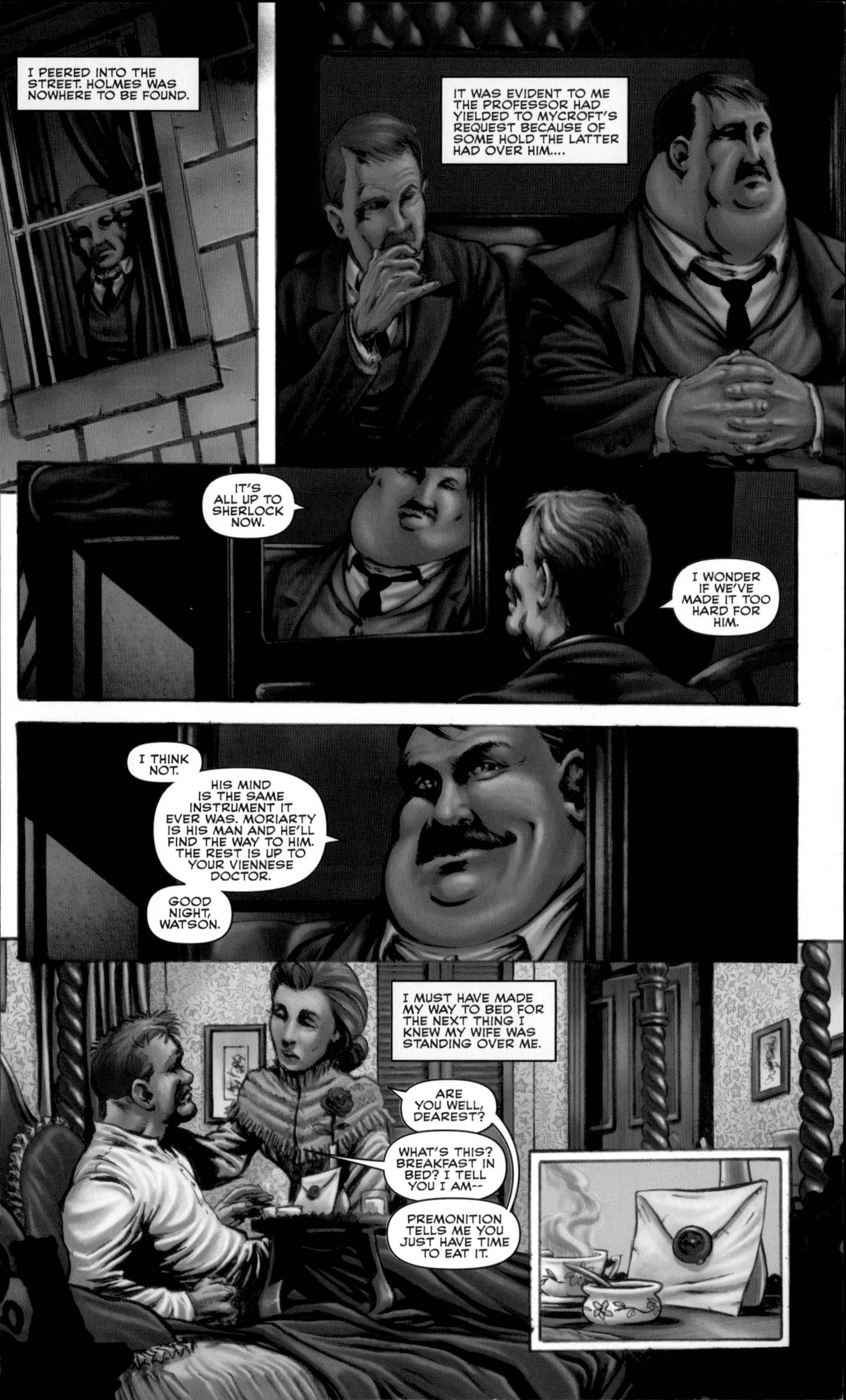
I PEERED INTO THE STREET. HOLMES WAS NOWHERE TO BE FOUND.
IT WAS EVIDENT TO ME THE PROFESSOR HAD YIELDED TO MYCROFT'S REQUEST BECAUSE OF SOME HOLD THE LATTER HAD OVER HIM....
IT'S ALL UP TO SHERLOCK NOW.
I WONDER IF WE'VE MADE IT TOO HARD FOR HIM.
I THINK NOT.
HIS MIND IS THE SAME INSTRUMENT IT EVER WAS. MORIARTY IS HIS MAN AND HE'LL FIND THE WAY TO HIM. THE REST IS UP TO YOUR VIENNESE DOCTOR.
GOOD NIGHT, WATSON.
I MUST HAVE MADE MY WAY TO BED FOR THE NEXT THING I KNEW MY WIFE WAS STANDING OVER ME.
ARE YOU WELL, DEAREST?
WHAT'S THIS? BREAKFAST IN BED? I TELL YOU I AM--
PREMONITION TELLS ME YOU JUST HAVE TIME TO EAT IT.

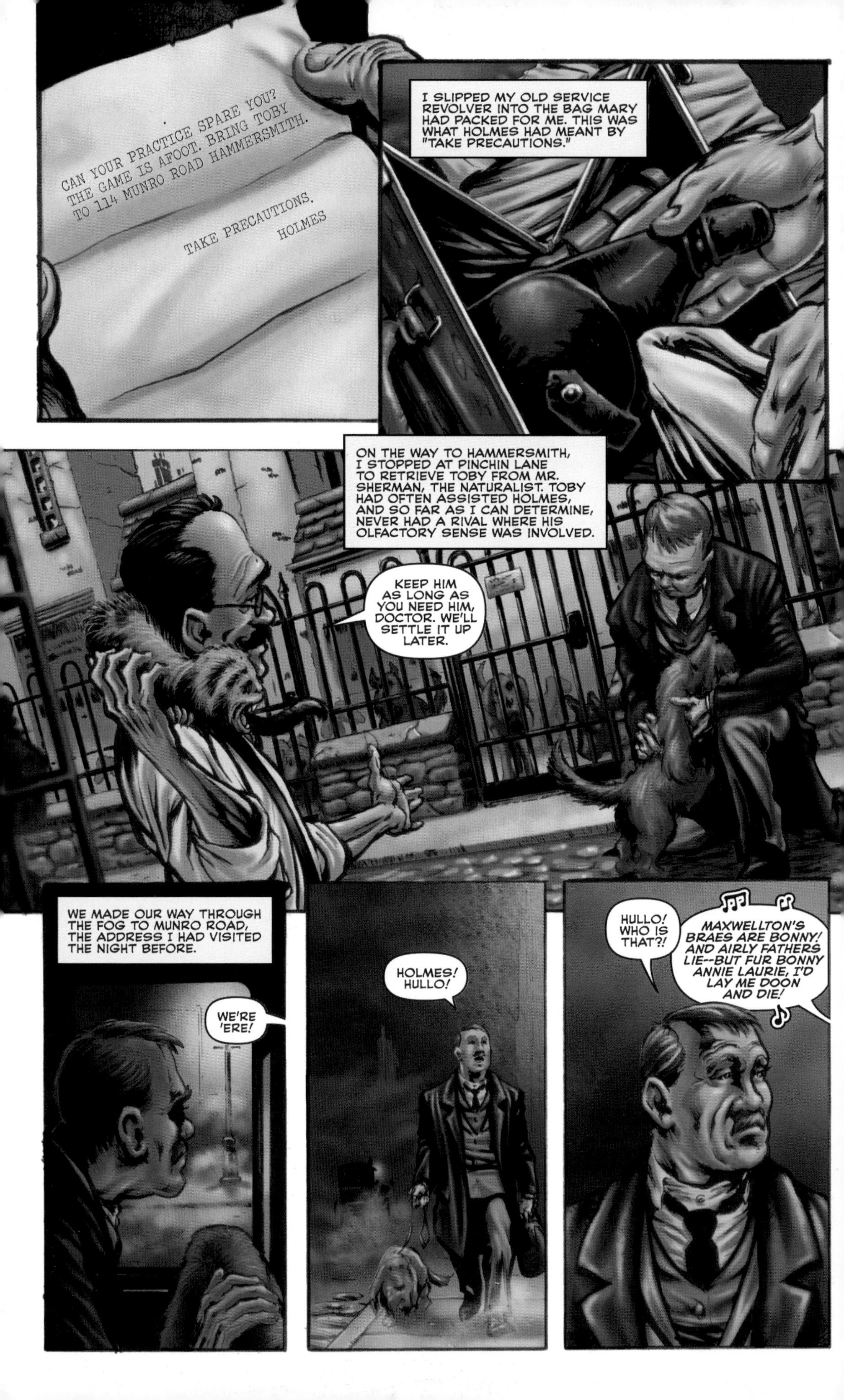
CAN YOUR PRACTICE SPARE YOU? THE GAME IS AFOOT. BRING TOBY TO 114 MUNRO ROAD HAMMERSMITH.
TAKE PRECAUTIONS.
HOLMES
I SLIPPED MY OLD SERVICE REVOLVER INTO THE BAG MARY HAD PACKED FOR ME. THIS WAS WHAT HOLMES HAD MEANT BY "TAKE PRECAUTIONS."
ON THE WAY TO HAMMERSMITH, I STOPPED AT PINCHIN LANE TO RETRIEVE TOBY FROM MR. SHERMAN, THE NATURALIST. TOBY HAD OFTEN ASSISTED HOLMES, AND SO FAR AS I CAN DETERMINE, NEVER HAD A RIVAL WHERE HIS OLFACTORY SENSE WAS INVOLVED.
KEEP HIM AS LONG AS YOU NEED HIM, DOCTOR. WE'LL SETTLE IT UP LATER.
WE MADE OUR WAY THROUGH THE FOG TO MUNRO ROAD, THE ADDRESS I HAD VISITED THE NIGHT BEFORE.
WE'RE 'ERE!
HOLMES! HULLO!
HULLO! WHO IS THAT?!
MAXWELLTON'S BRAES ARE BONNY! AND AIRLY FATHERS LIE--BUT FUR BONNY ANNIE LAURIE, I'D LAY ME DOON AND DIE!

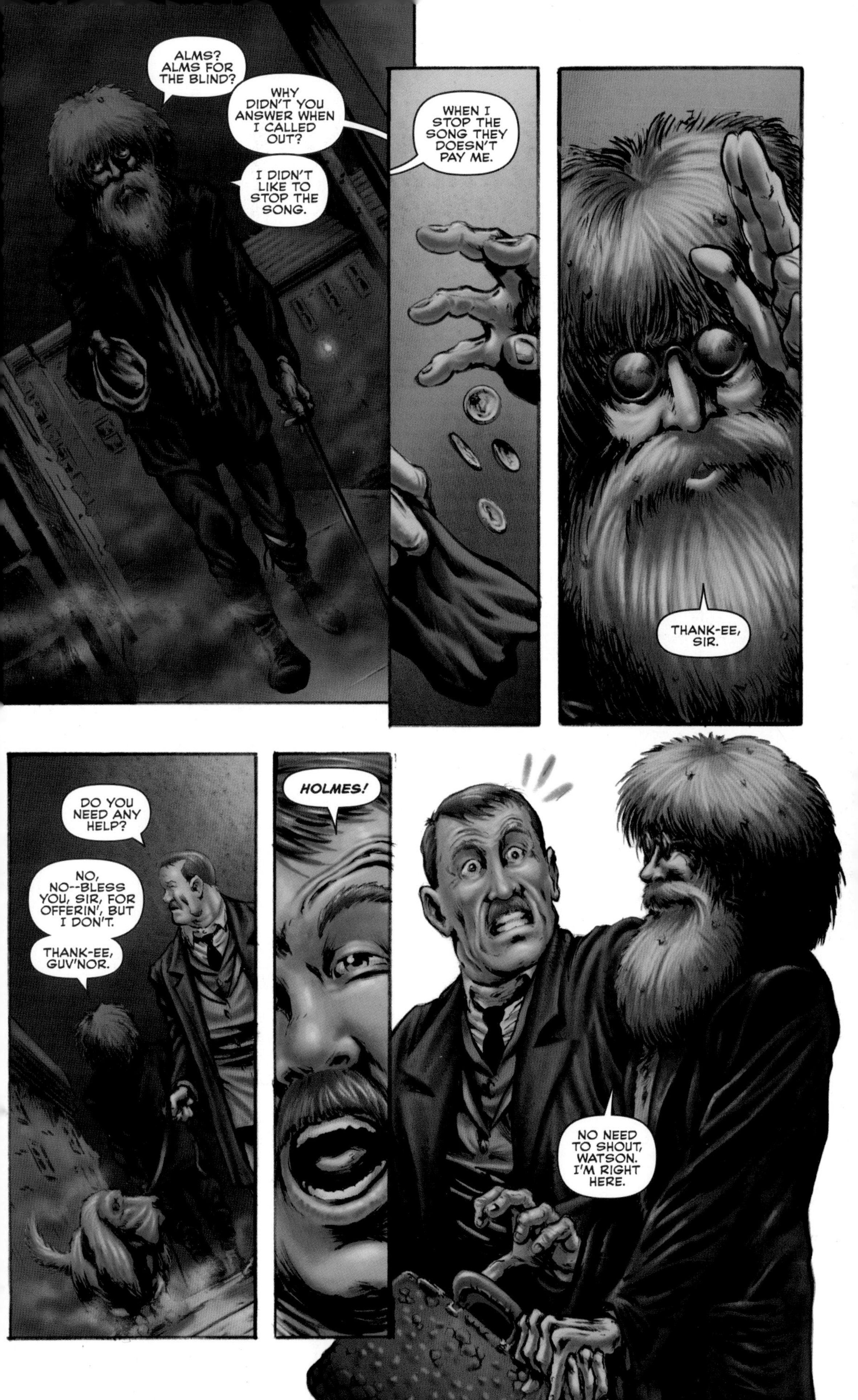
ALMS? ALMS FOR THE BLIND?
WHY DIDN'T YOU ANSWER WHEN I CALLED OUT?
I DIDN'T LIKE TO STOP THE SONG.
WHEN I STOP THE SONG THEY DOESN'T PAY ME.
THANK-EE, SIR.
DO YOU NEED ANY HELP?
NO, NO--BLESS YOU, SIR, FOR OFFERIN', BUT I DON'T.
THANK-EE, GUV'NOR.
HOLMES!
NO NEED TO SHOUT, WATSON. I'M RIGHT HERE.

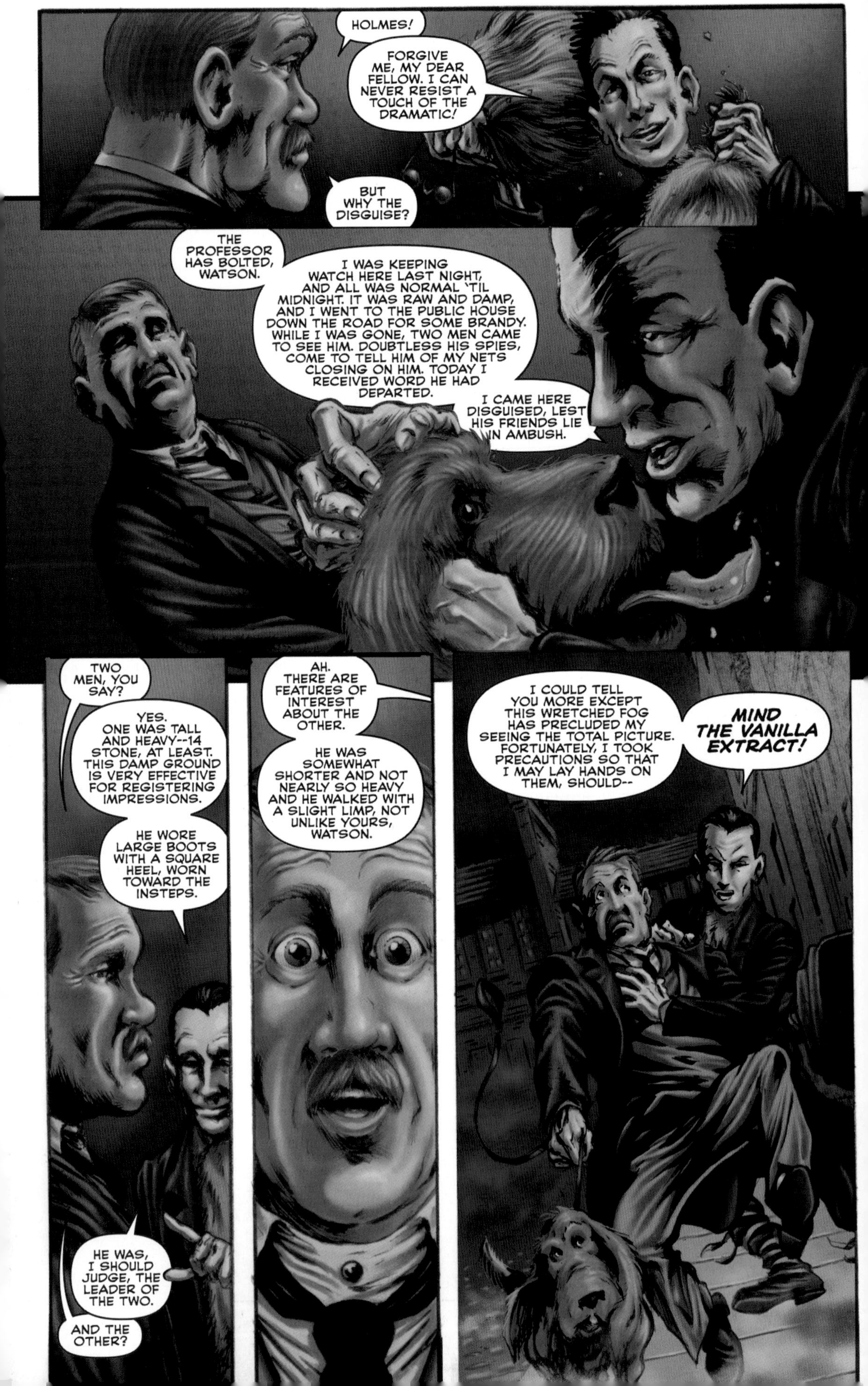
HOLMES!
FORGIVE ME, MY DEAR FELLOW. I CAN NEVER RESIST A TOUCH OF THE DRAMATIC!
BUT WHY THE DISGUISE?
THE PROFESSOR HAS BOLTED, WATSON.
I WAS KEEPING WATCH HERE LAST NIGHT, AND ALL WAS NORMAL 'TIL MIDNIGHT. IT WAS RAW AND DAMP, AND I WENT TO THE PUBLIC HOUSE DOWN THE ROAD FOR SOME BRANDY. WHILE I WAS GONE, TWO MEN CAME TO SEE HIM. DOUBTLESS HIS SPIES, COME TO TELL HIM OF MY NETS CLOSING ON HIM. TODAY I RECEIVED WORD HE HAD DEPARTED.
I CAME HERE DISGUISED, LEST HIS FRIENDS LIE IN AMBUSH.
TWO MEN, YOU SAY?
YES. ONE WAS TALL AND HEAVY--14 STONE, AT LEAST. THIS DAMP GROUND IS VERY EFFECTIVE FOR REGISTERING IMPRESSIONS.
HE WORE LARGE BOOTS WITH A SQUARE HEEL, WORN TOWARD THE INSTEPS.
HE WAS, I SHOULD JUDGE, THE LEADER OF THE TWO.
AND THE OTHER?
AH. THERE ARE FEATURES OF INTEREST ABOUT THE OTHER.
HE WAS SOMEWHAT SHORTER AND NOT NEARLY SO HEAVY AND HE WALKED WITH A SLIGHT LIMP, NOT UNLIKE YOURS, WATSON.
I COULD TELL YOU MORE EXCEPT THIS WRETCHED FOG HAS PRECLUDED MY SEEING THE TOTAL PICTURE. FORTUNATELY, I TOOK PRECAUTIONS SO THAT I MAY LAY HANDS ON THEM, SHOULD--
MIND THE VANILLA EXTRACT!

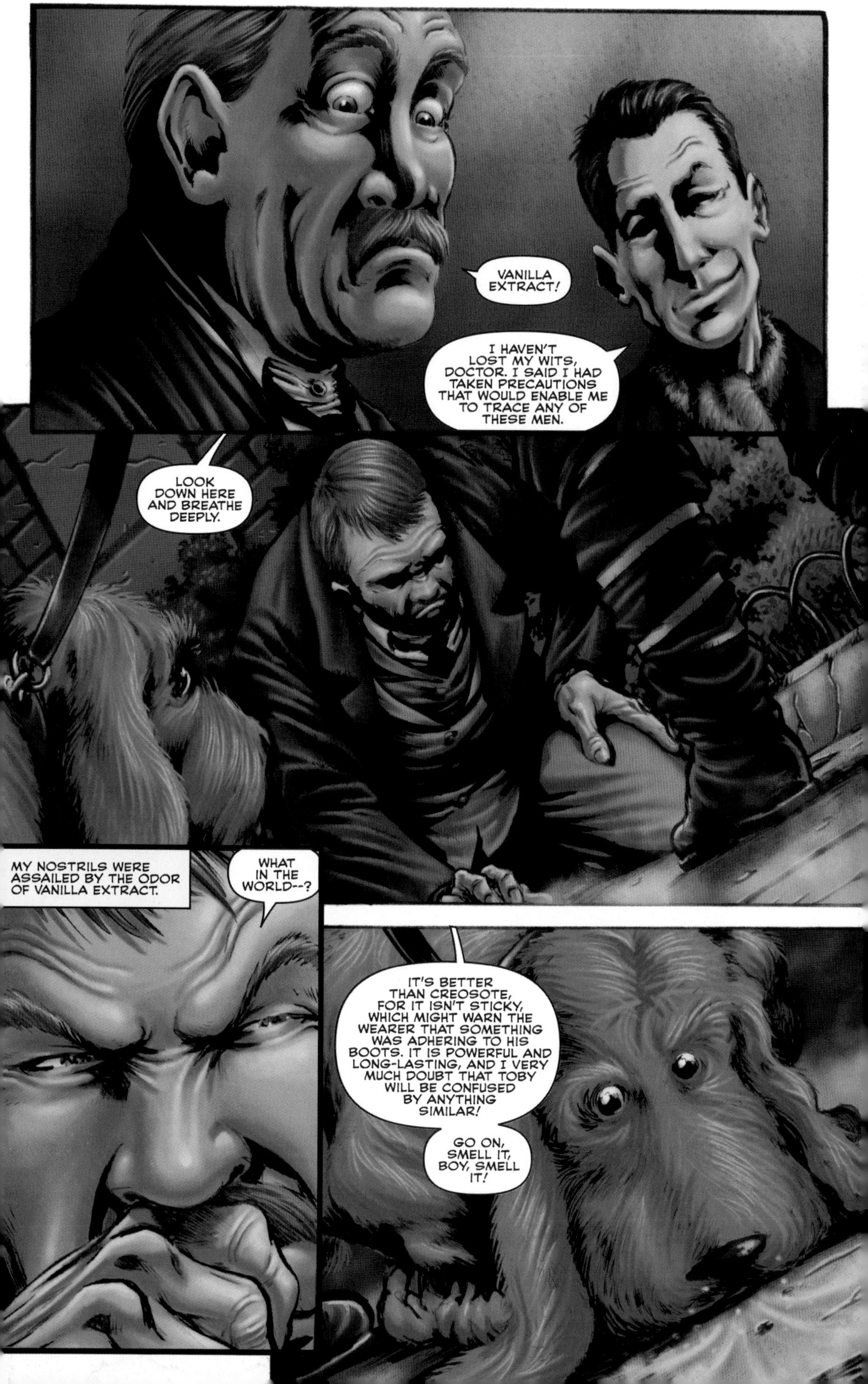
VANILLA EXTRACT!
I HAVEN'T LOST MY WITS, DOCTOR. I SAID I HAD TAKEN PRECAUTIONS THAT WOULD ENABLE ME TO TRACE ANY OF THESE MEN.
LOOK DOWN HERE AND BREATHE DEEPLY.
MY NOSTRILS WERE ASSAILED BY THE ODOR OF VANILLA EXTRACT.
WHAT IN THE WORLD--?
IT'S BETTER THAN CREOSOTE, FOR IT ISN'T STICKY, WHICH MIGHT WARN THE WEARER THAT SOMETHING WAS ADHERING TO HIS BOOTS. IT IS POWERFUL AND LONG-LASTING, AND I VERY MUCH DOUBT THAT TOBY WILL BE CONFUSED BY ANYTHING SIMILAR!
GO ON, SMELL IT, BOY, SMELL IT!

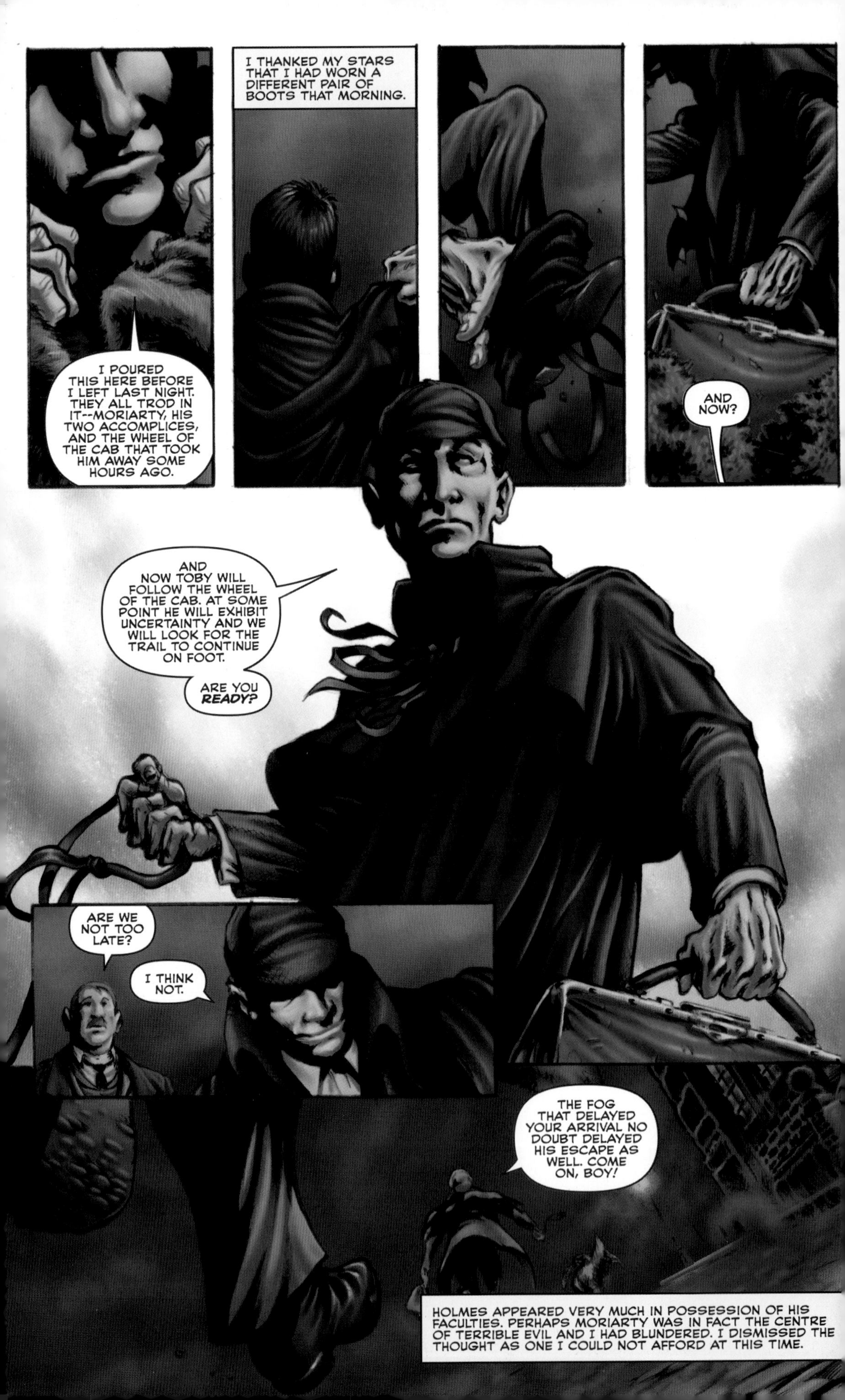
I POURED THIS HERE BEFORE I LEFT LAST NIGHT. THEY ALL TROD IN IT--MORIARTY, HIS TWO ACCOMPLICES, AND THE WHEEL OF THE CAB THAT TOOK HIM AWAY SOME HOURS AGO.
I THANKED MY STARS THAT I HAD WORN A DIFFERENT PAIR OF BOOTS THAT MORNING.
AND NOW?
AND NOW TOBY WILL FOLLOW THE WHEEL OF THE CAB. AT SOME POINT HE WILL EXHIBIT UNCERTAINTY AND WE WILL LOOK FOR THE TRAIL TO CONTINUE ON FOOT.
ARE YOU *READY?*
ARE WE NOT TOO LATE?
I THINK NOT.
THE FOG THAT DELAYED YOUR ARRIVAL NO DOUBT DELAYED HIS ESCAPE AS WELL. COME ON, BOY!
HOLMES APPEARED VERY MUCH IN POSSESSION OF HIS FACULTIES. PERHAPS MORIARTY WAS IN FACT THE CENTRE OF TERRIBLE EVIL AND I HAD BLUNDERED. I DISMISSED THE THOUGHT AS ONE I COULD NOT AFFORD AT THIS TIME.

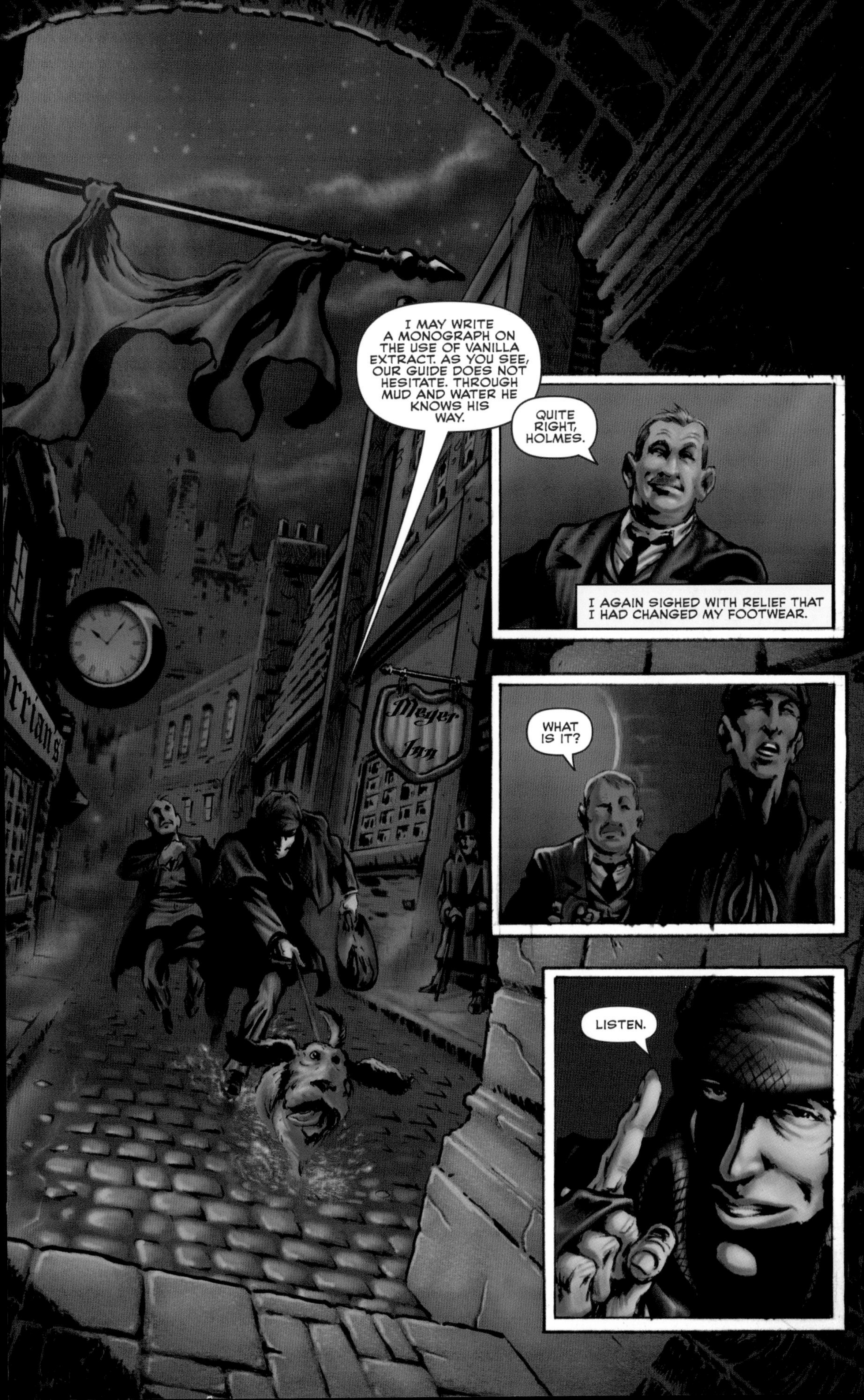
Meyer Inn
I MAY WRITE A MONOGRAPH ON THE USE OF VANILLA EXTRACT. AS YOU SEE, OUR GUIDE DOES NOT HESITATE. THROUGH MUD AND WATER HE KNOWS HIS WAY.
QUITE RIGHT, HOLMES.
I AGAIN SIGHED WITH RELIEF THAT I HAD CHANGED MY FOOTWEAR.
WHAT IS IT?
LISTEN.

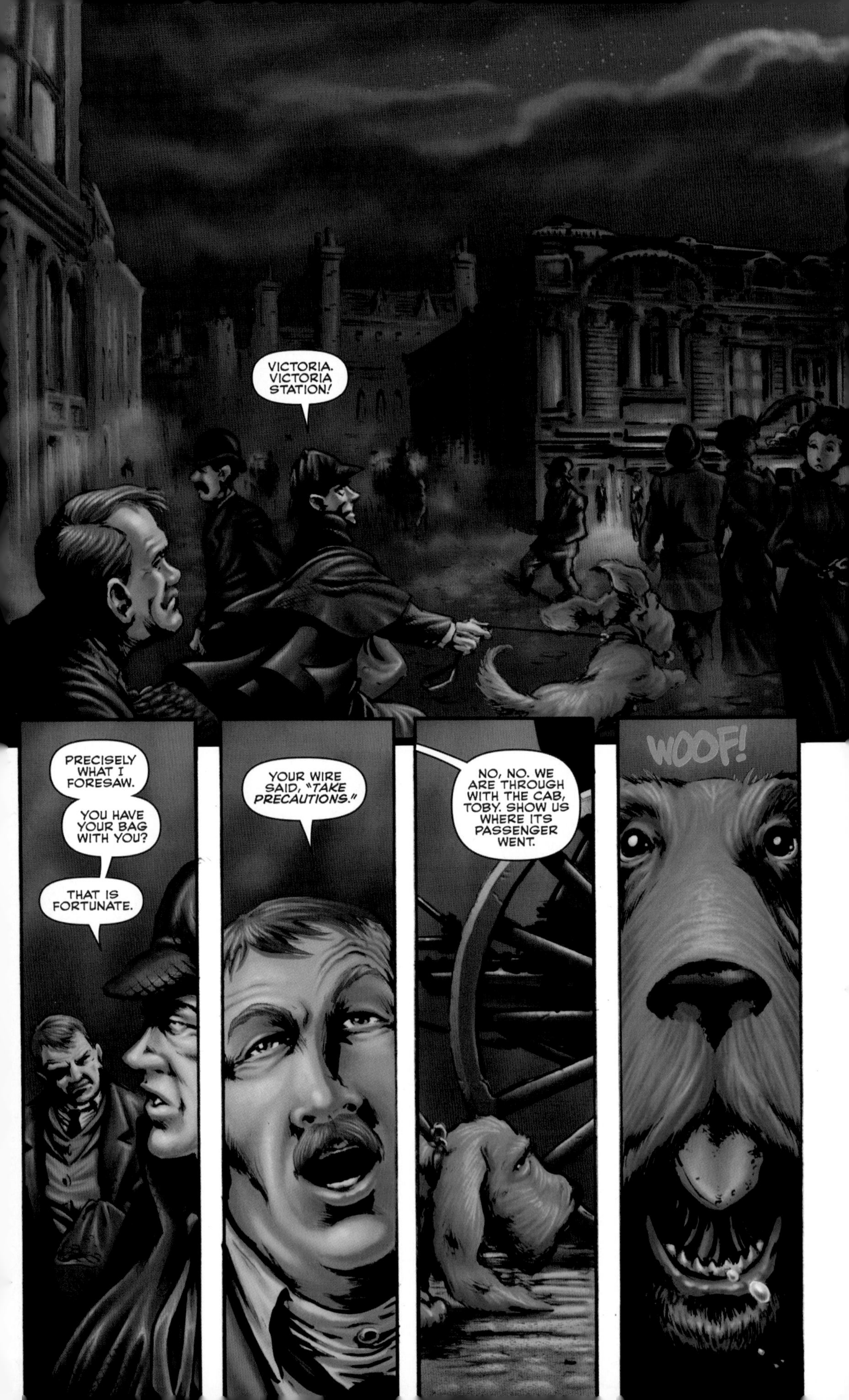
VICTORIA. VICTORIA STATION!
PRECISELY WHAT I FORESAW.
YOU HAVE YOUR BAG WITH YOU?
THAT IS FORTUNATE.
YOUR WIRE SAID, "TAKE PRECAUTIONS."
NO, NO. WE ARE THROUGH WITH THE CAB, TOBY. SHOW US WHERE ITS PASSENGER WENT.
WOOF!

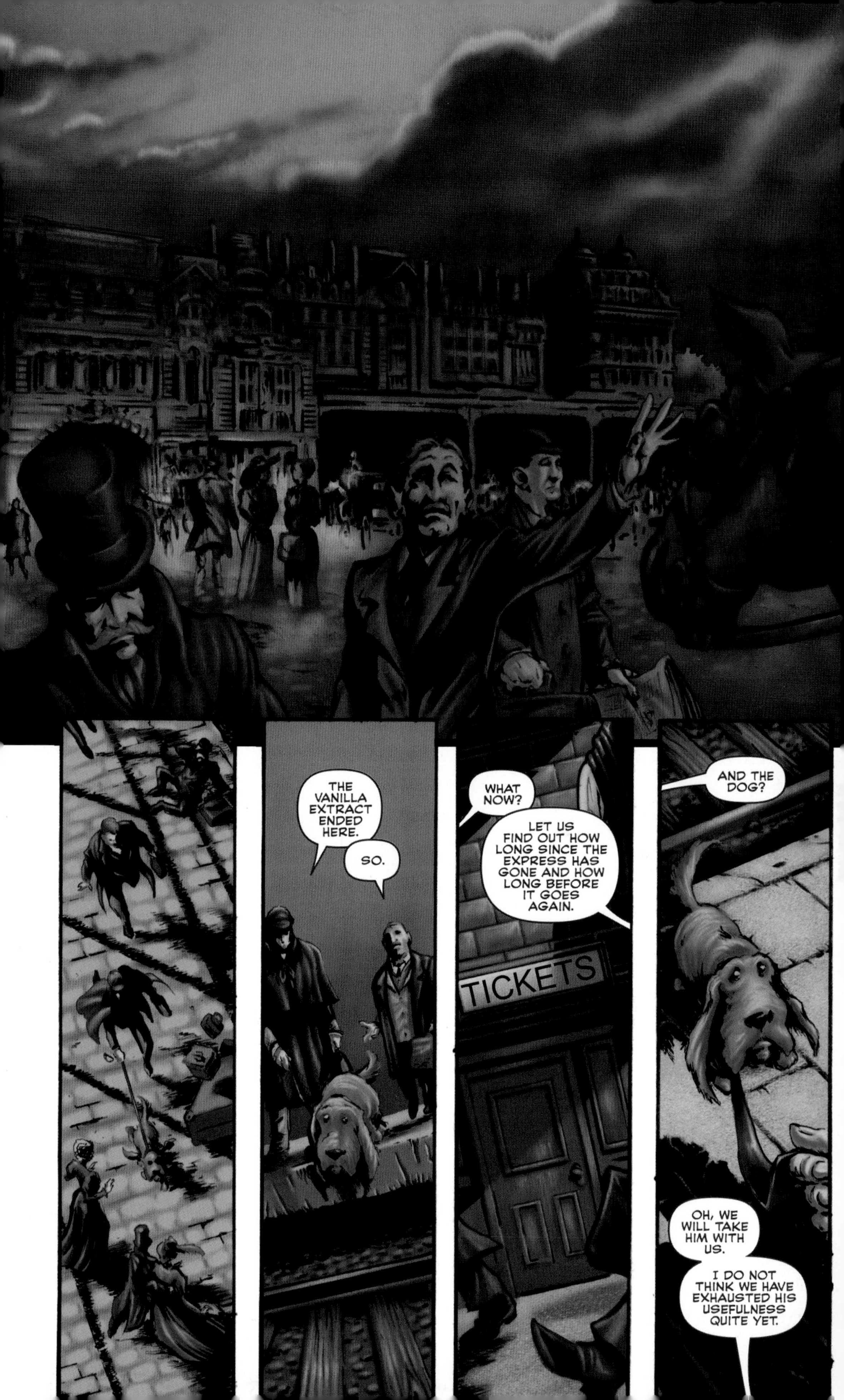
THE VANILLA EXTRACT ENDED HERE.
SO.
WHAT NOW?
LET US FIND OUT HOW LONG SINCE THE EXPRESS HAS GONE AND HOW LONG BEFORE IT GOES AGAIN.
TICKETS
AND THE DOG?
OH, WE WILL TAKE HIM WITH US.
I DO NOT THINK WE HAVE EXHAUSTED HIS USEFULNESS QUITE YET.

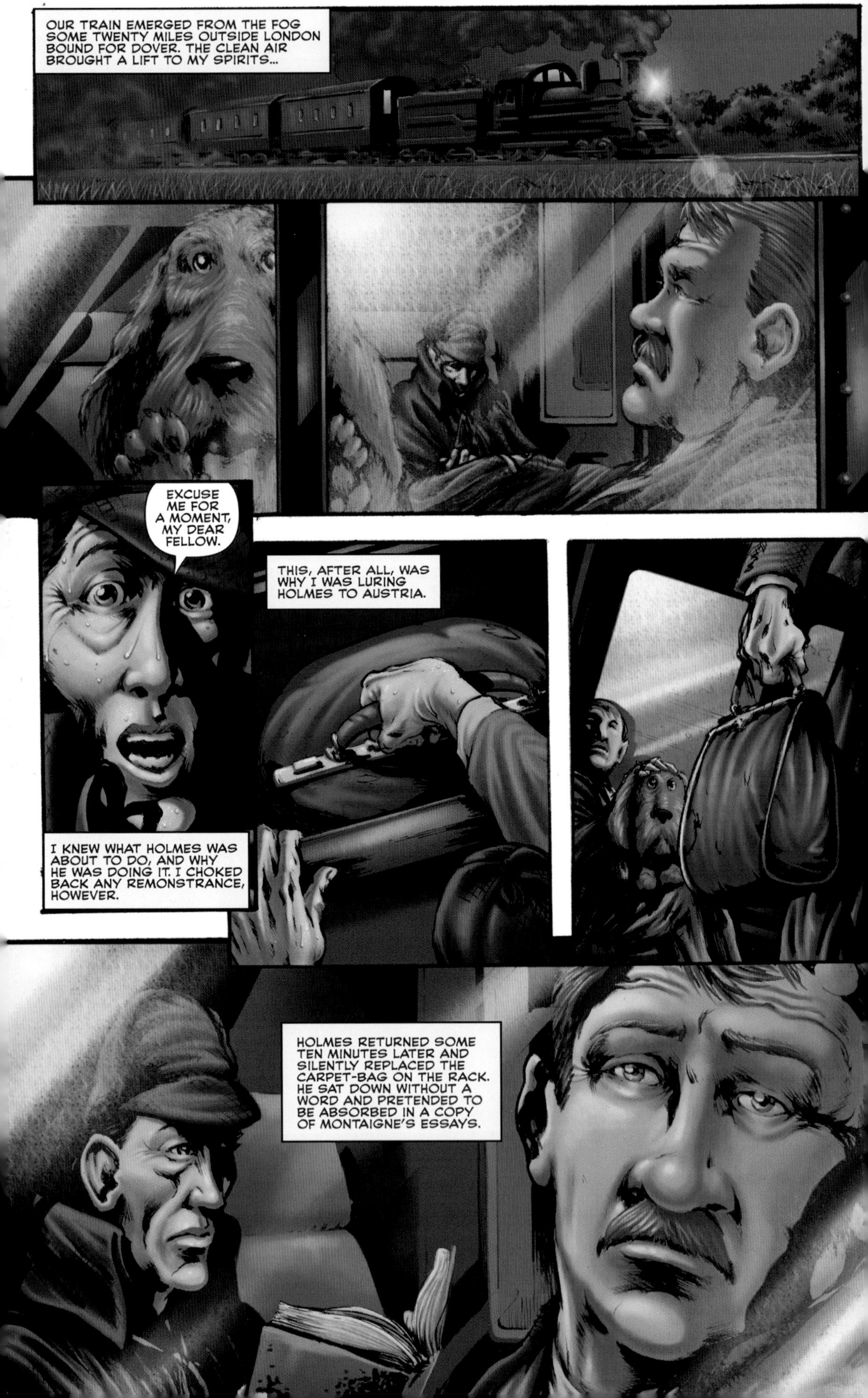

OUR TRAIN EMERGED FROM THE FOG SOME TWENTY MILES OUTSIDE LONDON BOUND FOR DOVER. THE CLEAN AIR BROUGHT A LIFT TO MY SPIRITS...
EXCUSE ME FOR A MOMENT, MY DEAR FELLOW.
THIS, AFTER ALL, WAS WHY I WAS LURING HOLMES TO AUSTRIA.
I KNEW WHAT HOLMES WAS ABOUT TO DO, AND WHY HE WAS DOING IT. I CHOKED BACK ANY REMONSTRANCE, HOWEVER.
HOLMES RETURNED SOME TEN MINUTES LATER AND SILENTLY REPLACED THE CARPET-BAG ON THE RACK. HE SAT DOWN WITHOUT A WORD AND PRETENDED TO BE ABSORBED IN A COPY OF MONTAIGNE'S ESSAYS.

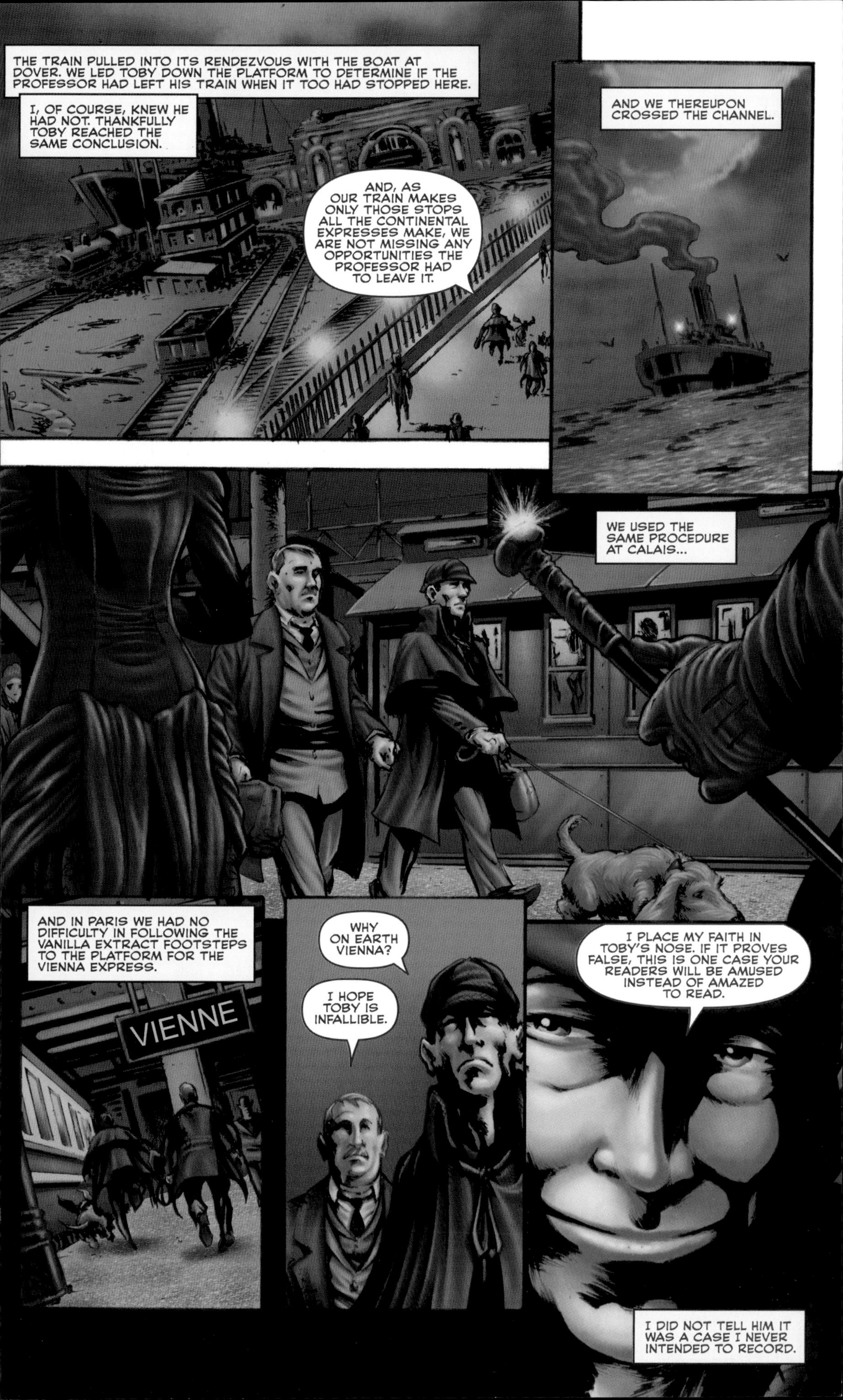
THE TRAIN PULLED INTO ITS RENDEZVOUS WITH THE BOAT AT DOVER. WE LED TOBY DOWN THE PLATFORM TO DETERMINE IF THE PROFESSOR HAD LEFT HIS TRAIN WHEN IT TOO HAD STOPPED HERE.
I, OF COURSE, KNEW HE HAD NOT. THANKFULLY TOBY REACHED THE SAME CONCLUSION.
AND, AS OUR TRAIN MAKES ONLY THOSE STOPS ALL THE CONTINENTAL EXPRESSES MAKE, WE ARE NOT MISSING ANY OPPORTUNITIES THE PROFESSOR HAD TO LEAVE IT.
AND WE THEREUPON CROSSED THE CHANNEL.
WE USED THE SAME PROCEDURE AT CALAIS...
AND IN PARIS WE HAD NO DIFFICULTY IN FOLLOWING THE VANILLA EXTRACT FOOTSTEPS TO THE PLATFORM FOR THE VIENNA EXPRESS.
VIENNE
WHY ON EARTH VIENNA?
I HOPE TOBY IS INFALLIBLE.
I PLACE MY FAITH IN TOBY'S NOSE. IF IT PROVES FALSE, THIS IS ONE CASE YOUR READERS WILL BE AMUSED INSTEAD OF AMAZED TO READ.
I DID NOT TELL HIM IT WAS A CASE I NEVER INTENDED TO RECORD.

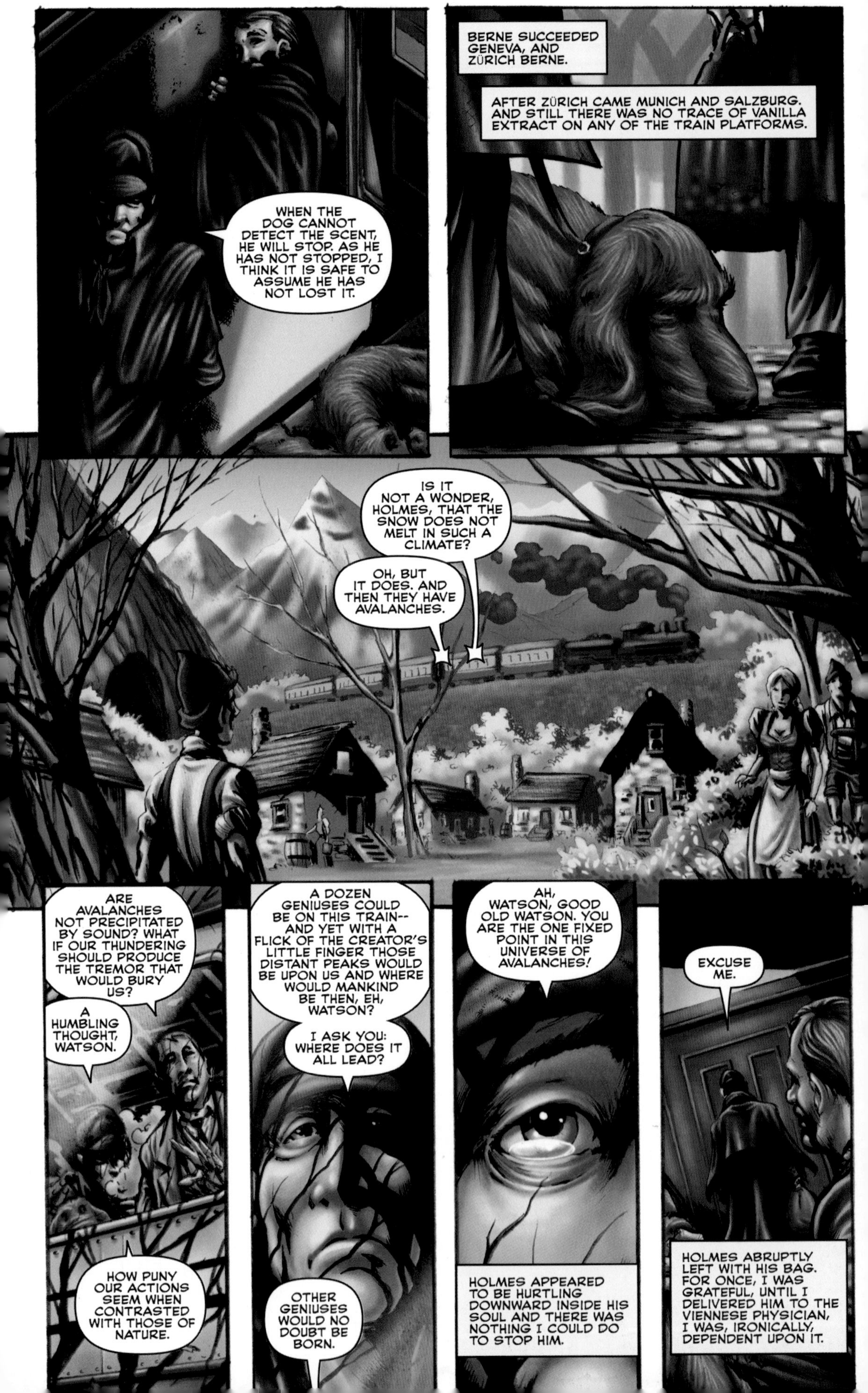
WHEN THE DOG CANNOT DETECT THE SCENT, HE WILL STOP. AS HE HAS NOT STOPPED, I THINK IT IS SAFE TO ASSUME HE HAS NOT LOST IT.
BERNE SUCCEEDED GENEVA, AND ZÜRICH BERNE.
AFTER ZÜRICH CAME MUNICH AND SALZBURG. AND STILL THERE WAS NO TRACE OF VANILLA EXTRACT ON ANY OF THE TRAIN PLATFORMS.
IS IT NOT A WONDER, HOLMES, THAT THE SNOW DOES NOT MELT IN SUCH A CLIMATE?
OH, BUT IT DOES. AND THEN THEY HAVE AVALANCHES.
ARE AVALANCHES NOT PRECIPITATED BY SOUND? WHAT IF OUR THUNDERING SHOULD PRODUCE THE TREMOR THAT WOULD BURY US?
A HUMBLING THOUGHT, WATSON.
HOW PUNY OUR ACTIONS SEEM WHEN CONTRASTED WITH THOSE OF NATURE.
A DOZEN GENIUSES COULD BE ON THIS TRAIN-- AND YET WITH A FLICK OF THE CREATOR'S LITTLE FINGER THOSE DISTANT PEAKS WOULD BE UPON US AND WHERE WOULD MANKIND BE THEN, EH, WATSON?
I ASK YOU: WHERE DOES IT ALL LEAD?
OTHER GENIUSES WOULD NO DOUBT BE BORN.
AH, WATSON, GOOD OLD WATSON. YOU ARE THE ONE FIXED POINT IN THIS UNIVERSE OF AVALANCHES!
HOLMES APPEARED TO BE HURTLING DOWNWARD INSIDE HIS SOUL AND THERE WAS NOTHING I COULD DO TO STOP HIM.
EXCUSE ME.
HOLMES ABRUPTLY LEFT WITH HIS BAG. FOR ONCE, I WAS GRATEFUL, UNTIL I DELIVERED HIM TO THE VIENNESE PHYSICIAN, I WAS, IRONICALLY, DEPENDENT UPON IT.

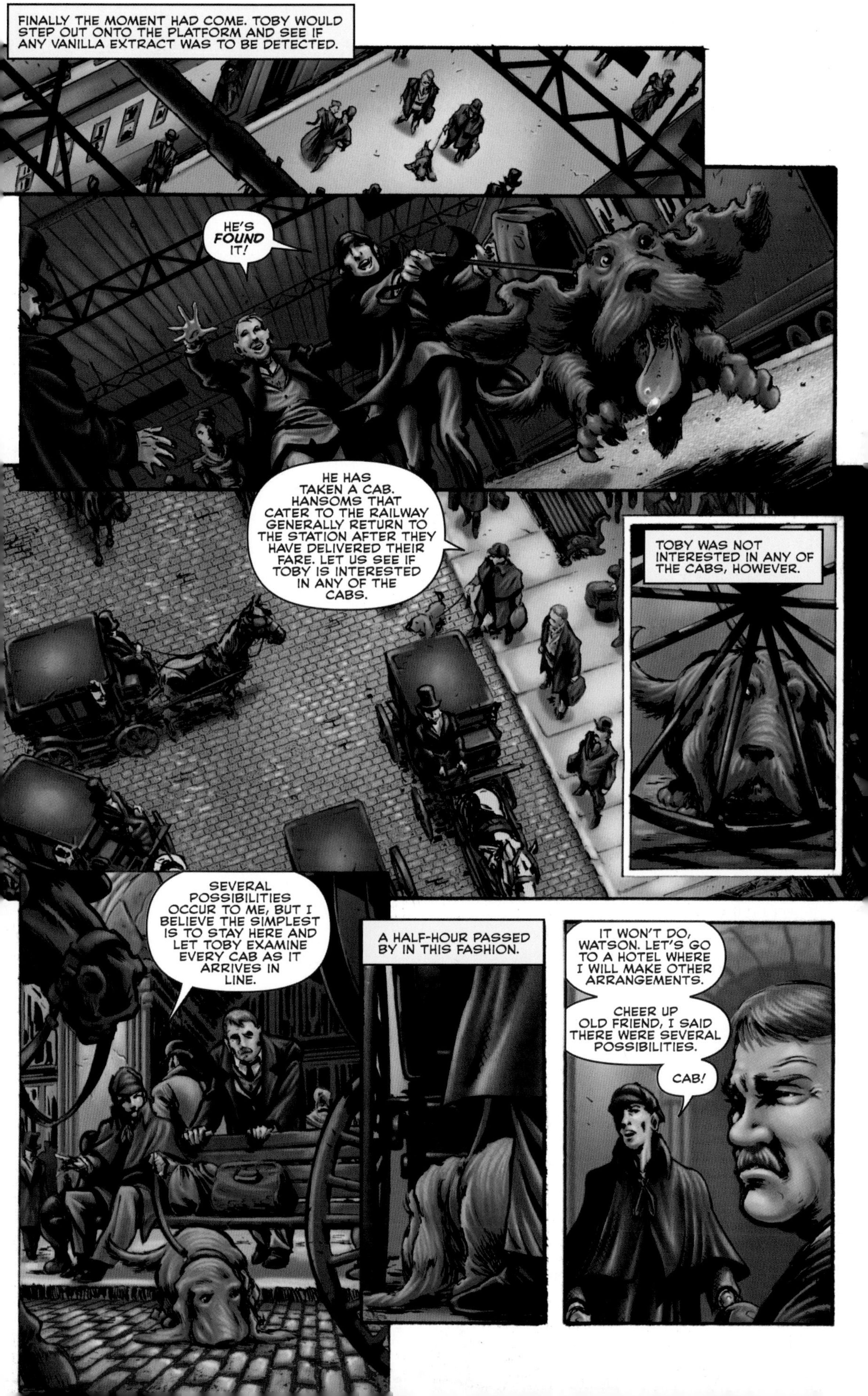
FINALLY THE MOMENT HAD COME. TOBY WOULD STEP OUT ONTO THE PLATFORM AND SEE IF ANY VANILLA EXTRACT WAS TO BE DETECTED.
HE'S *FOUND* IT!
HE HAS TAKEN A CAB. HANSOMS THAT CATER TO THE RAILWAY GENERALLY RETURN TO THE STATION AFTER THEY HAVE DELIVERED THEIR FARE. LET US SEE IF TOBY IS INTERESTED IN ANY OF THE CABS.
TOBY WAS NOT INTERESTED IN ANY OF THE CABS, HOWEVER.
SEVERAL POSSIBILITIES OCCUR TO ME, BUT I BELIEVE THE SIMPLEST IS TO STAY HERE AND LET TOBY EXAMINE EVERY CAB AS IT ARRIVES IN LINE.
A HALF-HOUR PASSED BY IN THIS FASHION.
IT WON'T DO, WATSON. LET'S GO TO A HOTEL WHERE I WILL MAKE OTHER ARRANGEMENTS.
CHEER UP OLD FRIEND, I SAID THERE WERE SEVERAL POSSIBILITIES.
CAB!

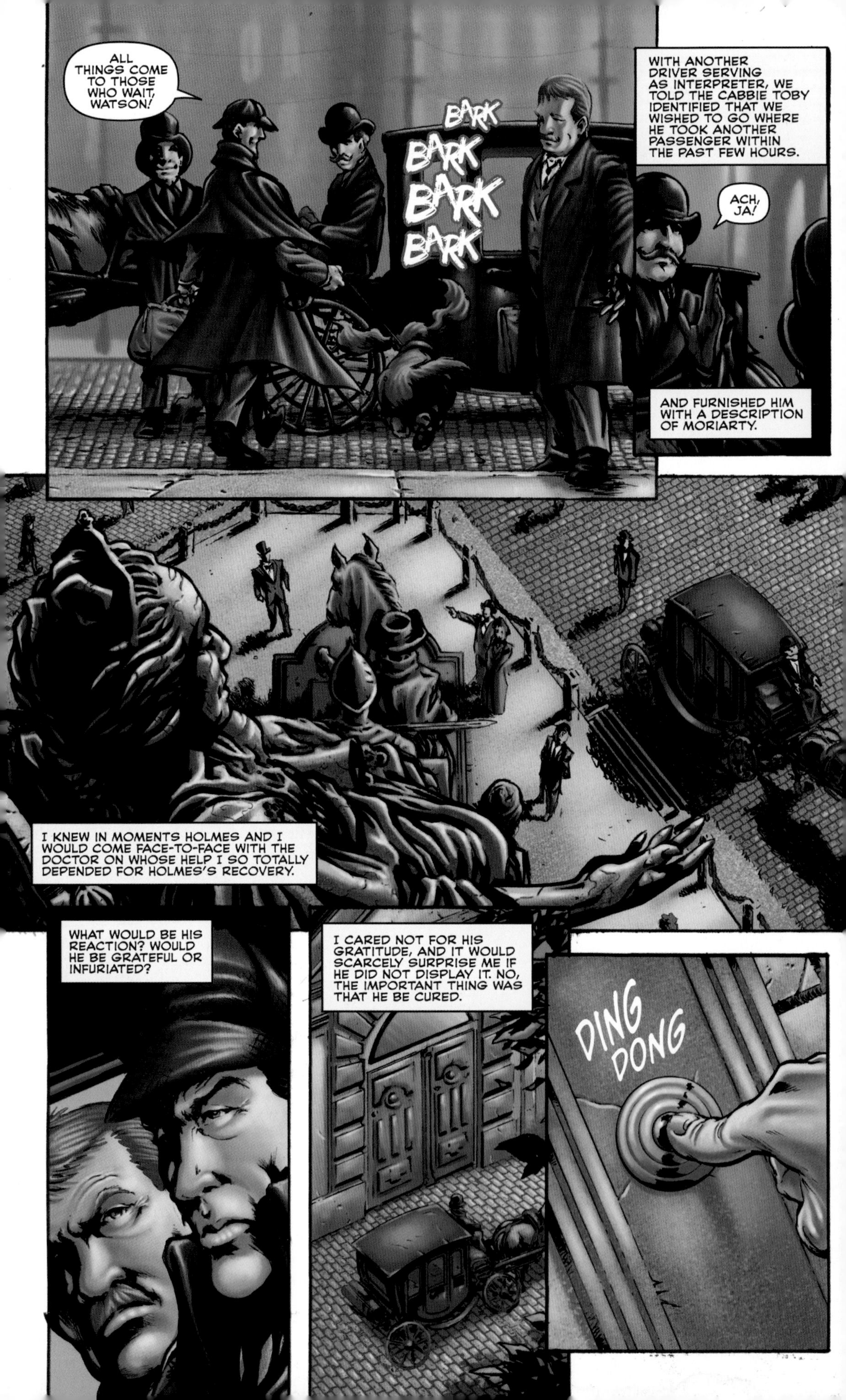

ALL THINGS COME TO THOSE WHO WAIT, WATSON!
BARK BARK BARK BARK
WITH ANOTHER DRIVER SERVING AS INTERPRETER, WE TOLD THE CABBIE TOBY IDENTIFIED THAT WE WISHED TO GO WHERE HE TOOK ANOTHER PASSENGER WITHIN THE PAST FEW HOURS.
ACH, JA!
AND FURNISHED HIM WITH A DESCRIPTION OF MORIARTY.
I KNEW IN MOMENTS HOLMES AND I WOULD COME FACE-TO-FACE WITH THE DOCTOR ON WHOSE HELP I SO TOTALLY DEPENDED FOR HOLMES'S RECOVERY.
WHAT WOULD BE HIS REACTION? WOULD HE BE GRATEFUL OR INFURIATED?
I CARED NOT FOR HIS GRATITUDE, AND IT WOULD SCARCELY SURPRISE ME IF HE DID NOT DISPLAY IT. NO, THE IMPORTANT THING WAS THAT HE BE CURED.
DING DONG

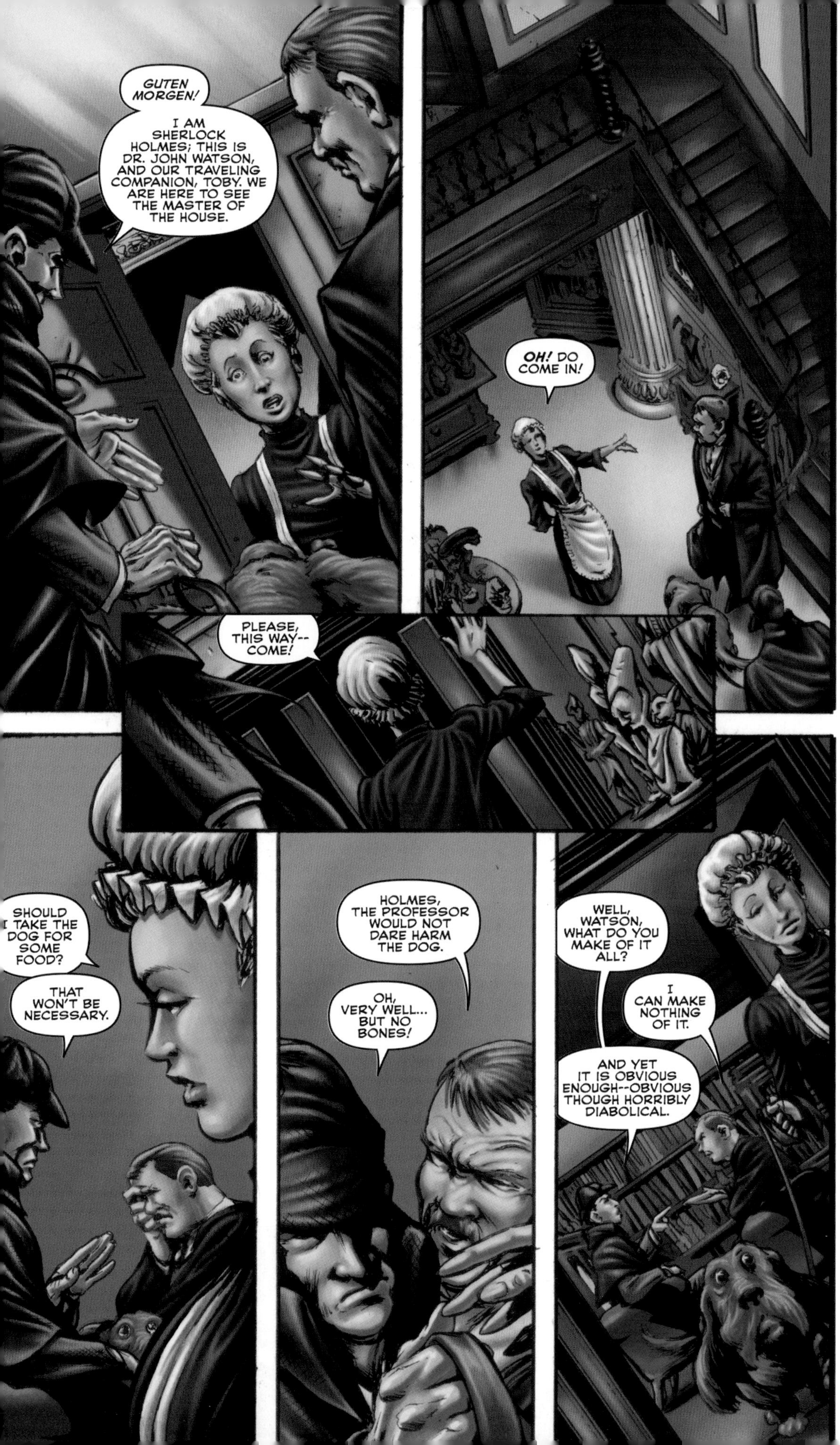
GUTEN MORGEN!
I AM SHERLOCK HOLMES; THIS IS DR. JOHN WATSON, AND OUR TRAVELING COMPANION, TOBY. WE ARE HERE TO SEE THE MASTER OF THE HOUSE.
OH! DO COME IN!
PLEASE, THIS WAY-- COME!
SHOULD I TAKE THE DOG FOR SOME FOOD?
THAT WON'T BE NECESSARY.
HOLMES, THE PROFESSOR WOULD NOT DARE HARM THE DOG.
OH, VERY WELL... BUT NO BONES!
WELL, WATSON, WHAT DO YOU MAKE OF IT ALL?
I CAN MAKE NOTHING OF IT.
AND YET IT IS OBVIOUS ENOUGH--OBVIOUS THOUGH HORRIBLY DIABOLICAL.

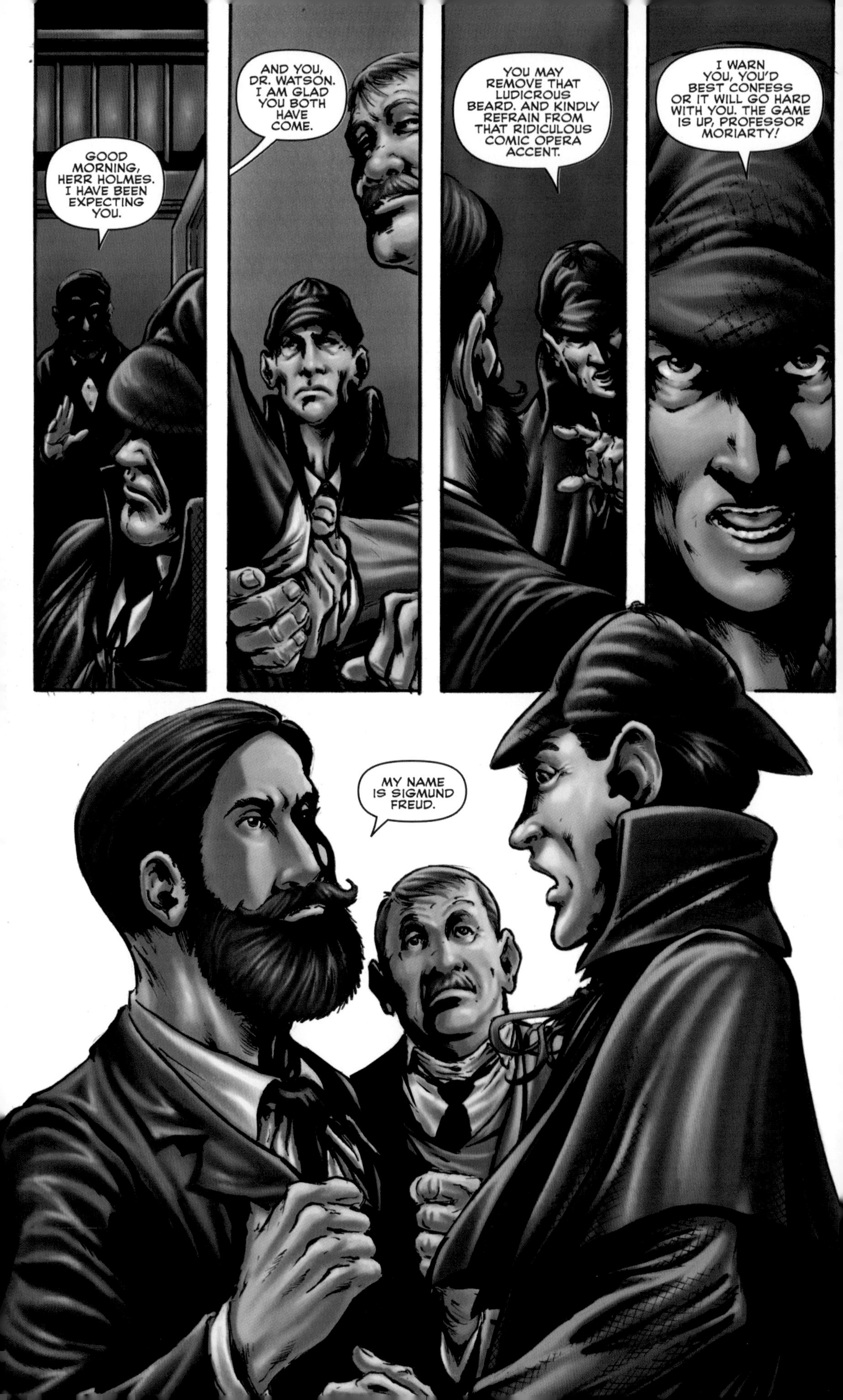
GOOD MORNING, HERR HOLMES. I HAVE BEEN EXPECTING YOU.
AND YOU, DR. WATSON. I AM GLAD YOU BOTH HAVE COME.
YOU MAY REMOVE THAT LUDICROUS BEARD. AND KINDLY REFRAIN FROM THAT RIDICULOUS COMIC OPERA ACCENT.
I WARN YOU, YOU'D BEST CONFESS OR IT WILL GO HARD WITH YOU. THE GAME IS UP, PROFESSOR MORIARTY!
MY NAME IS SIGMUND FREUD.

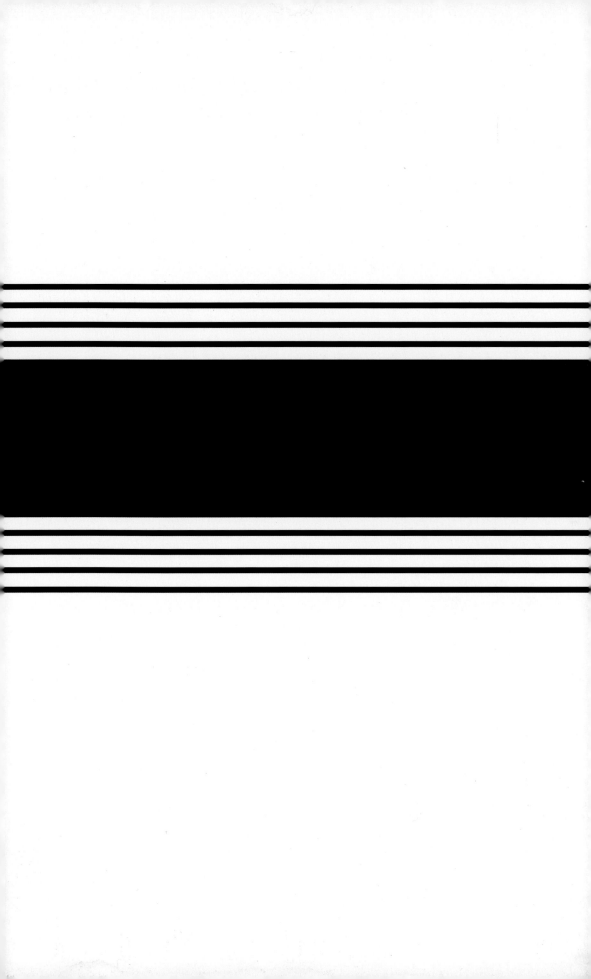

ART BY **KELLEY JONES**

COLORS BY **JAY FOTOS**

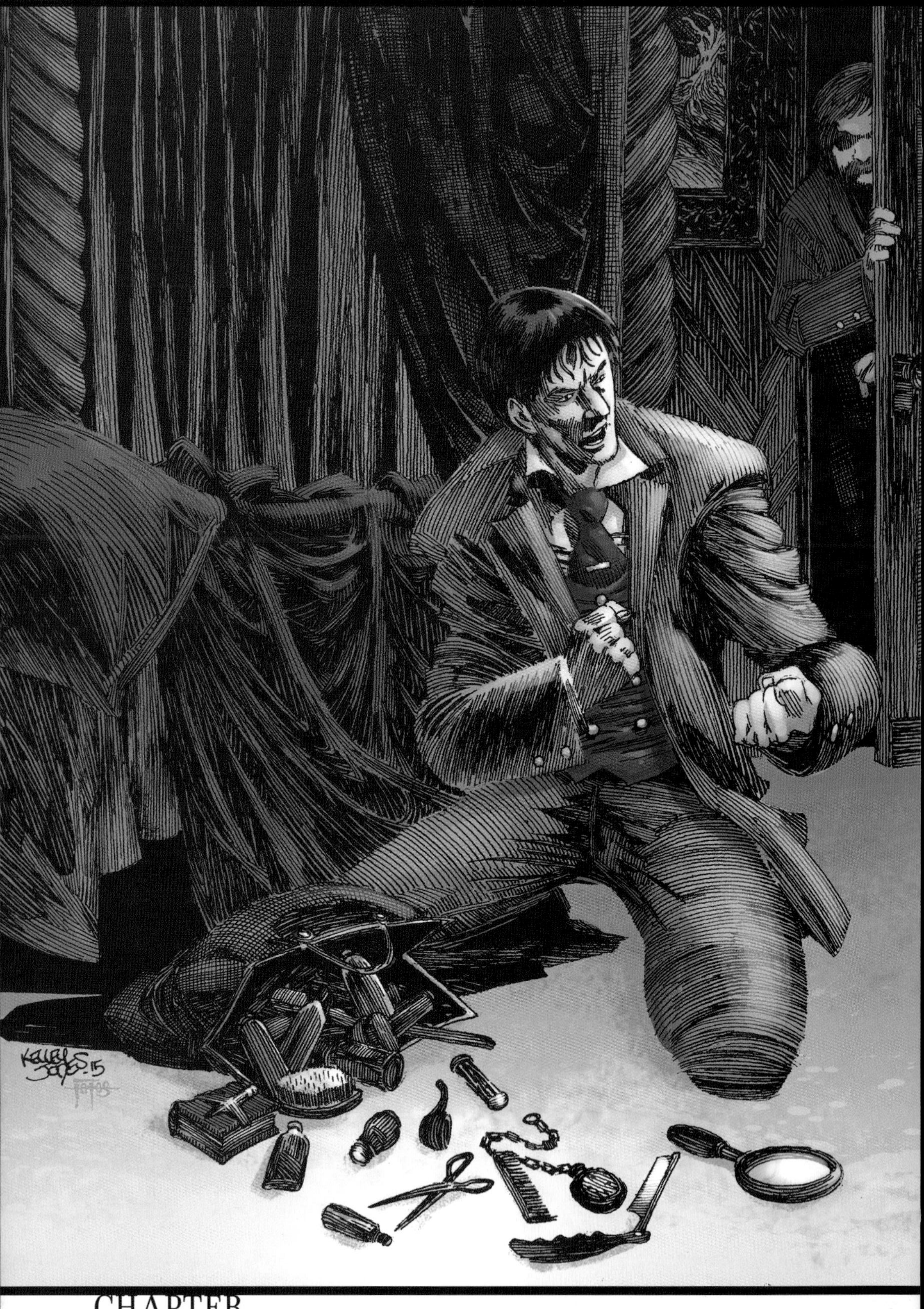

CHAPTER THREE

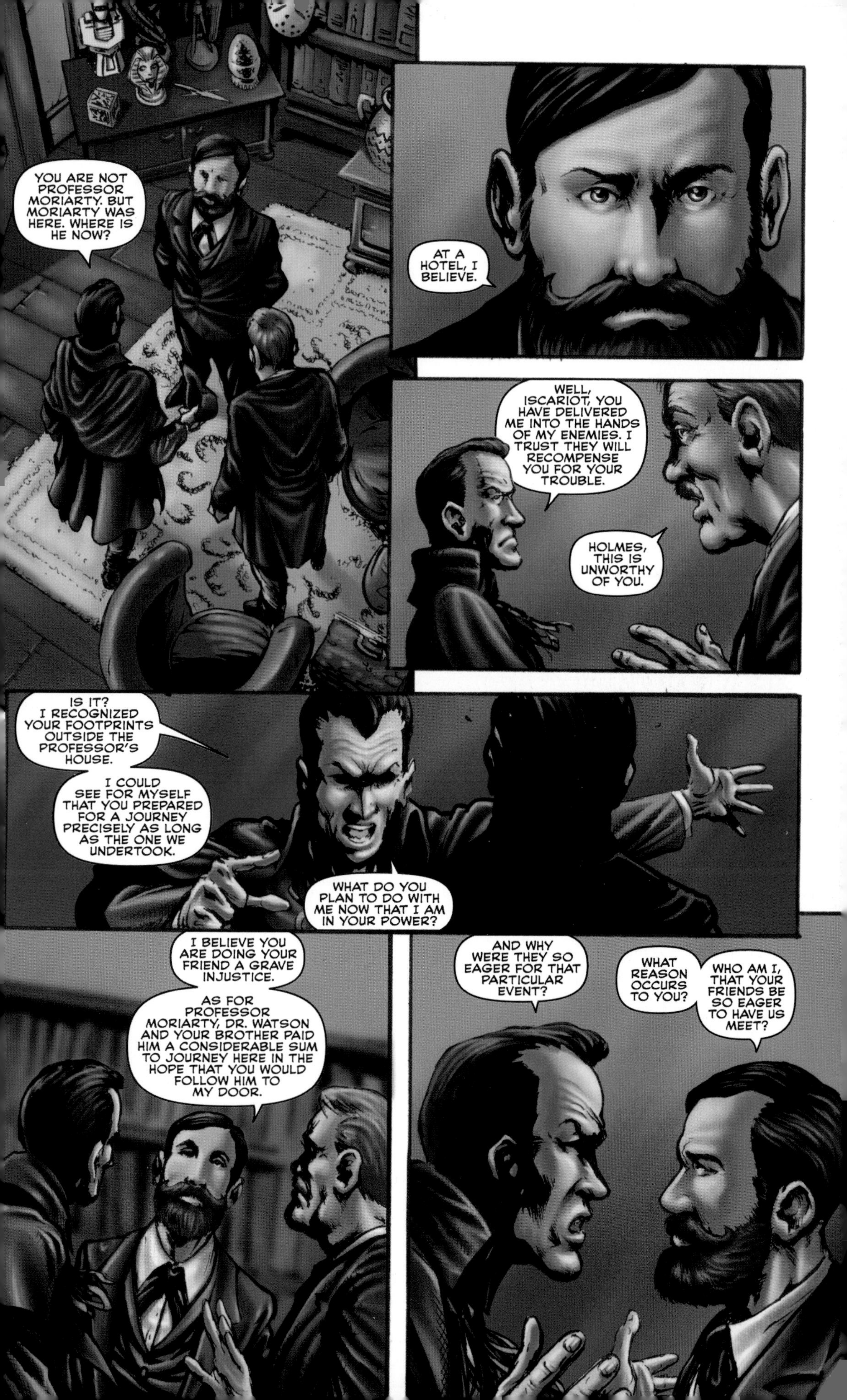
YOU ARE NOT PROFESSOR MORIARTY. BUT MORIARTY WAS HERE. WHERE IS HE NOW?
AT A HOTEL, I BELIEVE.
WELL, ISCARIOT, YOU HAVE DELIVERED ME INTO THE HANDS OF MY ENEMIES. I TRUST THEY WILL RECOMPENSE YOU FOR YOUR TROUBLE.
HOLMES, THIS IS UNWORTHY OF YOU.
IS IT? I RECOGNIZED YOUR FOOTPRINTS OUTSIDE THE PROFESSOR'S HOUSE.
I COULD SEE FOR MYSELF THAT YOU PREPARED FOR A JOURNEY PRECISELY AS LONG AS THE ONE WE UNDERTOOK.
WHAT DO YOU PLAN TO DO WITH ME NOW THAT I AM IN YOUR POWER?
I BELIEVE YOU ARE DOING YOUR FRIEND A GRAVE INJUSTICE.
AS FOR PROFESSOR MORIARTY, DR. WATSON AND YOUR BROTHER PAID HIM A CONSIDERABLE SUM TO JOURNEY HERE IN THE HOPE THAT YOU WOULD FOLLOW HIM TO MY DOOR.
AND WHY WERE THEY SO EAGER FOR THAT PARTICULAR EVENT?
WHAT REASON OCCURS TO YOU?
WHO AM I, THAT YOUR FRIENDS BE SO EAGER TO HAVE US MEET?

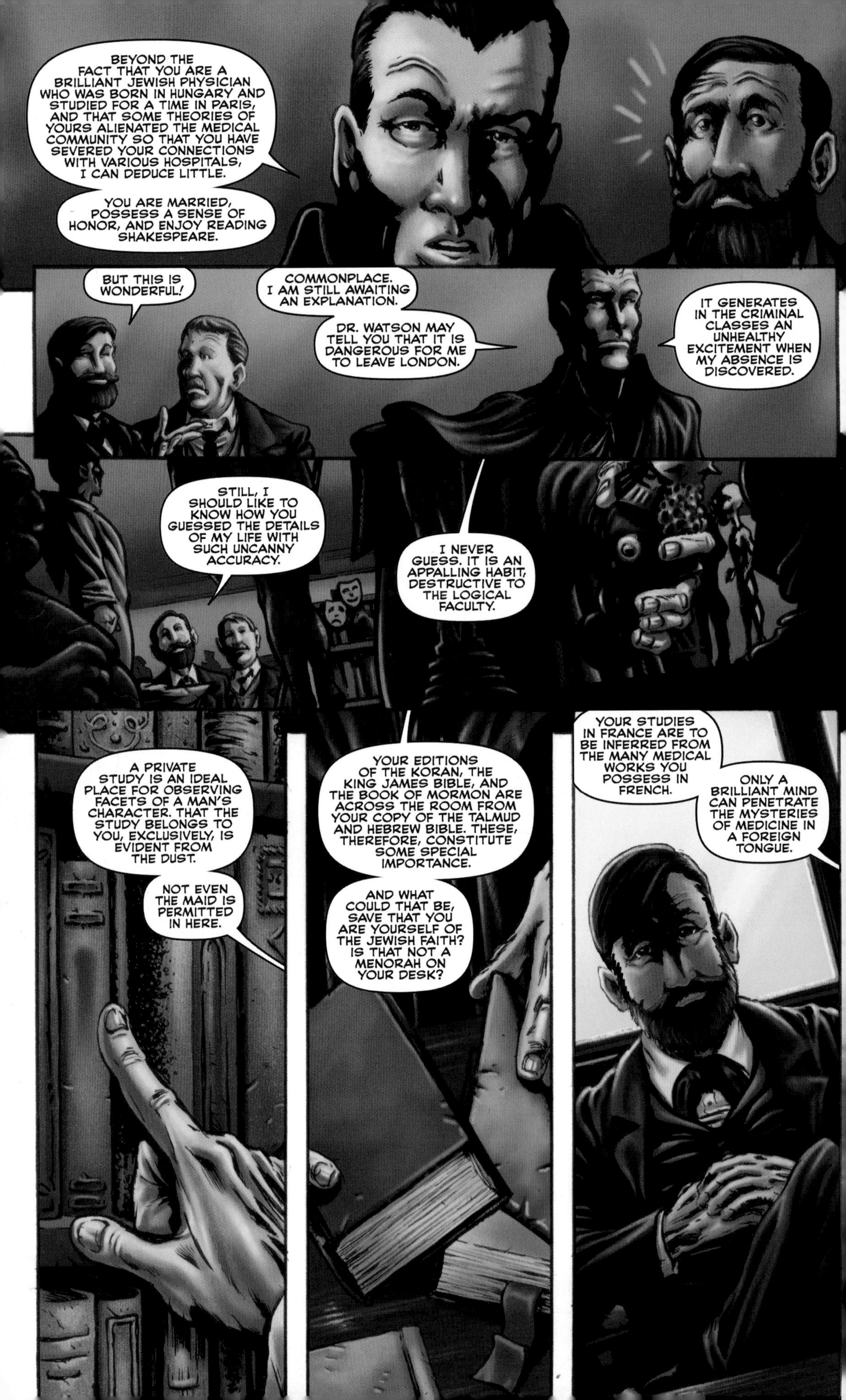
BEYOND THE FACT THAT YOU ARE A BRILLIANT JEWISH PHYSICIAN WHO WAS BORN IN HUNGARY AND STUDIED FOR A TIME IN PARIS, AND THAT SOME THEORIES OF YOURS ALIENATED THE MEDICAL COMMUNITY SO THAT YOU HAVE SEVERED YOUR CONNECTIONS WITH VARIOUS HOSPITALS, I CAN DEDUCE LITTLE.
YOU ARE MARRIED, POSSESS A SENSE OF HONOR, AND ENJOY READING SHAKESPEARE.
BUT THIS IS WONDERFUL!
COMMONPLACE. I AM STILL AWAITING AN EXPLANATION.
DR. WATSON MAY TELL YOU THAT IT IS DANGEROUS FOR ME TO LEAVE LONDON.
IT GENERATES IN THE CRIMINAL CLASSES AN UNHEALTHY EXCITEMENT WHEN MY ABSENCE IS DISCOVERED.
STILL, I SHOULD LIKE TO KNOW HOW YOU GUESSED THE DETAILS OF MY LIFE WITH SUCH UNCANNY ACCURACY.
I NEVER GUESS. IT IS AN APPALLING HABIT, DESTRUCTIVE TO THE LOGICAL FACULTY.
A PRIVATE STUDY IS AN IDEAL PLACE FOR OBSERVING FACETS OF A MAN'S CHARACTER. THAT THE STUDY BELONGS TO YOU, EXCLUSIVELY, IS EVIDENT FROM THE DUST.
NOT EVEN THE MAID IS PERMITTED IN HERE.
YOUR EDITIONS OF THE KORAN, THE KING JAMES BIBLE, AND THE BOOK OF MORMON ARE ACROSS THE ROOM FROM YOUR COPY OF THE TALMUD AND HEBREW BIBLE. THESE, THEREFORE, CONSTITUTE SOME SPECIAL IMPORTANCE.
AND WHAT COULD THAT BE, SAVE THAT YOU ARE YOURSELF OF THE JEWISH FAITH? IS THAT NOT A MENORAH ON YOUR DESK?
YOUR STUDIES IN FRANCE ARE TO BE INFERRED FROM THE MANY MEDICAL WORKS YOU POSSESS IN FRENCH.
ONLY A BRILLIANT MIND CAN PENETRATE THE MYSTERIES OF MEDICINE IN A FOREIGN TONGUE.

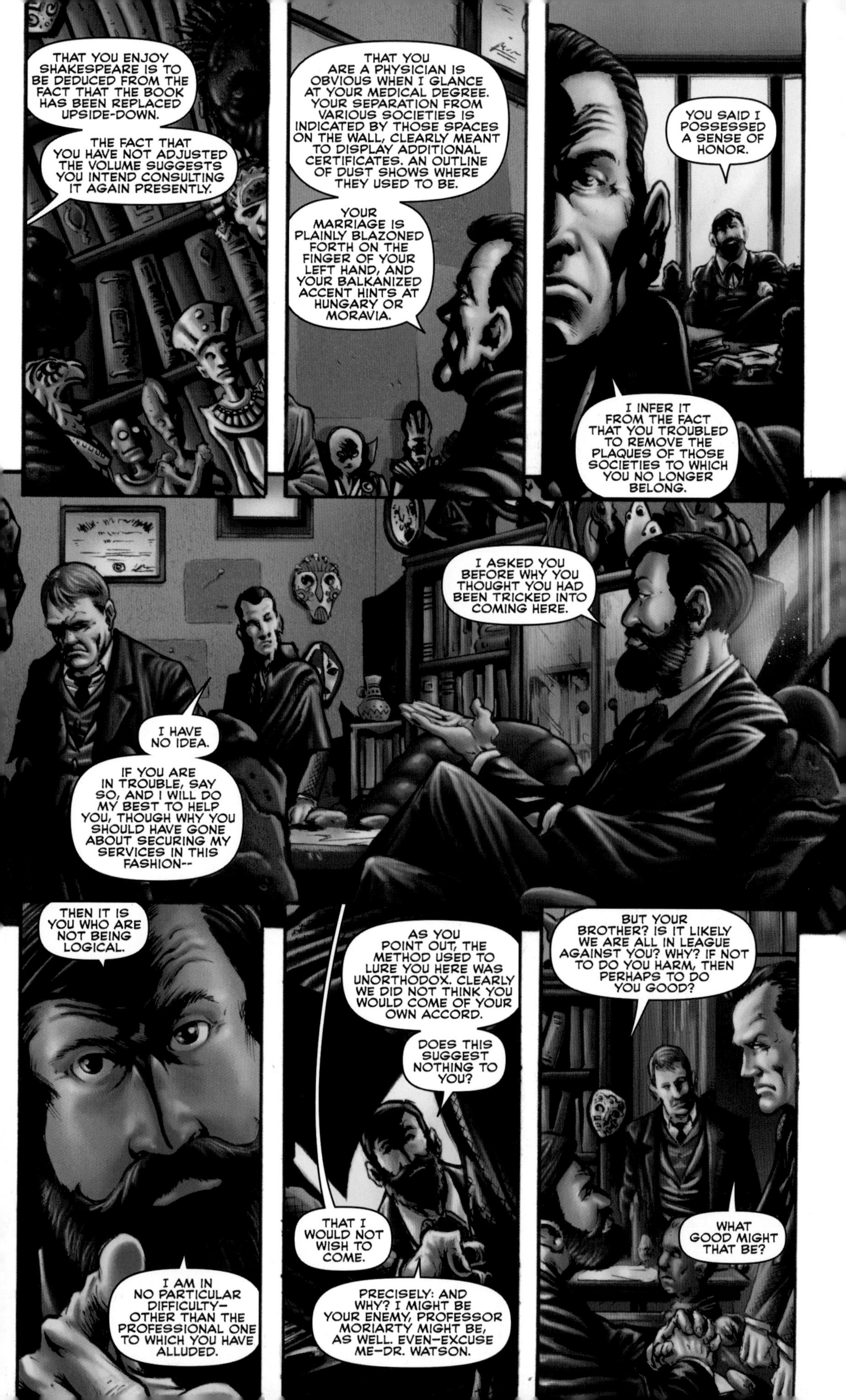
THAT YOU ENJOY SHAKESPEARE IS TO BE DEDUCED FROM THE FACT THAT THE BOOK HAS BEEN REPLACED UPSIDE-DOWN.
THE FACT THAT YOU HAVE NOT ADJUSTED THE VOLUME SUGGESTS YOU INTEND CONSULTING IT AGAIN PRESENTLY.
THAT YOU ARE A PHYSICIAN IS OBVIOUS WHEN I GLANCE AT YOUR MEDICAL DEGREE. YOUR SEPARATION FROM VARIOUS SOCIETIES IS INDICATED BY THOSE SPACES ON THE WALL, CLEARLY MEANT TO DISPLAY ADDITIONAL CERTIFICATES. AN OUTLINE OF DUST SHOWS WHERE THEY USED TO BE.
YOUR MARRIAGE IS PLAINLY BLAZONED FORTH ON THE FINGER OF YOUR LEFT HAND, AND YOUR BALKANIZED ACCENT HINTS AT HUNGARY OR MORAVIA.
YOU SAID I POSSESSED A SENSE OF HONOR.
I INFER IT FROM THE FACT THAT YOU TROUBLED TO REMOVE THE PLAQUES OF THOSE SOCIETIES TO WHICH YOU NO LONGER BELONG.
I ASKED YOU BEFORE WHY YOU THOUGHT YOU HAD BEEN TRICKED INTO COMING HERE.
I HAVE NO IDEA.
IF YOU ARE IN TROUBLE, SAY SO, AND I WILL DO MY BEST TO HELP YOU, THOUGH WHY YOU SHOULD HAVE GONE ABOUT SECURING MY SERVICES IN THIS FASHION--
THEN IT IS YOU WHO ARE NOT BEING LOGICAL.
I AM IN NO PARTICULAR DIFFICULTY--OTHER THAN THE PROFESSIONAL ONE TO WHICH YOU HAVE ALLUDED.
AS YOU POINT OUT, THE METHOD USED TO LURE YOU HERE WAS UNORTHODOX. CLEARLY WE DID NOT THINK YOU WOULD COME OF YOUR OWN ACCORD.
DOES THIS SUGGEST NOTHING TO YOU?
THAT I WOULD NOT WISH TO COME.
PRECISELY: AND WHY? I MIGHT BE YOUR ENEMY, PROFESSOR MORIARTY MIGHT BE, AS WELL. EVEN--EXCUSE ME--DR. WATSON.
BUT YOUR BROTHER? IS IT LIKELY WE ARE ALL IN LEAGUE AGAINST YOU? WHY? IF NOT TO DO YOU HARM, THEN PERHAPS TO DO YOU GOOD?
WHAT GOOD MIGHT THAT BE?

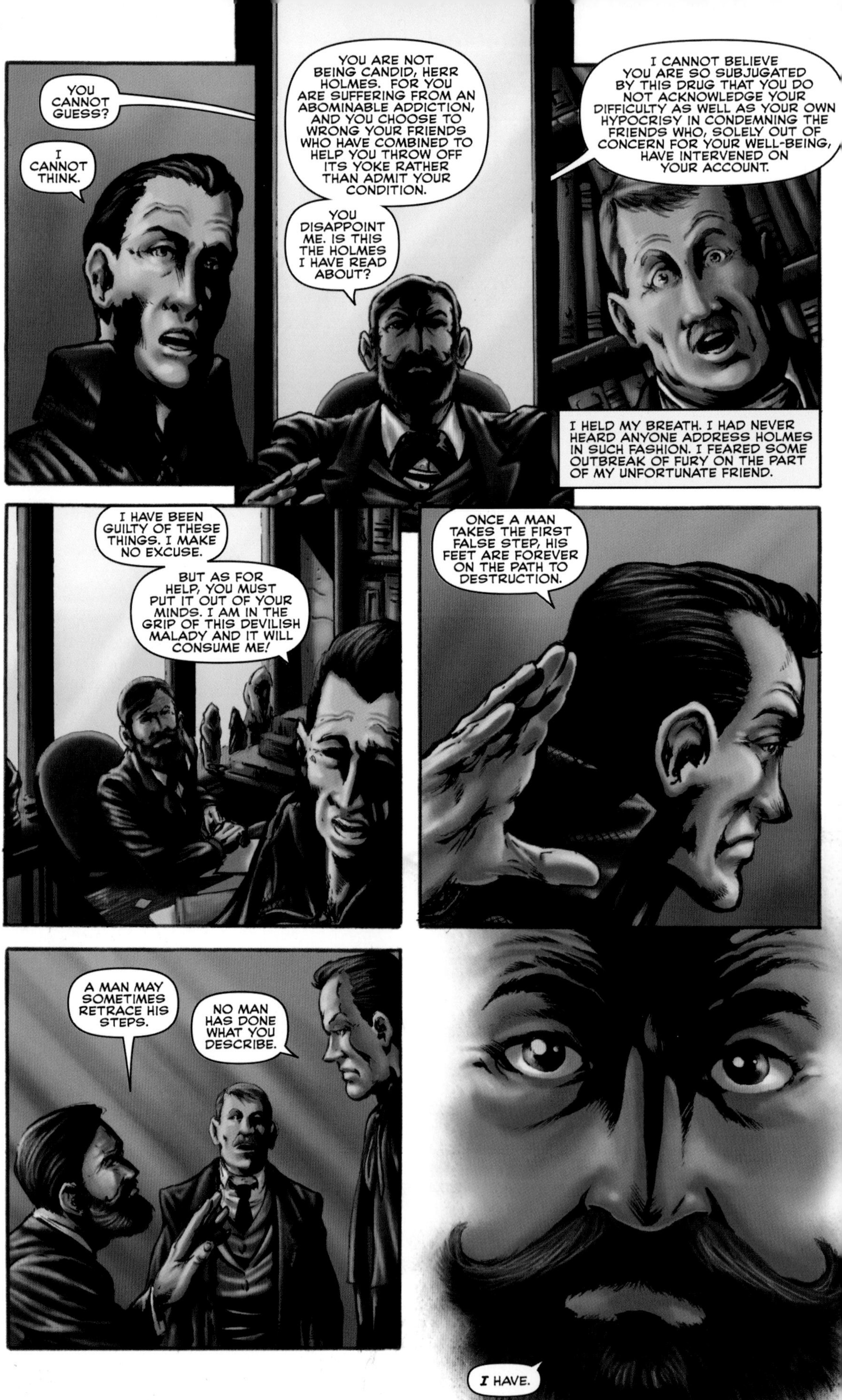
YOU CANNOT GUESS?
I CANNOT THINK.
YOU ARE NOT BEING CANDID, HERR HOLMES. FOR YOU ARE SUFFERING FROM AN ABOMINABLE ADDICTION, AND YOU CHOOSE TO WRONG YOUR FRIENDS WHO HAVE COMBINED TO HELP YOU THROW OFF ITS YOKE RATHER THAN ADMIT YOUR CONDITION.
YOU DISAPPOINT ME. IS THIS THE HOLMES I HAVE READ ABOUT?
I CANNOT BELIEVE YOU ARE SO SUBJUGATED BY THIS DRUG THAT YOU DO NOT ACKNOWLEDGE YOUR DIFFICULTY AS WELL AS YOUR OWN HYPOCRISY IN CONDEMNING THE FRIENDS WHO, SOLELY OUT OF CONCERN FOR YOUR WELL-BEING, HAVE INTERVENED ON YOUR ACCOUNT.
I HELD MY BREATH. I HAD NEVER HEARD ANYONE ADDRESS HOLMES IN SUCH FASHION. I FEARED SOME OUTBREAK OF FURY ON THE PART OF MY UNFORTUNATE FRIEND.
I HAVE BEEN GUILTY OF THESE THINGS. I MAKE NO EXCUSE.
BUT AS FOR HELP, YOU MUST PUT IT OUT OF YOUR MINDS. I AM IN THE GRIP OF THIS DEVILISH MALADY AND IT WILL CONSUME ME!
ONCE A MAN TAKES THE FIRST FALSE STEP, HIS FEET ARE FOREVER ON THE PATH TO DESTRUCTION.
A MAN MAY SOMETIMES RETRACE HIS STEPS.
NO MAN HAS DONE WHAT YOU DESCRIBE.
I HAVE.

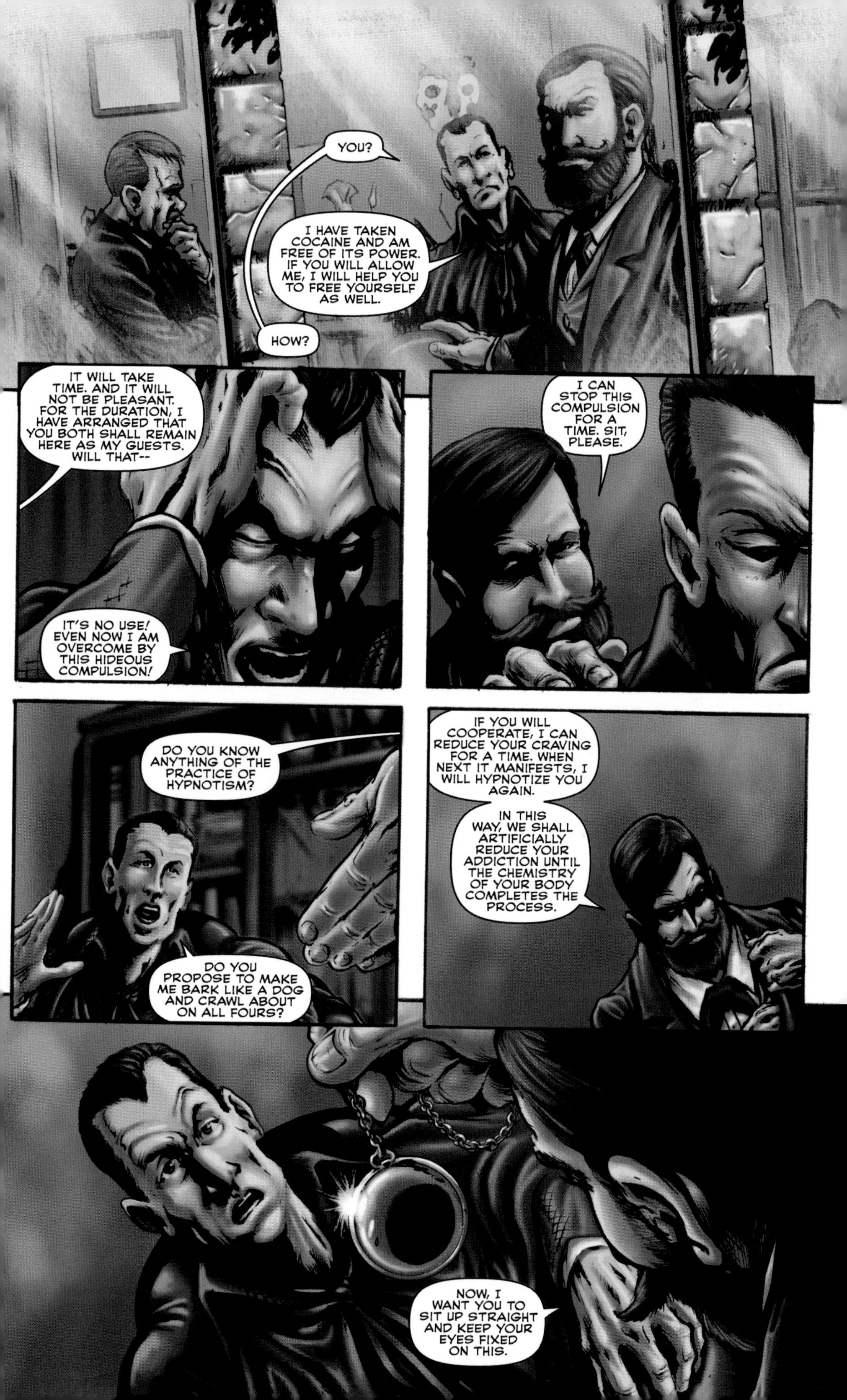
YOU?
I HAVE TAKEN COCAINE AND AM FREE OF ITS POWER. IF YOU WILL ALLOW ME, I WILL HELP YOU TO FREE YOURSELF AS WELL.
HOW?
IT WILL TAKE TIME. AND IT WILL NOT BE PLEASANT. FOR THE DURATION, I HAVE ARRANGED THAT YOU BOTH SHALL REMAIN HERE AS MY GUESTS. WILL THAT--
IT'S NO USE! EVEN NOW I AM OVERCOME BY THIS HIDEOUS COMPULSION!
I CAN STOP THIS COMPULSION FOR A TIME. SIT, PLEASE.
DO YOU KNOW ANYTHING OF THE PRACTICE OF HYPNOTISM?
DO YOU PROPOSE TO MAKE ME BARK LIKE A DOG AND CRAWL ABOUT ON ALL FOURS?
IF YOU WILL COOPERATE, I CAN REDUCE YOUR CRAVING FOR A TIME. WHEN NEXT IT MANIFESTS, I WILL HYPNOTIZE YOU AGAIN.
IN THIS WAY, WE SHALL ARTIFICIALLY REDUCE YOUR ADDICTION UNTIL THE CHEMISTRY OF YOUR BODY COMPLETES THE PROCESS.
NOW, I WANT YOU TO SIT UP STRAIGHT AND KEEP YOUR EYES FIXED ON THIS.

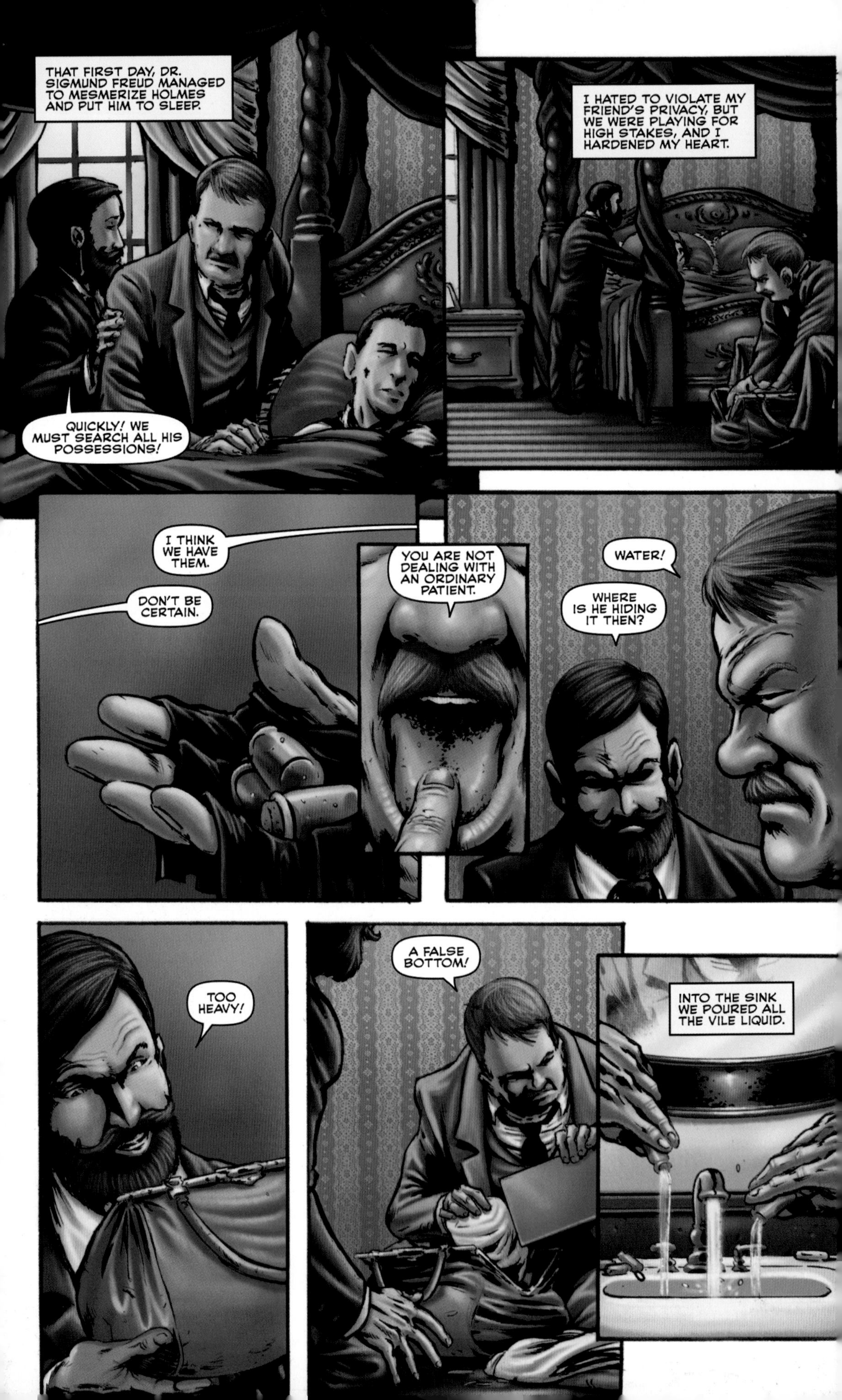

THAT FIRST DAY, DR. SIGMUND FREUD MANAGED TO MESMERIZE HOLMES AND PUT HIM TO SLEEP.
QUICKLY! WE MUST SEARCH ALL HIS POSSESSIONS!
I HATED TO VIOLATE MY FRIEND'S PRIVACY, BUT WE WERE PLAYING FOR HIGH STAKES, AND I HARDENED MY HEART.
I THINK WE HAVE THEM.
DON'T BE CERTAIN.
YOU ARE NOT DEALING WITH AN ORDINARY PATIENT.
WATER!
WHERE IS HE HIDING IT THEN?
TOO HEAVY!
A FALSE BOTTOM!
INTO THE SINK WE POURED ALL THE VILE LIQUID.

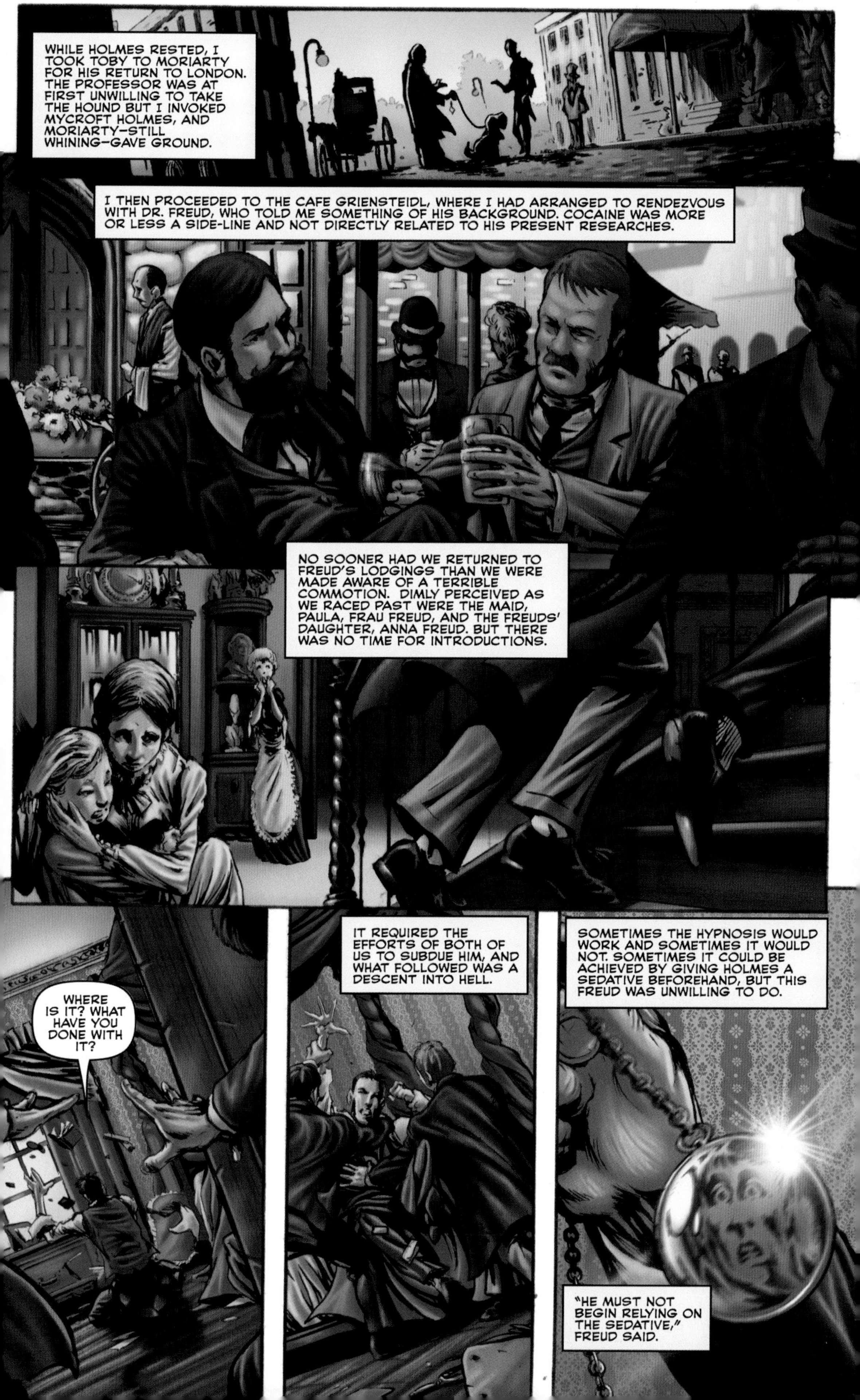

WHILE HOLMES RESTED, I TOOK TOBY TO MORIARTY FOR HIS RETURN TO LONDON. THE PROFESSOR WAS AT FIRST UNWILLING TO TAKE THE HOUND BUT I INVOKED MYCROFT HOLMES, AND MORIARTY—STILL WHINING—GAVE GROUND.
I THEN PROCEEDED TO THE CAFE GRIENSTEIDL, WHERE I HAD ARRANGED TO RENDEZVOUS WITH DR. FREUD, WHO TOLD ME SOMETHING OF HIS BACKGROUND. COCAINE WAS MORE OR LESS A SIDE-LINE AND NOT DIRECTLY RELATED TO HIS PRESENT RESEARCHES.
NO SOONER HAD WE RETURNED TO FREUD'S LODGINGS THAN WE WERE MADE AWARE OF A TERRIBLE COMMOTION. DIMLY PERCEIVED AS WE RACED PAST WERE THE MAID, PAULA, FRAU FREUD, AND THE FREUDS' DAUGHTER, ANNA FREUD. BUT THERE WAS NO TIME FOR INTRODUCTIONS.
WHERE IS IT? WHAT HAVE YOU DONE WITH IT?
IT REQUIRED THE EFFORTS OF BOTH OF US TO SUBDUE HIM, AND WHAT FOLLOWED WAS A DESCENT INTO HELL.
SOMETIMES THE HYPNOSIS WOULD WORK AND SOMETIMES IT WOULD NOT. SOMETIMES IT COULD BE ACHIEVED BY GIVING HOLMES A SEDATIVE BEFOREHAND, BUT THIS FREUD WAS UNWILLING TO DO.
"HE MUST NOT BEGIN RELYING ON THE SEDATIVE," FREUD SAID.

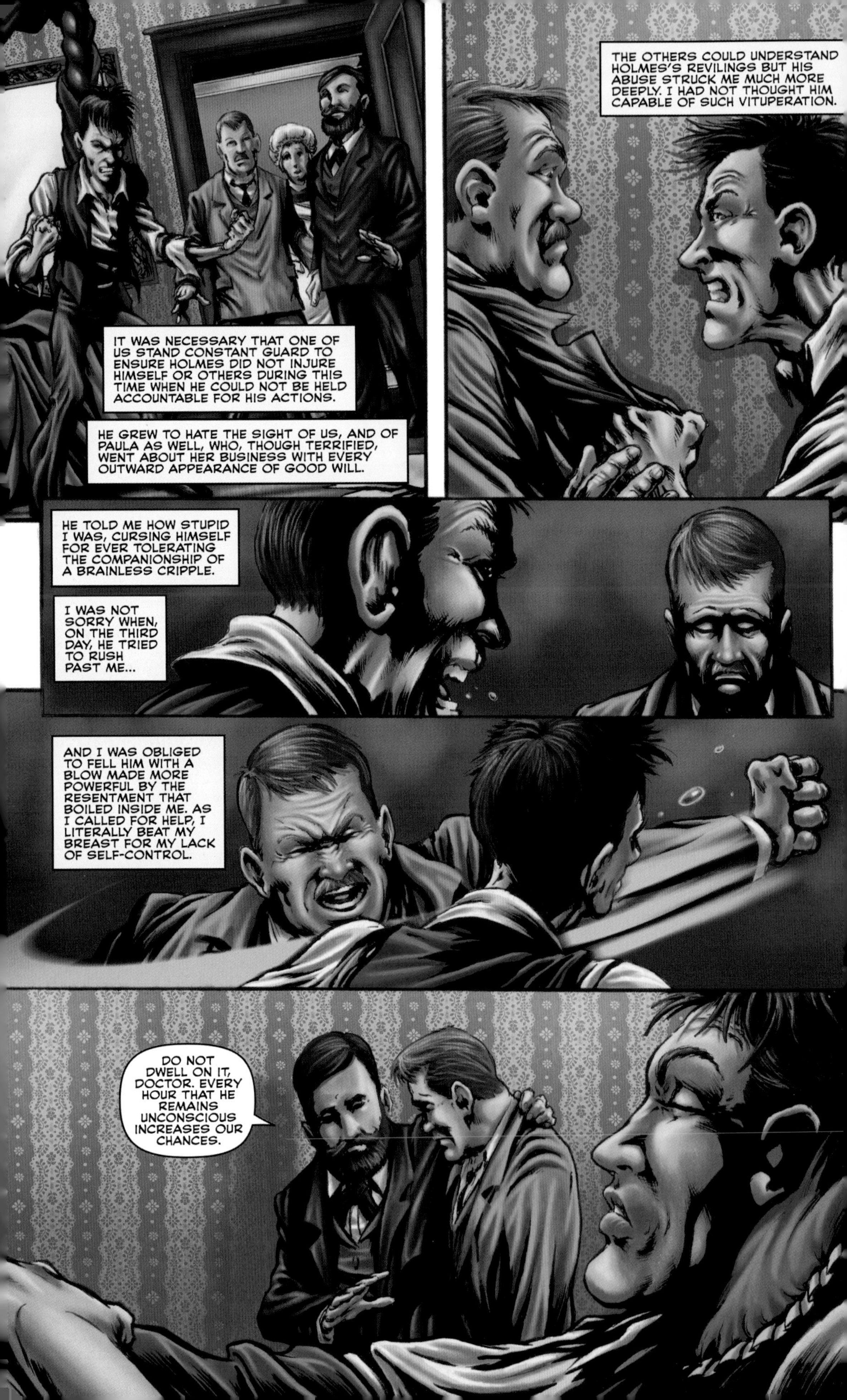
IT WAS NECESSARY THAT ONE OF US STAND CONSTANT GUARD TO ENSURE HOLMES DID NOT INJURE HIMSELF OR OTHERS DURING THIS TIME WHEN HE COULD NOT BE HELD ACCOUNTABLE FOR HIS ACTIONS.
HE GREW TO HATE THE SIGHT OF US, AND OF PAULA AS WELL, WHO, THOUGH TERRIFIED, WENT ABOUT HER BUSINESS WITH EVERY OUTWARD APPEARANCE OF GOOD WILL.
THE OTHERS COULD UNDERSTAND HOLMES'S REVILINGS BUT HIS ABUSE STRUCK ME MUCH MORE DEEPLY. I HAD NOT THOUGHT HIM CAPABLE OF SUCH VITUPERATION.
HE TOLD ME HOW STUPID I WAS, CURSING HIMSELF FOR EVER TOLERATING THE COMPANIONSHIP OF A BRAINLESS CRIPPLE.
I WAS NOT SORRY WHEN, ON THE THIRD DAY, HE TRIED TO RUSH PAST ME...
AND I WAS OBLIGED TO FELL HIM WITH A BLOW MADE MORE POWERFUL BY THE RESENTMENT THAT BOILED INSIDE ME. AS I CALLED FOR HELP, I LITERALLY BEAT MY BREAST FOR MY LACK OF SELF-CONTROL.
DO NOT DWELL ON IT, DOCTOR. EVERY HOUR THAT HE REMAINS UNCONSCIOUS INCREASES OUR CHANCES.

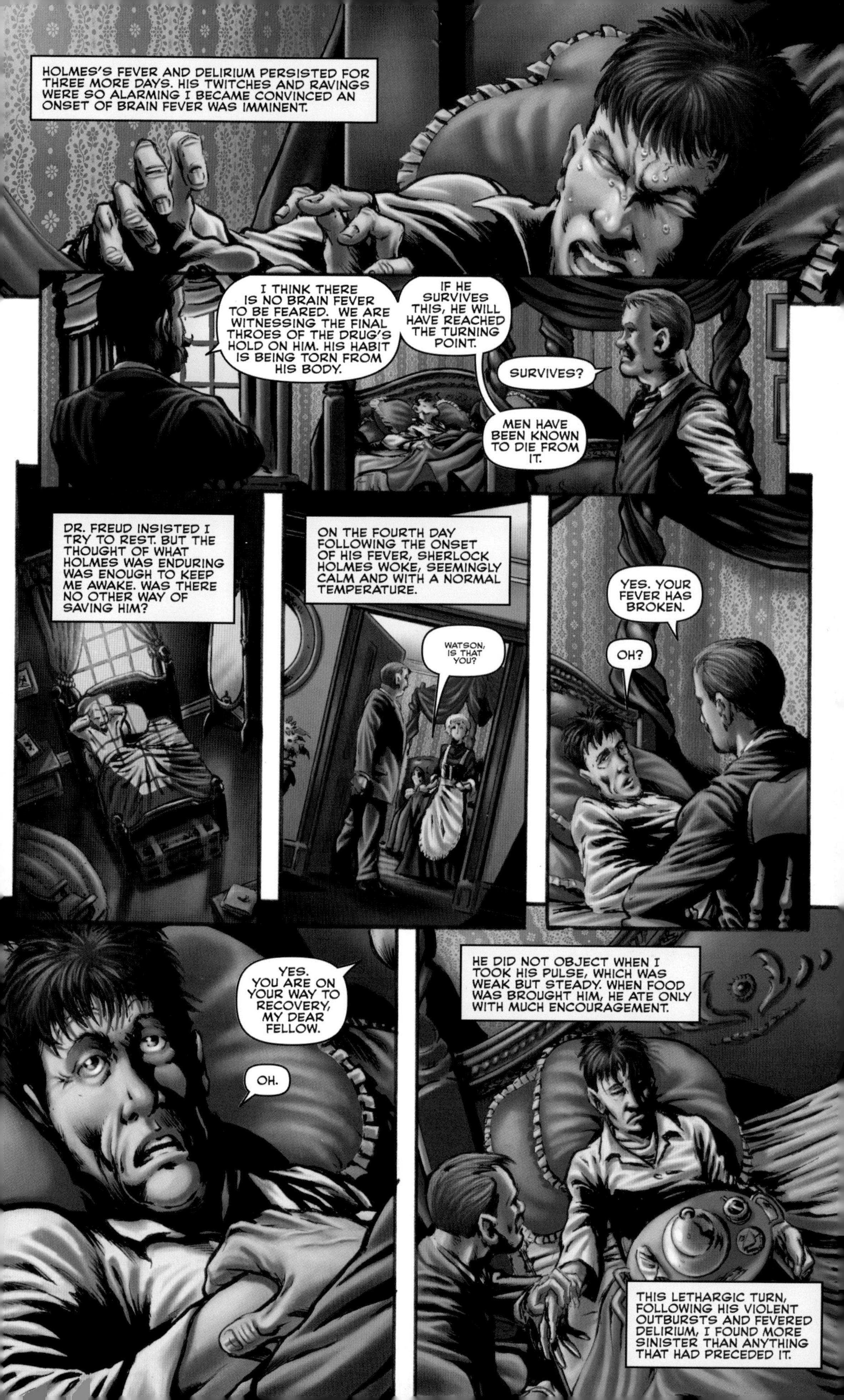
HOLMES'S FEVER AND DELIRIUM PERSISTED FOR THREE MORE DAYS. HIS TWITCHES AND RAVINGS WERE SO ALARMING I BECAME CONVINCED AN ONSET OF BRAIN FEVER WAS IMMINENT.
I THINK THERE IS NO BRAIN FEVER TO BE FEARED. WE ARE WITNESSING THE FINAL THROES OF THE DRUG'S HOLD ON HIM. HIS HABIT IS BEING TORN FROM HIS BODY.
IF HE SURVIVES THIS, HE WILL HAVE REACHED THE TURNING POINT.
SURVIVES?
MEN HAVE BEEN KNOWN TO DIE FROM IT.
DR. FREUD INSISTED I TRY TO REST. BUT THE THOUGHT OF WHAT HOLMES WAS ENDURING WAS ENOUGH TO KEEP ME AWAKE. WAS THERE NO OTHER WAY OF SAVING HIM?
ON THE FOURTH DAY FOLLOWING THE ONSET OF HIS FEVER, SHERLOCK HOLMES WOKE, SEEMINGLY CALM AND WITH A NORMAL TEMPERATURE.
WATSON, IS THAT YOU?
YES. YOUR FEVER HAS BROKEN.
OH?
YES. YOU ARE ON YOUR WAY TO RECOVERY, MY DEAR FELLOW.
OH.
HE DID NOT OBJECT WHEN I TOOK HIS PULSE, WHICH WAS WEAK BUT STEADY. WHEN FOOD WAS BROUGHT HIM, HE ATE ONLY WITH MUCH ENCOURAGEMENT.
THIS LETHARGIC TURN, FOLLOWING HIS VIOLENT OUTBURSTS AND FEVERED DELIRIUM, I FOUND MORE SINISTER THAN ANYTHING THAT HAD PRECEDED IT.

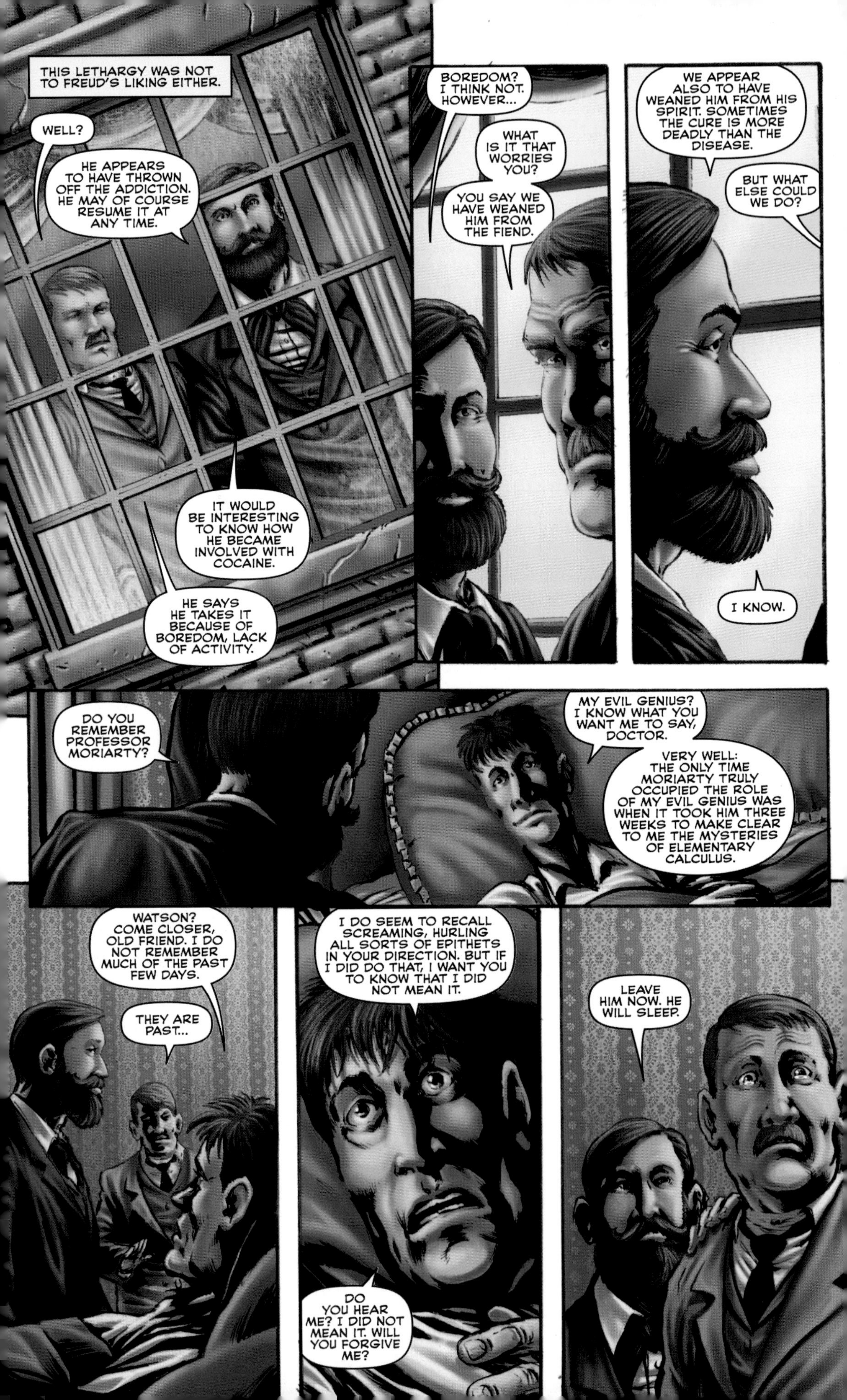
THIS LETHARGY WAS NOT TO FREUD'S LIKING EITHER.
WELL?
HE APPEARS TO HAVE THROWN OFF THE ADDICTION. HE MAY OF COURSE RESUME IT AT ANY TIME.
IT WOULD BE INTERESTING TO KNOW HOW HE BECAME INVOLVED WITH COCAINE.
HE SAYS HE TAKES IT BECAUSE OF BOREDOM, LACK OF ACTIVITY.
BOREDOM? I THINK NOT. HOWEVER...
WHAT IS IT THAT WORRIES YOU?
YOU SAY WE HAVE WEANED HIM FROM THE FIEND.
WE APPEAR ALSO TO HAVE WEANED HIM FROM HIS SPIRIT. SOMETIMES THE CURE IS MORE DEADLY THAN THE DISEASE.
BUT WHAT ELSE COULD WE DO?
I KNOW.
DO YOU REMEMBER PROFESSOR MORIARTY?
MY EVIL GENIUS? I KNOW WHAT YOU WANT ME TO SAY, DOCTOR.
VERY WELL: THE ONLY TIME MORIARTY TRULY OCCUPIED THE ROLE OF MY EVIL GENIUS WAS WHEN IT TOOK HIM THREE WEEKS TO MAKE CLEAR TO ME THE MYSTERIES OF ELEMENTARY CALCULUS.
WATSON? COME CLOSER, OLD FRIEND. I DO NOT REMEMBER MUCH OF THE PAST FEW DAYS.
THEY ARE PAST...
I DO SEEM TO RECALL SCREAMING, HURLING ALL SORTS OF EPITHETS IN YOUR DIRECTION. BUT IF I DID DO THAT, I WANT YOU TO KNOW THAT I DID NOT MEAN IT.
DO YOU HEAR ME? I DID NOT MEAN IT. WILL YOU FORGIVE ME?
LEAVE HIM NOW. HE WILL SLEEP.

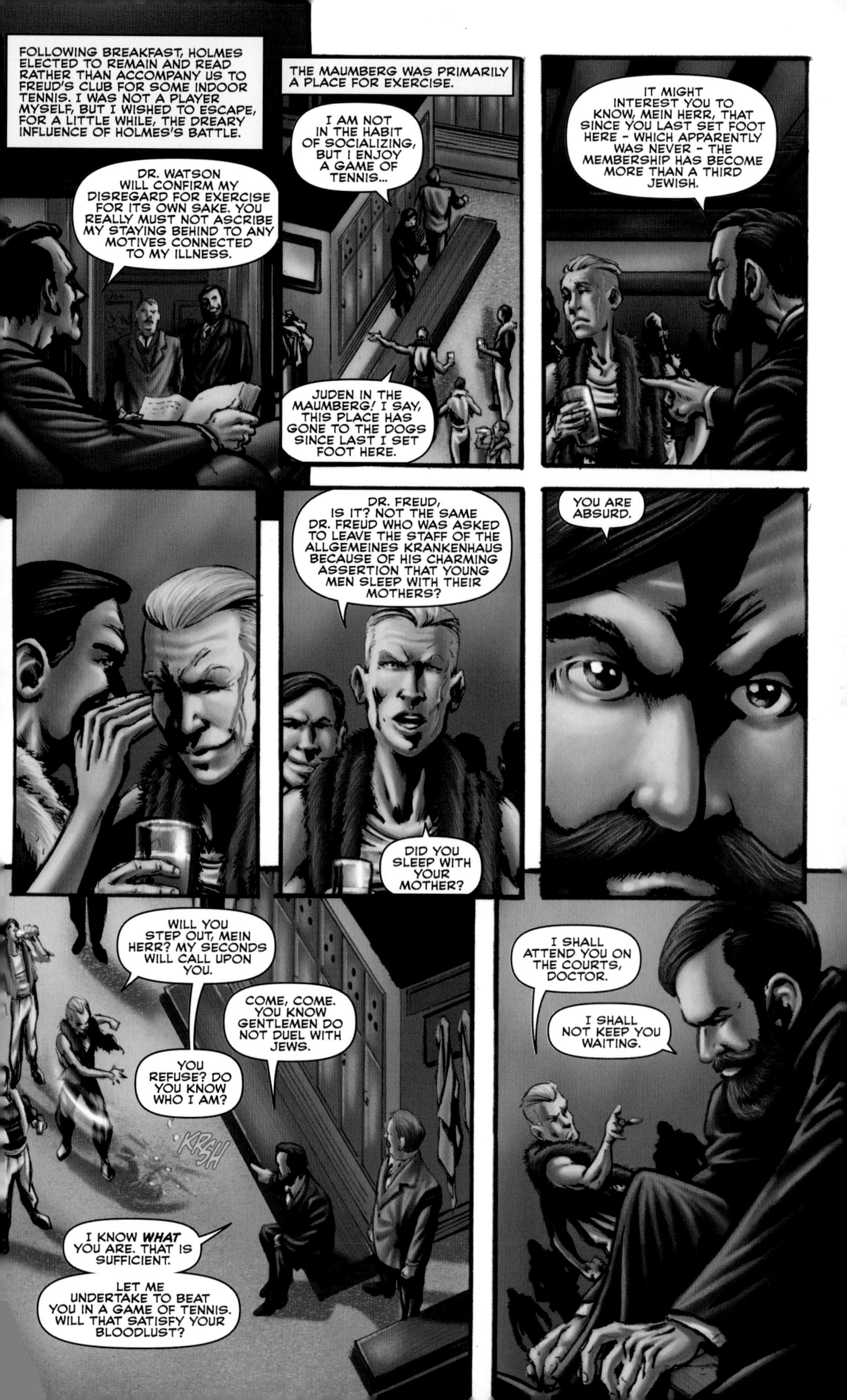
FOLLOWING BREAKFAST, HOLMES ELECTED TO REMAIN AND READ RATHER THAN ACCOMPANY US TO FREUD'S CLUB FOR SOME INDOOR TENNIS. I WAS NOT A PLAYER MYSELF, BUT I WISHED TO ESCAPE, FOR A LITTLE WHILE, THE DREARY INFLUENCE OF HOLMES'S BATTLE.
DR. WATSON WILL CONFIRM MY DISREGARD FOR EXERCISE FOR ITS OWN SAKE. YOU REALLY MUST NOT ASCRIBE MY STAYING BEHIND TO ANY MOTIVES CONNECTED TO MY ILLNESS.
THE MAUMBERG WAS PRIMARILY A PLACE FOR EXERCISE.
I AM NOT IN THE HABIT OF SOCIALIZING, BUT I ENJOY A GAME OF TENNIS...
JUDEN IN THE MAUMBERG! I SAY, THIS PLACE HAS GONE TO THE DOGS SINCE LAST I SET FOOT HERE.
IT MIGHT INTEREST YOU TO KNOW, MEIN HERR, THAT SINCE YOU LAST SET FOOT HERE - WHICH APPARENTLY WAS NEVER - THE MEMBERSHIP HAS BECOME MORE THAN A THIRD JEWISH.
DR. FREUD, IS IT? NOT THE SAME DR. FREUD WHO WAS ASKED TO LEAVE THE STAFF OF THE ALLGEMEINES KRANKENHAUS BECAUSE OF HIS CHARMING ASSERTION THAT YOUNG MEN SLEEP WITH THEIR MOTHERS?
DID YOU SLEEP WITH YOUR MOTHER?
YOU ARE ABSURD.
WILL YOU STEP OUT, MEIN HERR? MY SECONDS WILL CALL UPON YOU.
COME, COME. YOU KNOW GENTLEMEN DO NOT DUEL WITH JEWS.
YOU REFUSE? DO YOU KNOW WHO I AM?
KRSH
I KNOW WHAT YOU ARE. THAT IS SUFFICIENT.
LET ME UNDERTAKE TO BEAT YOU IN A GAME OF TENNIS. WILL THAT SATISFY YOUR BLOODLUST?
I SHALL ATTEND YOU ON THE COURTS, DOCTOR.
I SHALL NOT KEEP YOU WAITING.

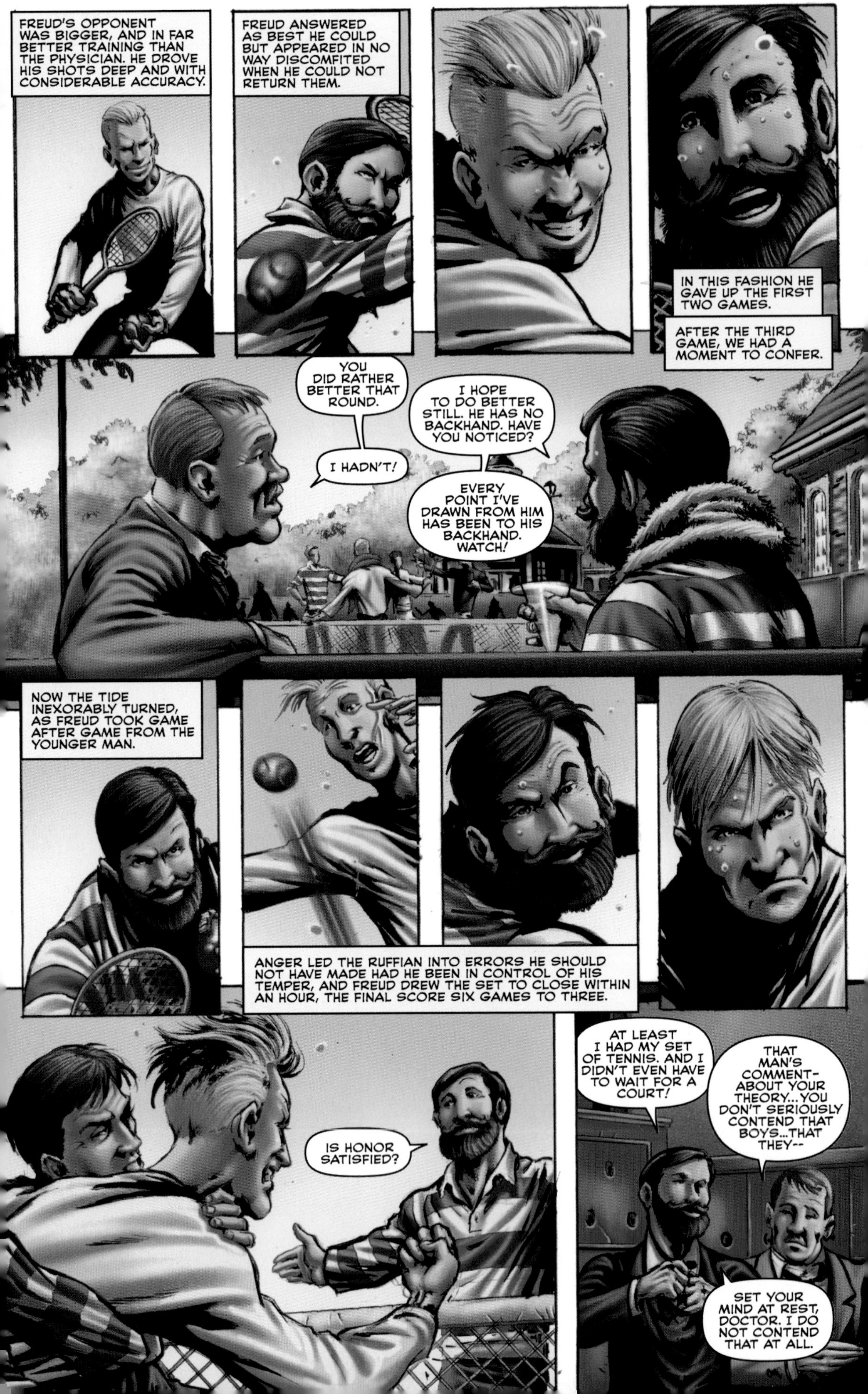
FREUD'S OPPONENT WAS BIGGER, AND IN FAR BETTER TRAINING THAN THE PHYSICIAN. HE DROVE HIS SHOTS DEEP AND WITH CONSIDERABLE ACCURACY.
FREUD ANSWERED AS BEST HE COULD BUT APPEARED IN NO WAY DISCOMFITED WHEN HE COULD NOT RETURN THEM.
IN THIS FASHION HE GAVE UP THE FIRST TWO GAMES.
AFTER THE THIRD GAME, WE HAD A MOMENT TO CONFER.
YOU DID RATHER BETTER THAT ROUND.
I HOPE TO DO BETTER STILL. HE HAS NO BACKHAND. HAVE YOU NOTICED?
I HADN'T!
EVERY POINT I'VE DRAWN FROM HIM HAS BEEN TO HIS BACKHAND. WATCH!
NOW THE TIDE INEXORABLY TURNED, AS FREUD TOOK GAME AFTER GAME FROM THE YOUNGER MAN.
ANGER LED THE RUFFIAN INTO ERRORS HE SHOULD NOT HAVE MADE HAD HE BEEN IN CONTROL OF HIS TEMPER, AND FREUD DREW THE SET TO CLOSE WITHIN AN HOUR, THE FINAL SCORE SIX GAMES TO THREE.
IS HONOR SATISFIED?
AT LEAST I HAD MY SET OF TENNIS. AND I DIDN'T EVEN HAVE TO WAIT FOR A COURT!
THAT MAN'S COMMENT-ABOUT YOUR THEORY...YOU DON'T SERIOUSLY CONTEND THAT BOYS...THAT THEY--
SET YOUR MIND AT REST, DOCTOR. I DO NOT CONTEND THAT AT ALL.

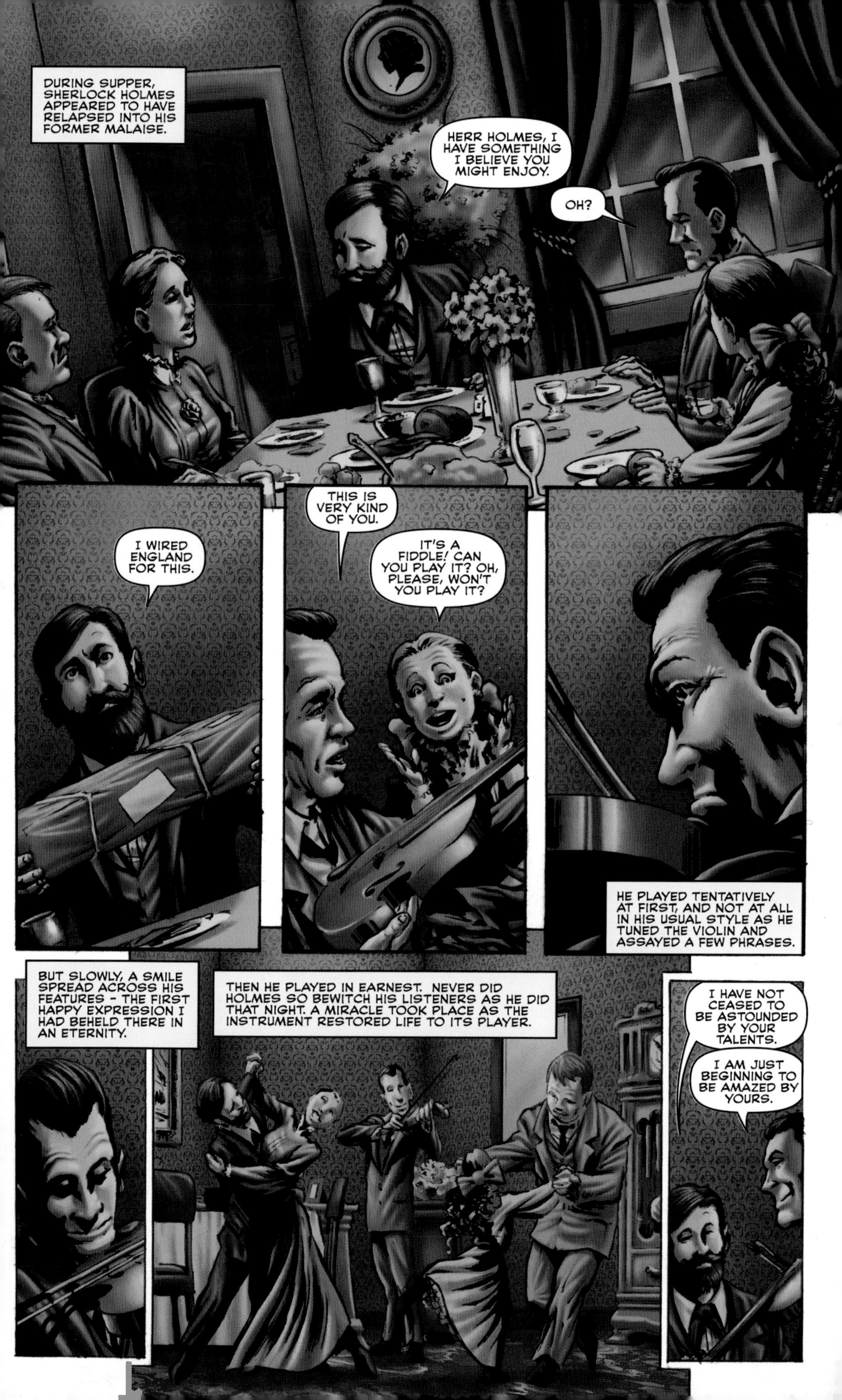
DURING SUPPER, SHERLOCK HOLMES APPEARED TO HAVE RELAPSED INTO HIS FORMER MALAISE.
HERR HOLMES, I HAVE SOMETHING I BELIEVE YOU MIGHT ENJOY.
OH?
I WIRED ENGLAND FOR THIS.
THIS IS VERY KIND OF YOU.
IT'S A FIDDLE! CAN YOU PLAY IT? OH, PLEASE, WON'T YOU PLAY IT?
HE PLAYED TENTATIVELY AT FIRST, AND NOT AT ALL IN HIS USUAL STYLE AS HE TUNED THE VIOLIN AND ASSAYED A FEW PHRASES.
BUT SLOWLY, A SMILE SPREAD ACROSS HIS FEATURES - THE FIRST HAPPY EXPRESSION I HAD BEHELD THERE IN AN ETERNITY.
THEN HE PLAYED IN EARNEST. NEVER DID HOLMES SO BEWITCH HIS LISTENERS AS HE DID THAT NIGHT. A MIRACLE TOOK PLACE AS THE INSTRUMENT RESTORED LIFE TO ITS PLAYER.
I HAVE NOT CEASED TO BE ASTOUNDED BY YOUR TALENTS.
I AM JUST BEGINNING TO BE AMAZED BY YOURS.

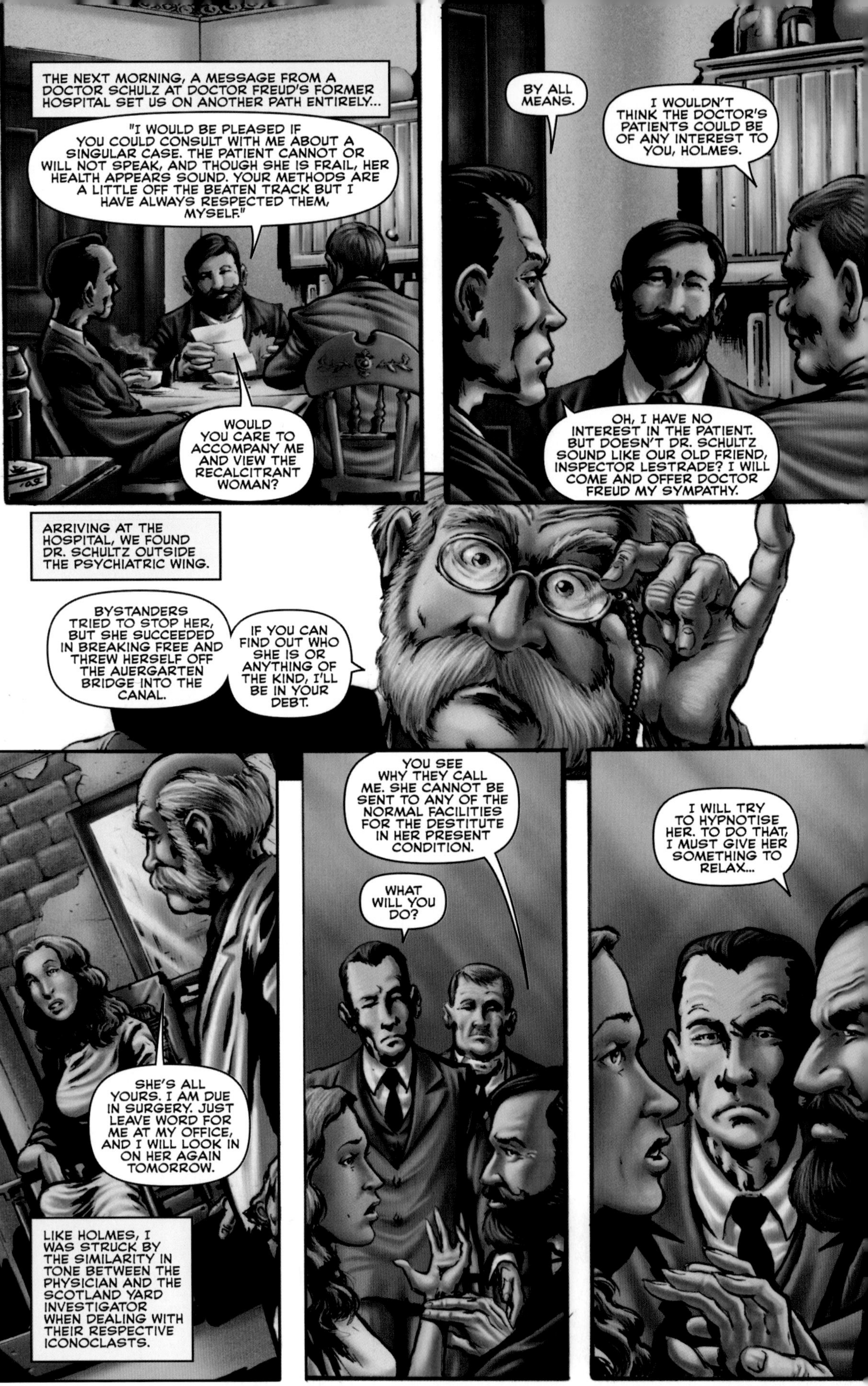

THE NEXT MORNING, A MESSAGE FROM A DOCTOR SCHULZ AT DOCTOR FREUD'S FORMER HOSPITAL SET US ON ANOTHER PATH ENTIRELY...
"I WOULD BE PLEASED IF YOU COULD CONSULT WITH ME ABOUT A SINGULAR CASE. THE PATIENT CANNOT OR WILL NOT SPEAK, AND THOUGH SHE IS FRAIL, HER HEALTH APPEARS SOUND. YOUR METHODS ARE A LITTLE OFF THE BEATEN TRACK BUT I HAVE ALWAYS RESPECTED THEM, MYSELF."
WOULD YOU CARE TO ACCOMPANY ME AND VIEW THE RECALCITRANT WOMAN?
BY ALL MEANS.
I WOULDN'T THINK THE DOCTOR'S PATIENTS COULD BE OF ANY INTEREST TO YOU, HOLMES.
OH, I HAVE NO INTEREST IN THE PATIENT. BUT DOESN'T DR. SCHULTZ SOUND LIKE OUR OLD FRIEND, INSPECTOR LESTRADE? I WILL COME AND OFFER DOCTOR FREUD MY SYMPATHY.
ARRIVING AT THE HOSPITAL, WE FOUND DR. SCHULTZ OUTSIDE THE PSYCHIATRIC WING.
BYSTANDERS TRIED TO STOP HER, BUT SHE SUCCEEDED IN BREAKING FREE AND THREW HERSELF OFF THE AUERGARTEN BRIDGE INTO THE CANAL.
IF YOU CAN FIND OUT WHO SHE IS OR ANYTHING OF THE KIND, I'LL BE IN YOUR DEBT.
SHE'S ALL YOURS. I AM DUE IN SURGERY. JUST LEAVE WORD FOR ME AT MY OFFICE, AND I WILL LOOK IN ON HER AGAIN TOMORROW.
LIKE HOLMES, I WAS STRUCK BY THE SIMILARITY IN TONE BETWEEN THE PHYSICIAN AND THE SCOTLAND YARD INVESTIGATOR WHEN DEALING WITH THEIR RESPECTIVE ICONOCLASTS.
YOU SEE WHY THEY CALL ME. SHE CANNOT BE SENT TO ANY OF THE NORMAL FACILITIES FOR THE DESTITUTE IN HER PRESENT CONDITION.
WHAT WILL YOU DO?
I WILL TRY TO HYPNOTISE HER. TO DO THAT, I MUST GIVE HER SOMETHING TO RELAX...

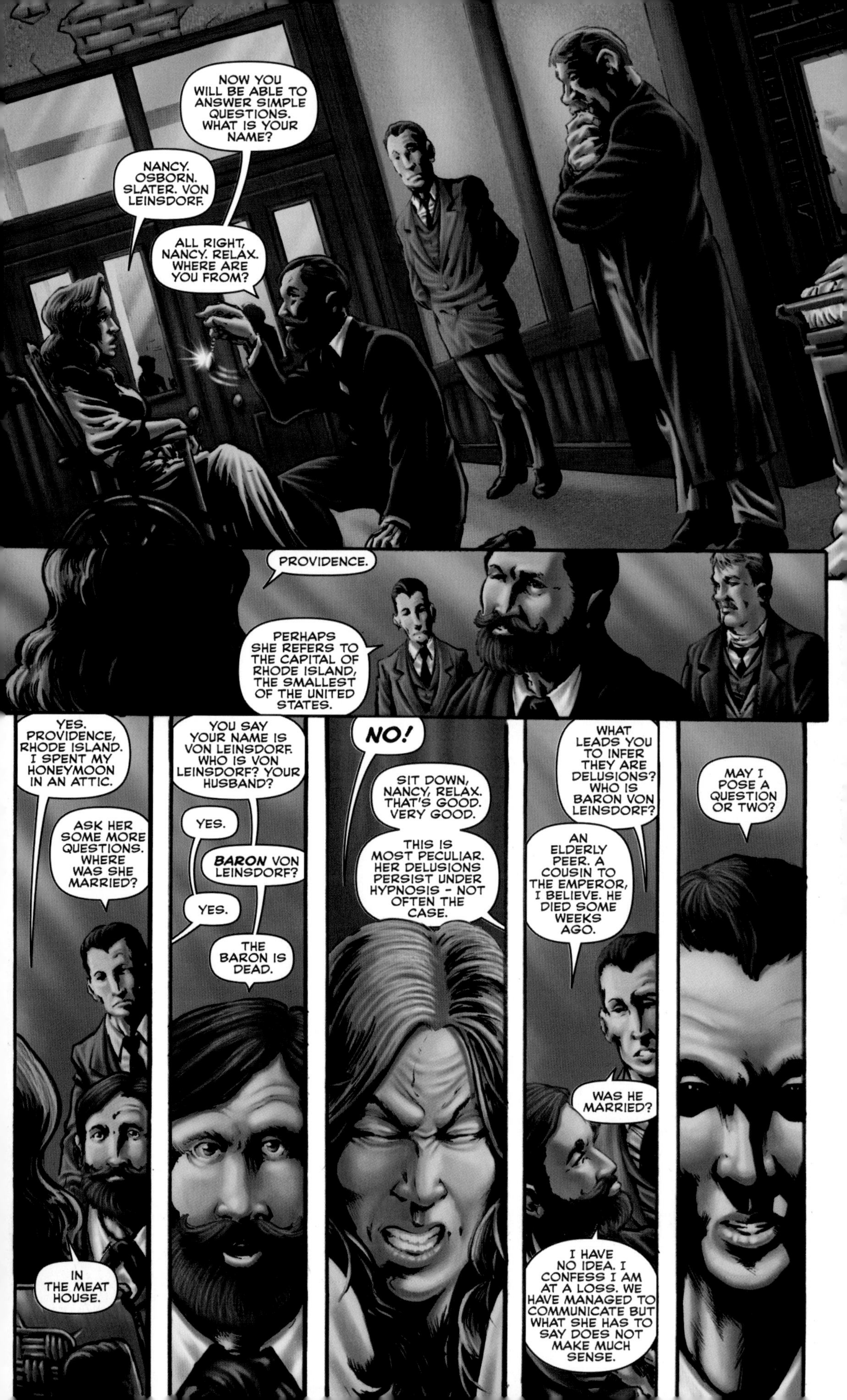
NOW YOU WILL BE ABLE TO ANSWER SIMPLE QUESTIONS. WHAT IS YOUR NAME?
NANCY. OSBORN. SLATER. VON LEINSDORF.
ALL RIGHT, NANCY. RELAX. WHERE ARE YOU FROM?
PROVIDENCE.
PERHAPS SHE REFERS TO THE CAPITAL OF RHODE ISLAND, THE SMALLEST OF THE UNITED STATES.
YES. PROVIDENCE, RHODE ISLAND. I SPENT MY HONEYMOON IN AN ATTIC.
ASK HER SOME MORE QUESTIONS. WHERE WAS SHE MARRIED?
IN THE MEAT HOUSE.
YOU SAY YOUR NAME IS VON LEINSDORF. WHO IS VON LEINSDORF? YOUR HUSBAND?
YES.
BARON VON LEINSDORF?
YES.
THE BARON IS DEAD.
NO!
SIT DOWN, NANCY, RELAX. THAT'S GOOD. VERY GOOD.
THIS IS MOST PECULIAR. HER DELUSIONS PERSIST UNDER HYPNOSIS - NOT OFTEN THE CASE.
WHAT LEADS YOU TO INFER THEY ARE DELUSIONS? WHO IS BARON VON LEINSDORF?
AN ELDERLY PEER. A COUSIN TO THE EMPEROR, I BELIEVE. HE DIED SOME WEEKS AGO.
WAS HE MARRIED?
I HAVE NO IDEA. I CONFESS I AM AT A LOSS. WE HAVE MANAGED TO COMMUNICATE BUT WHAT SHE HAS TO SAY DOES NOT MAKE MUCH SENSE.
MAY I POSE A QUESTION OR TWO?

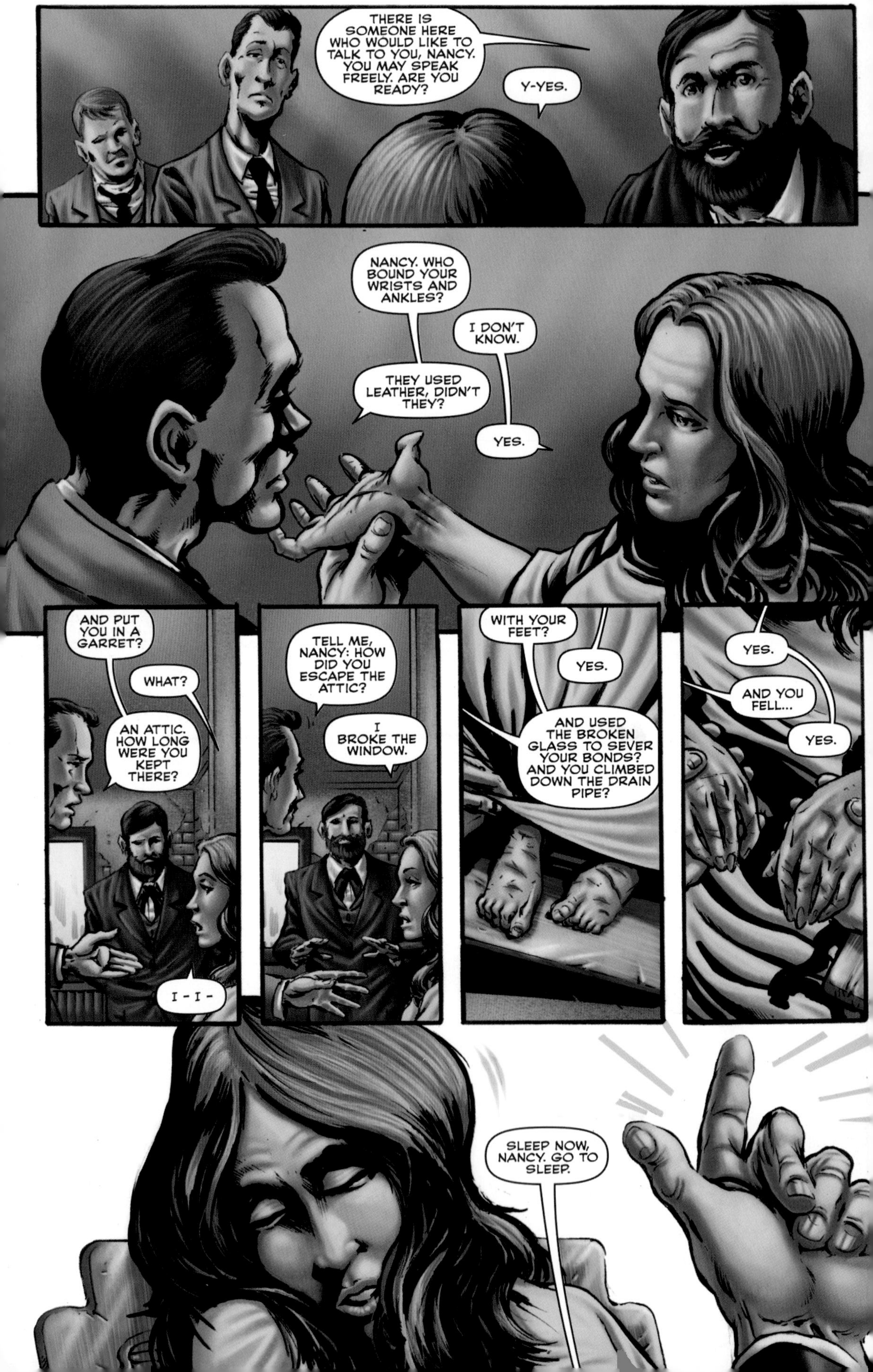
THERE IS SOMEONE HERE WHO WOULD LIKE TO TALK TO YOU, NANCY. YOU MAY SPEAK FREELY. ARE YOU READY?
Y-YES.
NANCY. WHO BOUND YOUR WRISTS AND ANKLES?
I DON'T KNOW.
THEY USED LEATHER, DIDN'T THEY?
YES.
AND PUT YOU IN A GARRET?
WHAT?
AN ATTIC. HOW LONG WERE YOU KEPT THERE?
I - I -
TELL ME, NANCY: HOW DID YOU ESCAPE THE ATTIC?
I BROKE THE WINDOW.
WITH YOUR FEET?
YES.
AND USED THE BROKEN GLASS TO SEVER YOUR BONDS? AND YOU CLIMBED DOWN THE DRAIN PIPE?
YES.
AND YOU FELL...
YES.
SLEEP NOW, NANCY. GO TO SLEEP.

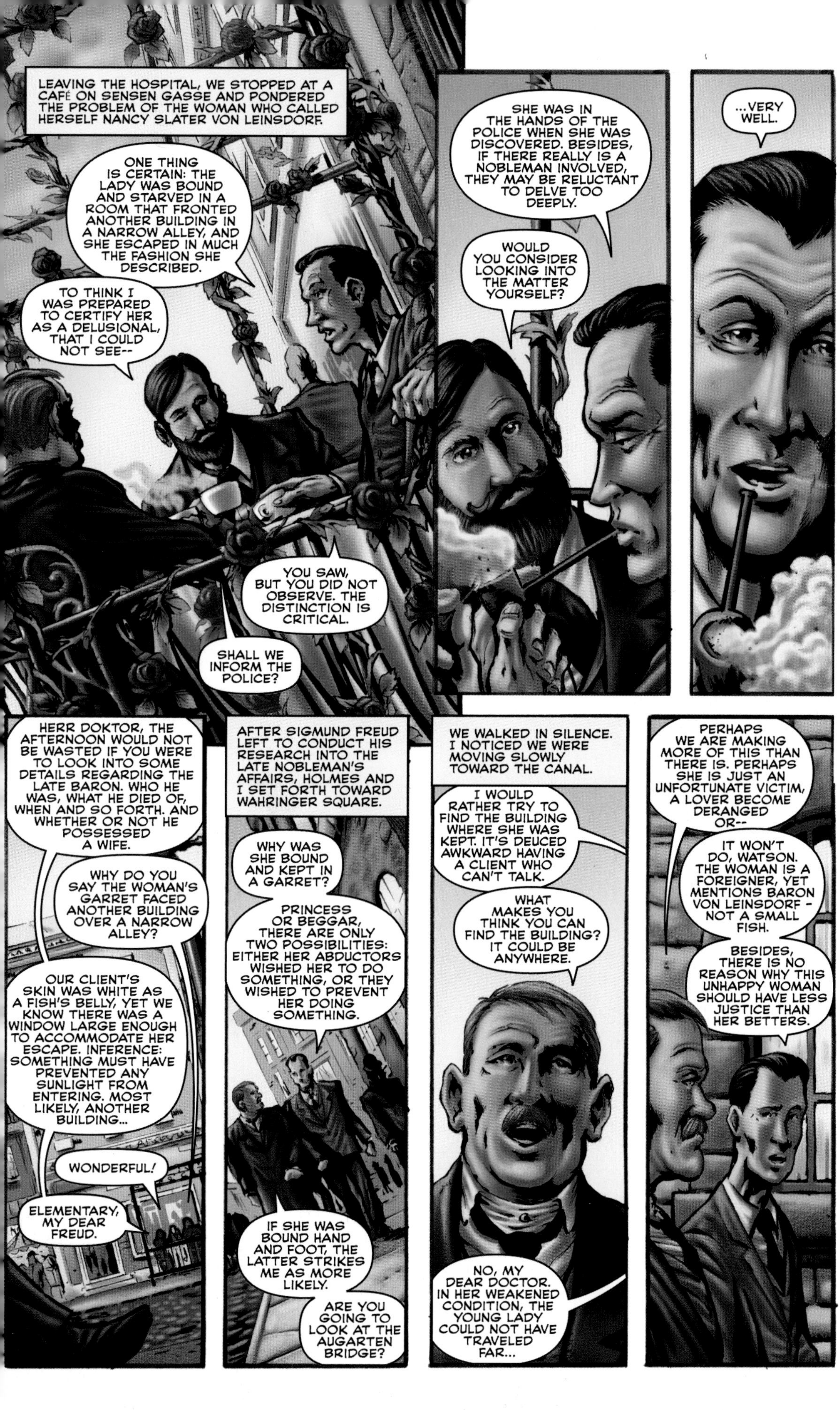
LEAVING THE HOSPITAL, WE STOPPED AT A CAFÉ ON SENSEN GASSE AND PONDERED THE PROBLEM OF THE WOMAN WHO CALLED HERSELF NANCY SLATER VON LEINSDORF.
ONE THING IS CERTAIN: THE LADY WAS BOUND AND STARVED IN A ROOM THAT FRONTED ANOTHER BUILDING IN A NARROW ALLEY, AND SHE ESCAPED IN MUCH THE FASHION SHE DESCRIBED.
TO THINK I WAS PREPARED TO CERTIFY HER AS A DELUSIONAL, THAT I COULD NOT SEE--
YOU SAW, BUT YOU DID NOT OBSERVE. THE DISTINCTION IS CRITICAL.
SHALL WE INFORM THE POLICE?
SHE WAS IN THE HANDS OF THE POLICE WHEN SHE WAS DISCOVERED. BESIDES, IF THERE REALLY IS A NOBLEMAN INVOLVED, THEY MAY BE RELUCTANT TO DELVE TOO DEEPLY.
WOULD YOU CONSIDER LOOKING INTO THE MATTER YOURSELF?
...VERY WELL.
HERR DOKTOR, THE AFTERNOON WOULD NOT BE WASTED IF YOU WERE TO LOOK INTO SOME DETAILS REGARDING THE LATE BARON. WHO HE WAS, WHAT HE DIED OF, WHEN AND SO FORTH. AND WHETHER OR NOT HE POSSESSED A WIFE.
WHY DO YOU SAY THE WOMAN'S GARRET FACED ANOTHER BUILDING OVER A NARROW ALLEY?
OUR CLIENT'S SKIN WAS WHITE AS A FISH'S BELLY, YET WE KNOW THERE WAS A WINDOW LARGE ENOUGH TO ACCOMMODATE HER ESCAPE. INFERENCE: SOMETHING MUST HAVE PREVENTED ANY SUNLIGHT FROM ENTERING. MOST LIKELY, ANOTHER BUILDING...
WONDERFUL!
ELEMENTARY, MY DEAR FREUD.
AFTER SIGMUND FREUD LEFT TO CONDUCT HIS RESEARCH INTO THE LATE NOBLEMAN'S AFFAIRS, HOLMES AND I SET FORTH TOWARD WAHRINGER SQUARE.
WHY WAS SHE BOUND AND KEPT IN A GARRET?
PRINCESS OR BEGGAR, THERE ARE ONLY TWO POSSIBILITIES: EITHER HER ABDUCTORS WISHED HER TO DO SOMETHING, OR THEY WISHED TO PREVENT HER DOING SOMETHING.
IF SHE WAS BOUND HAND AND FOOT, THE LATTER STRIKES ME AS MORE LIKELY.
ARE YOU GOING TO LOOK AT THE AUGARTEN BRIDGE?
WE WALKED IN SILENCE. I NOTICED WE WERE MOVING SLOWLY TOWARD THE CANAL.
I WOULD RATHER TRY TO FIND THE BUILDING WHERE SHE WAS KEPT. IT'S DEUCED AWKWARD HAVING A CLIENT WHO CAN'T TALK.
WHAT MAKES YOU THINK YOU CAN FIND THE BUILDING? IT COULD BE ANYWHERE.
NO, MY DEAR DOCTOR. IN HER WEAKENED CONDITION, THE YOUNG LADY COULD NOT HAVE TRAVELED FAR...
PERHAPS WE ARE MAKING MORE OF THIS THAN THERE IS. PERHAPS SHE IS JUST AN UNFORTUNATE VICTIM, A LOVER BECOME DERANGED OR--
IT WON'T DO, WATSON. THE WOMAN IS A FOREIGNER, YET MENTIONS BARON VON LEINSDORF - NOT A SMALL FISH.
BESIDES, THERE IS NO REASON WHY THIS UNHAPPY WOMAN SHOULD HAVE LESS JUSTICE THAN HER BETTERS.

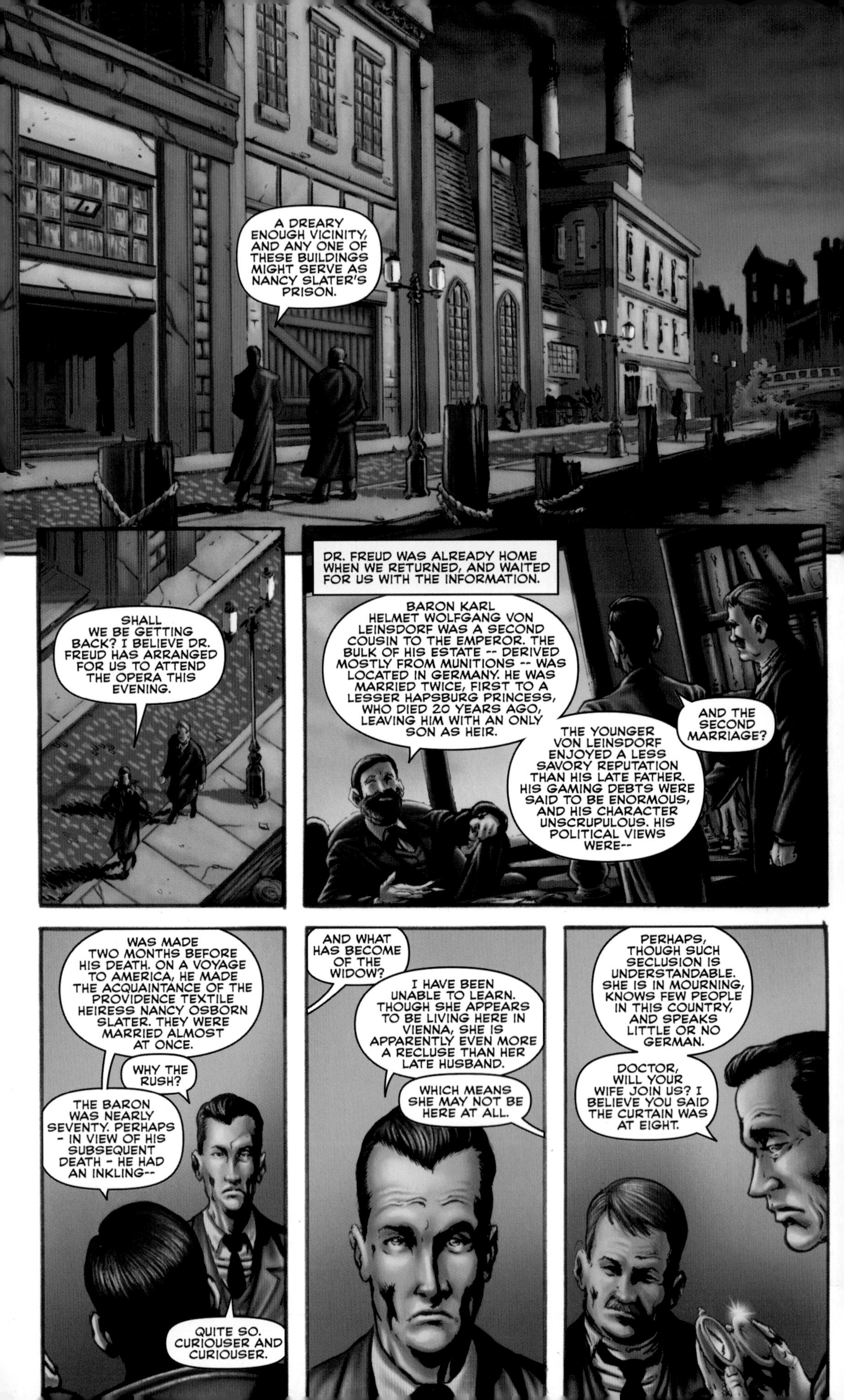
A DREARY ENOUGH VICINITY, AND ANY ONE OF THESE BUILDINGS MIGHT SERVE AS NANCY SLATER'S PRISON.
SHALL WE BE GETTING BACK? I BELIEVE DR. FREUD HAS ARRANGED FOR US TO ATTEND THE OPERA THIS EVENING.
DR. FREUD WAS ALREADY HOME WHEN WE RETURNED, AND WAITED FOR US WITH THE INFORMATION.
BARON KARL HELMET WOLFGANG VON LEINSDORF WAS A SECOND COUSIN TO THE EMPEROR. THE BULK OF HIS ESTATE -- DERIVED MOSTLY FROM MUNITIONS -- WAS LOCATED IN GERMANY. HE WAS MARRIED TWICE, FIRST TO A LESSER HAPSBURG PRINCESS, WHO DIED 20 YEARS AGO, LEAVING HIM WITH AN ONLY SON AS HEIR.
THE YOUNGER VON LEINSDORF ENJOYED A LESS SAVORY REPUTATION THAN HIS LATE FATHER. HIS GAMING DEBTS WERE SAID TO BE ENORMOUS, AND HIS CHARACTER UNSCRUPULOUS. HIS POLITICAL VIEWS WERE--
AND THE SECOND MARRIAGE?
WAS MADE TWO MONTHS BEFORE HIS DEATH. ON A VOYAGE TO AMERICA, HE MADE THE ACQUAINTANCE OF THE PROVIDENCE TEXTILE HEIRESS NANCY OSBORN SLATER. THEY WERE MARRIED ALMOST AT ONCE.
WHY THE RUSH?
THE BARON WAS NEARLY SEVENTY. PERHAPS - IN VIEW OF HIS SUBSEQUENT DEATH - HE HAD AN INKLING--
QUITE SO. CURIOUSER AND CURIOUSER.
AND WHAT HAS BECOME OF THE WIDOW?
I HAVE BEEN UNABLE TO LEARN. THOUGH SHE APPEARS TO BE LIVING HERE IN VIENNA, SHE IS APPARENTLY EVEN MORE A RECLUSE THAN HER LATE HUSBAND.
WHICH MEANS SHE MAY NOT BE HERE AT ALL.
PERHAPS, THOUGH SUCH SECLUSION IS UNDERSTANDABLE. SHE IS IN MOURNING, KNOWS FEW PEOPLE IN THIS COUNTRY, AND SPEAKS LITTLE OR NO GERMAN.
DOCTOR, WILL YOUR WIFE JOIN US? I BELIEVE YOU SAID THE CURTAIN WAS AT EIGHT.

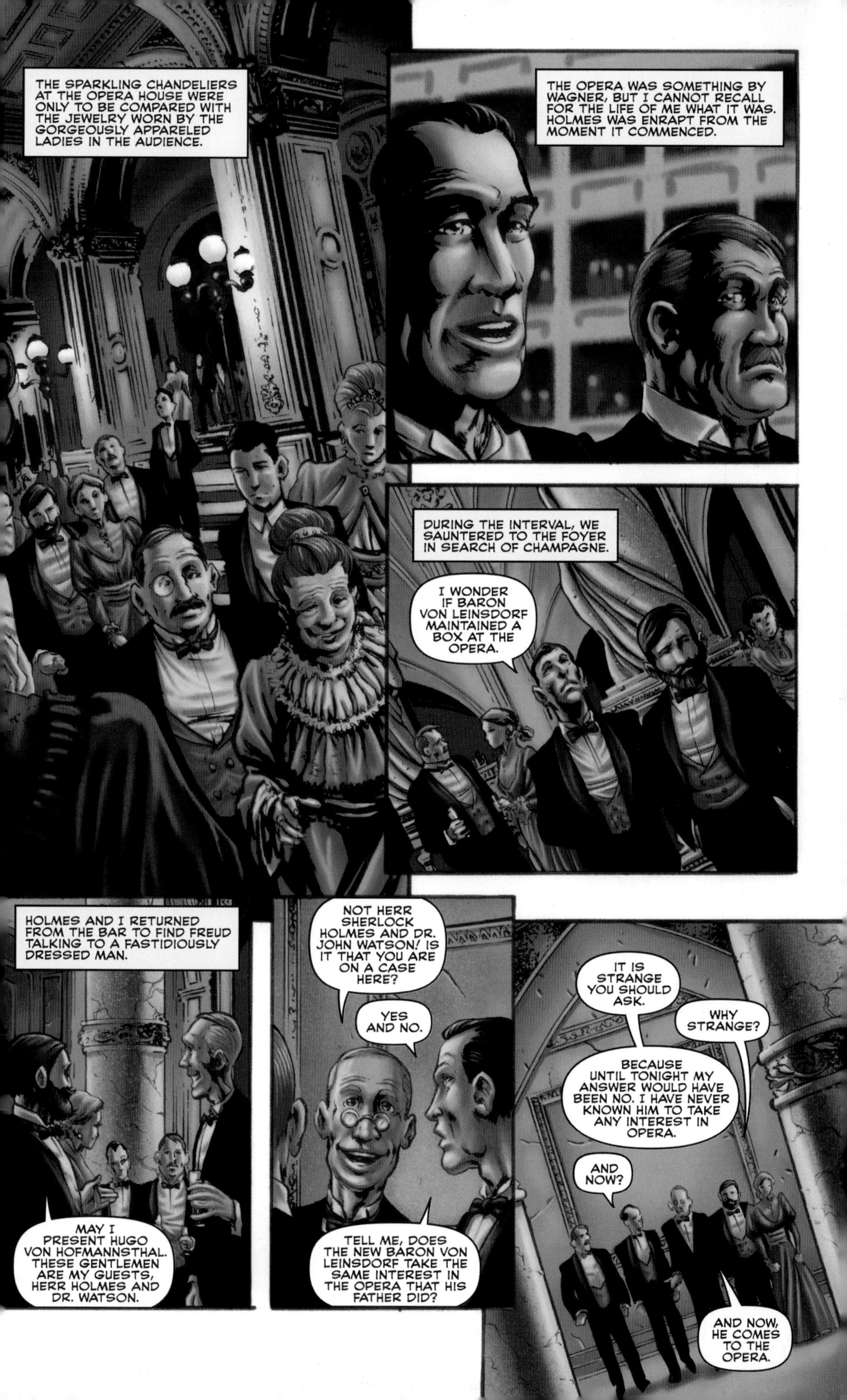
THE SPARKLING CHANDELIERS AT THE OPERA HOUSE WERE ONLY TO BE COMPARED WITH THE JEWELRY WORN BY THE GORGEOUSLY APPARELED LADIES IN THE AUDIENCE.
THE OPERA WAS SOMETHING BY WAGNER, BUT I CANNOT RECALL FOR THE LIFE OF ME WHAT IT WAS. HOLMES WAS ENRAPT FROM THE MOMENT IT COMMENCED.
DURING THE INTERVAL, WE SAUNTERED TO THE FOYER IN SEARCH OF CHAMPAGNE.
I WONDER IF BARON VON LEINSDORF MAINTAINED A BOX AT THE OPERA.
HOLMES AND I RETURNED FROM THE BAR TO FIND FREUD TALKING TO A FASTIDIOUSLY DRESSED MAN.
MAY I PRESENT HUGO VON HOFMANNSTHAL. THESE GENTLEMEN ARE MY GUESTS, HERR HOLMES AND DR. WATSON.
NOT HERR SHERLOCK HOLMES AND DR. JOHN WATSON! IS IT THAT YOU ARE ON A CASE HERE?
YES AND NO.
TELL ME, DOES THE NEW BARON VON LEINSDORF TAKE THE SAME INTEREST IN THE OPERA THAT HIS FATHER DID?
IT IS STRANGE YOU SHOULD ASK.
WHY STRANGE?
BECAUSE UNTIL TONIGHT MY ANSWER WOULD HAVE BEEN NO. I HAVE NEVER KNOWN HIM TO TAKE ANY INTEREST IN OPERA.
AND NOW?
AND NOW, HE COMES TO THE OPERA.

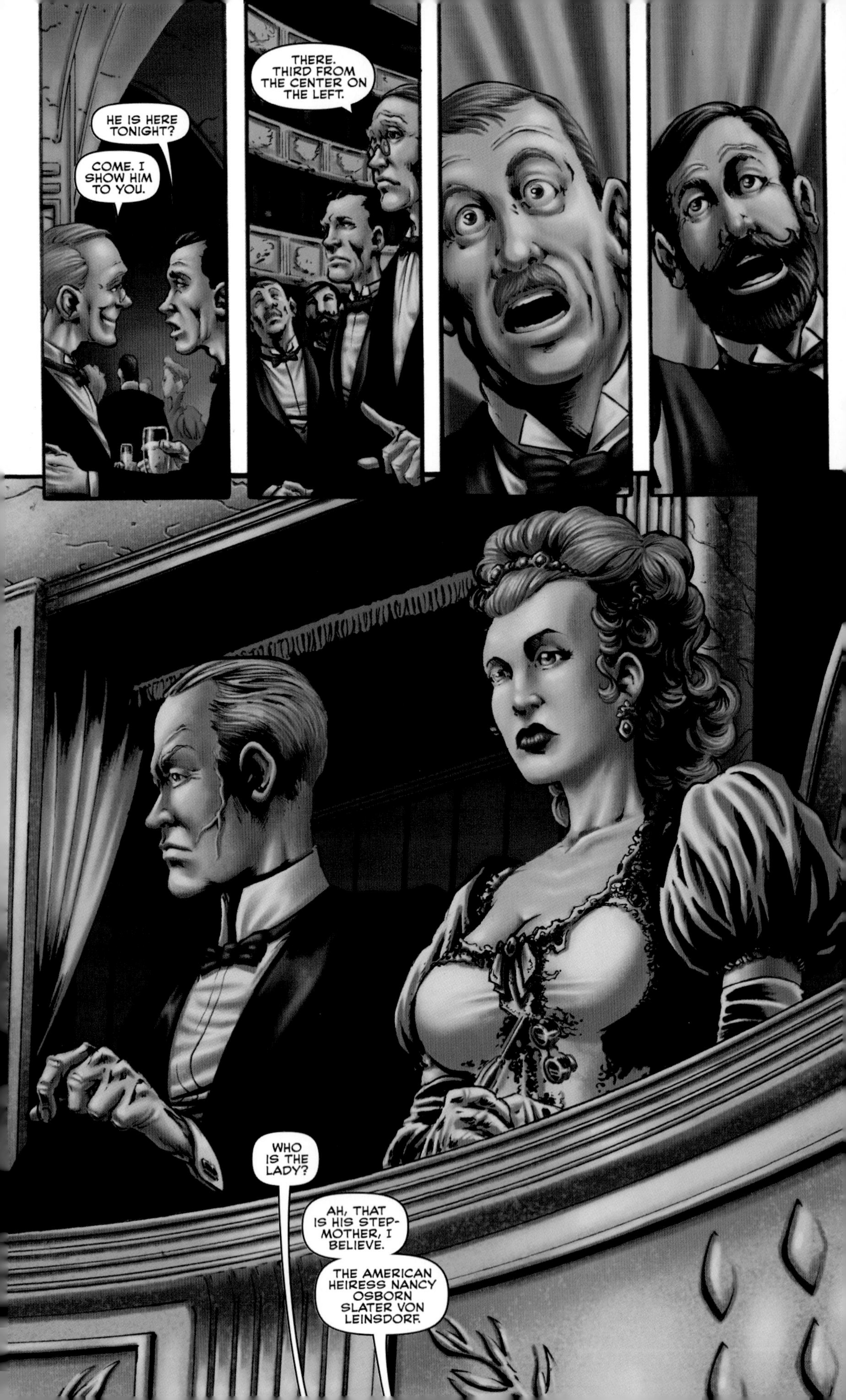
HE IS HERE TONIGHT?
COME. I SHOW HIM TO YOU.
THERE. THIRD FROM THE CENTER ON THE LEFT.
WHO IS THE LADY?
AH, THAT IS HIS STEP-MOTHER, I BELIEVE.
THE AMERICAN HEIRESS NANCY OSBORN SLATER VON LEINSDORF.

ART BY
KELLEY JONES

COLORS BY
JAY FOTOS

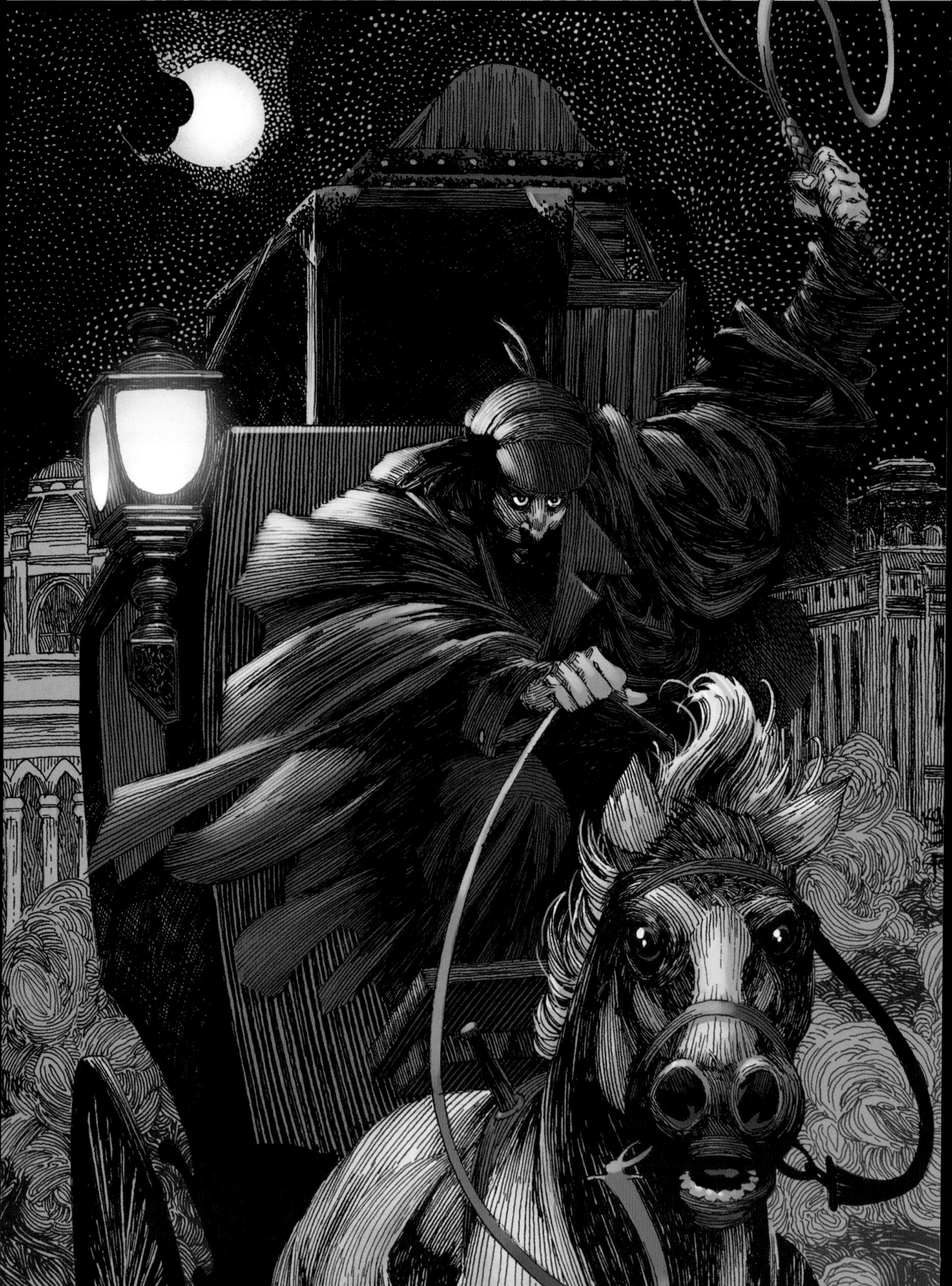

CHAPTER
FOUR

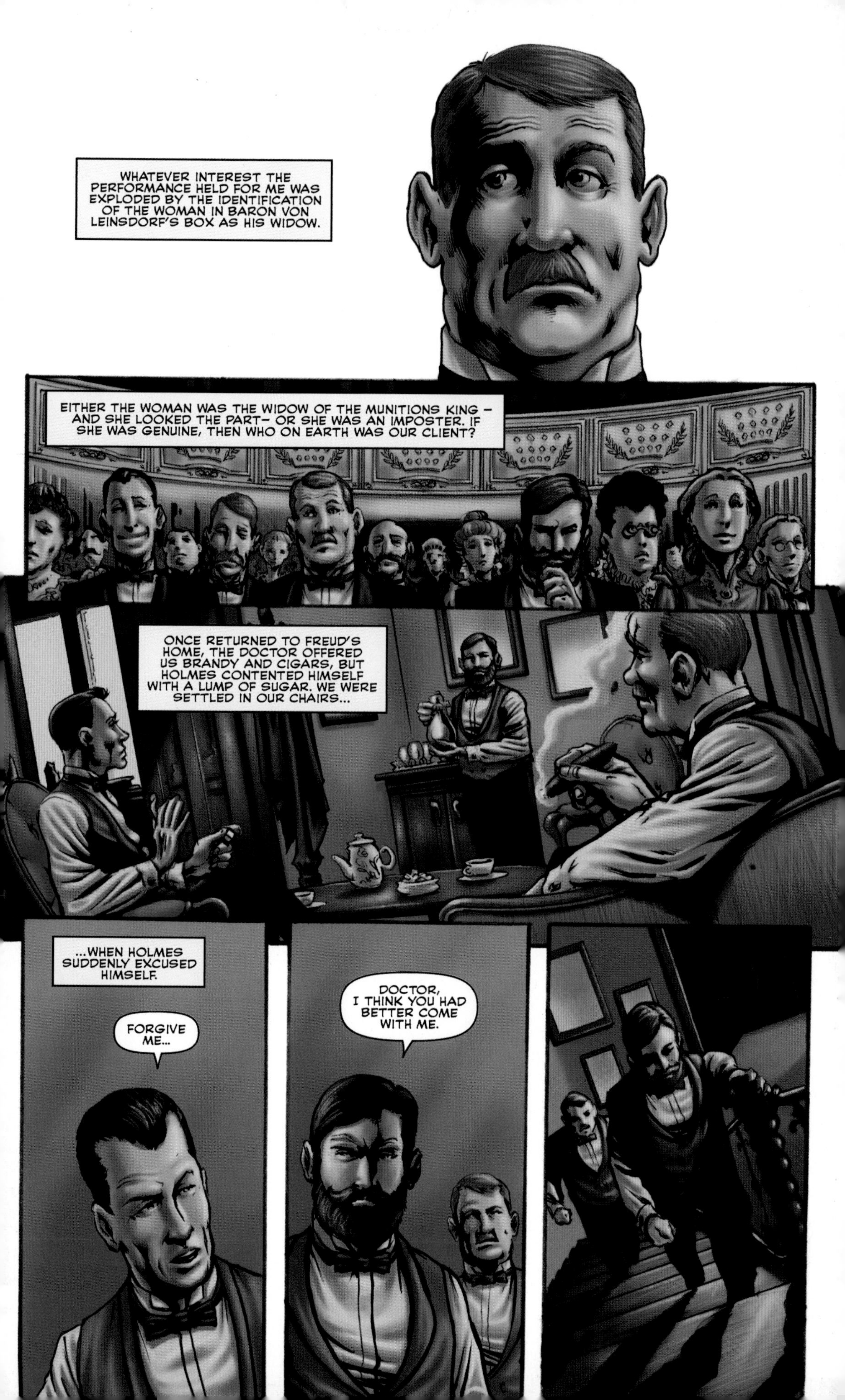
WHATEVER INTEREST THE PERFORMANCE HELD FOR ME WAS EXPLODED BY THE IDENTIFICATION OF THE WOMAN IN BARON VON LEINSDORF'S BOX AS HIS WIDOW.
EITHER THE WOMAN WAS THE WIDOW OF THE MUNITIONS KING – AND SHE LOOKED THE PART– OR SHE WAS AN IMPOSTER. IF SHE WAS GENUINE, THEN WHO ON EARTH WAS OUR CLIENT?
ONCE RETURNED TO FREUD'S HOME, THE DOCTOR OFFERED US BRANDY AND CIGARS, BUT HOLMES CONTENTED HIMSELF WITH A LUMP OF SUGAR. WE WERE SETTLED IN OUR CHAIRS...
...WHEN HOLMES SUDDENLY EXCUSED HIMSELF.
FORGIVE ME...
DOCTOR, I THINK YOU HAD BETTER COME WITH ME.

I WAS JUST CONSIDERING IT.

SO YOUR LUMP OF SUGAR INFORMED ME.

PONDER WELL: YOU CANNOT BE OF SERVICE TO US OR THE LADY YOU UNDERTOOK TO HELP IF YOU REVERT TO THIS PRACTICE NOW.

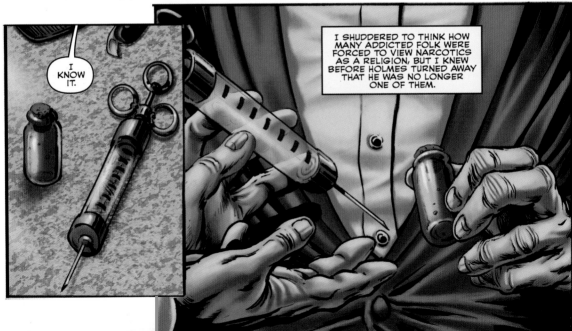

I KNOW IT.

I SHUDDERED TO THINK HOW MANY ADDICTED FOLK WERE FORCED TO VIEW NARCOTICS AS A RELIGION, BUT I KNEW BEFORE HOLMES TURNED AWAY THAT HE WAS NO LONGER ONE OF THEM.

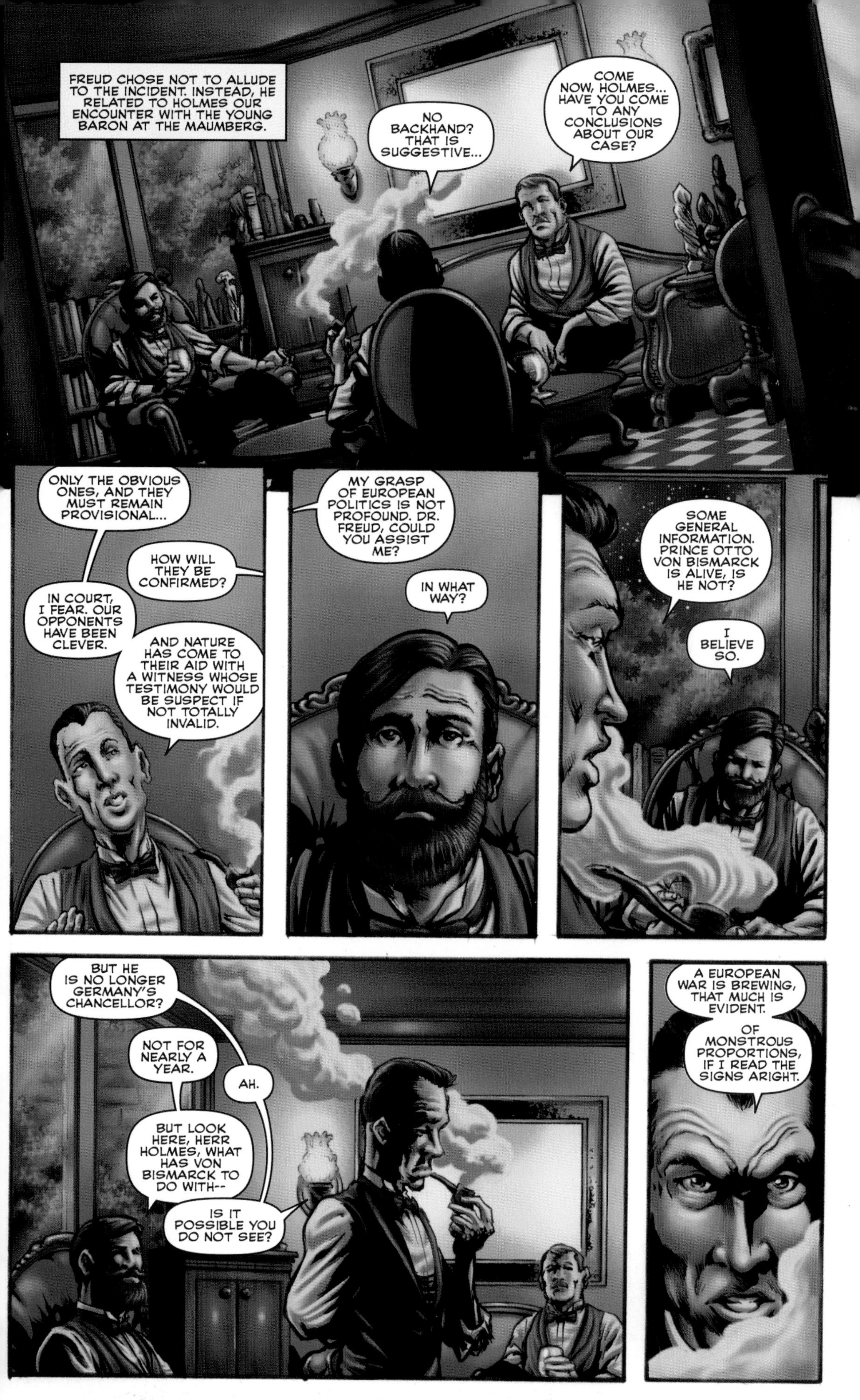
FREUD CHOSE NOT TO ALLUDE TO THE INCIDENT. INSTEAD, HE RELATED TO HOLMES OUR ENCOUNTER WITH THE YOUNG BARON AT THE MAUMBERG.
NO BACKHAND? THAT IS SUGGESTIVE...
COME NOW, HOLMES... HAVE YOU COME TO ANY CONCLUSIONS ABOUT OUR CASE?
ONLY THE OBVIOUS ONES, AND THEY MUST REMAIN PROVISIONAL...
HOW WILL THEY BE CONFIRMED?
IN COURT, I FEAR. OUR OPPONENTS HAVE BEEN CLEVER.
AND NATURE HAS COME TO THEIR AID WITH A WITNESS WHOSE TESTIMONY WOULD BE SUSPECT IF NOT TOTALLY INVALID.
MY GRASP OF EUROPEAN POLITICS IS NOT PROFOUND. DR. FREUD, COULD YOU ASSIST ME?
IN WHAT WAY?
SOME GENERAL INFORMATION. PRINCE OTTO VON BISMARCK IS ALIVE, IS HE NOT?
I BELIEVE SO.
BUT HE IS NO LONGER GERMANY'S CHANCELLOR?
NOT FOR NEARLY A YEAR.
AH.
BUT LOOK HERE, HERR HOLMES, WHAT HAS VON BISMARCK TO DO WITH--
IS IT POSSIBLE YOU DO NOT SEE?
A EUROPEAN WAR IS BREWING, THAT MUCH IS EVIDENT.
OF MONSTROUS PROPORTIONS, IF I READ THE SIGNS ARIGHT.

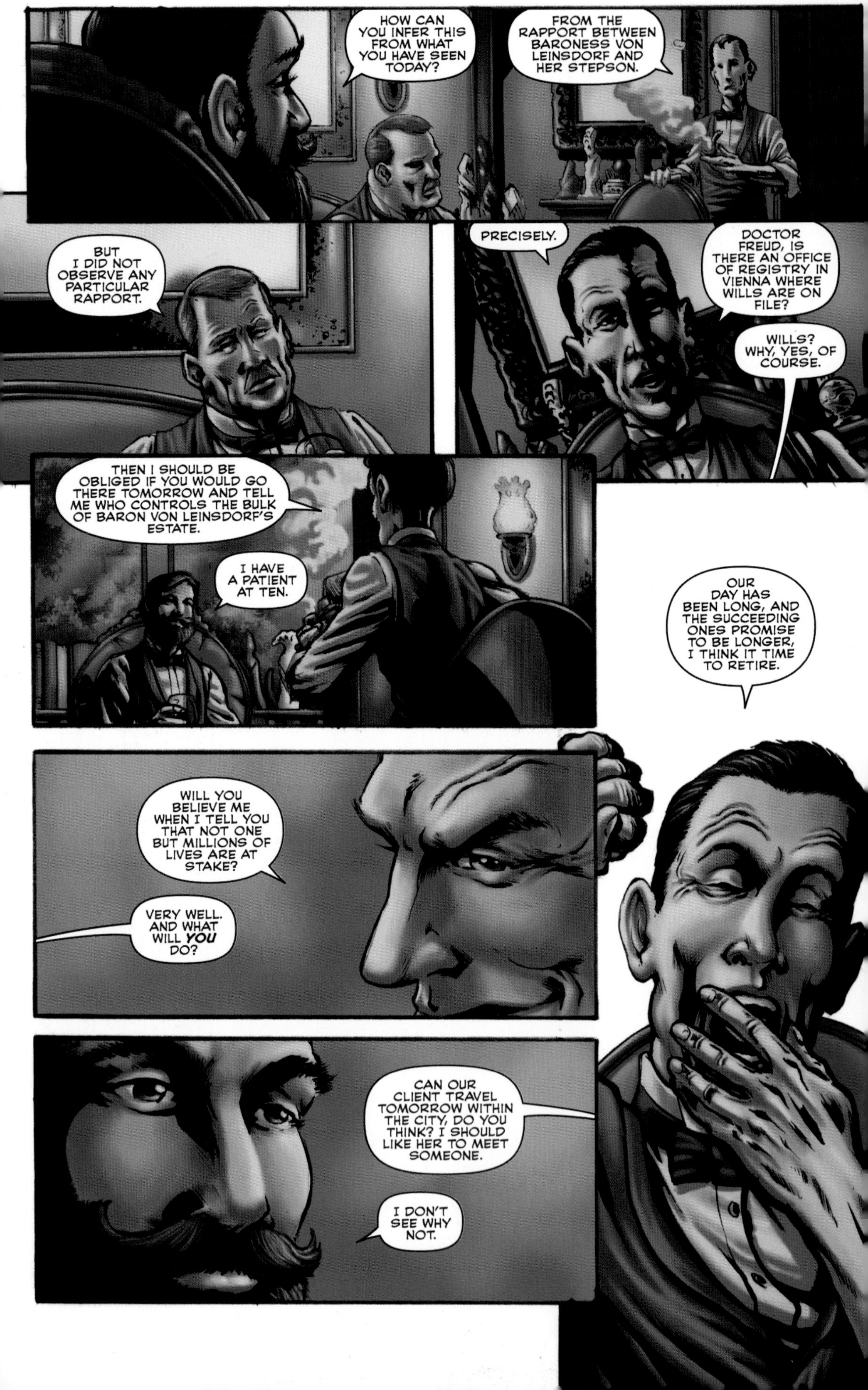
HOW CAN YOU INFER THIS FROM WHAT YOU HAVE SEEN TODAY?
FROM THE RAPPORT BETWEEN BARONESS VON LEINSDORF AND HER STEPSON.
BUT I DID NOT OBSERVE ANY PARTICULAR RAPPORT.
PRECISELY.
DOCTOR FREUD, IS THERE AN OFFICE OF REGISTRY IN VIENNA WHERE WILLS ARE ON FILE?
WILLS? WHY, YES, OF COURSE.
THEN I SHOULD BE OBLIGED IF YOU WOULD GO THERE TOMORROW AND TELL ME WHO CONTROLS THE BULK OF BARON VON LEINSDORF'S ESTATE.
I HAVE A PATIENT AT TEN.
OUR DAY HAS BEEN LONG, AND THE SUCCEEDING ONES PROMISE TO BE LONGER, I THINK IT TIME TO RETIRE.
WILL YOU BELIEVE ME WHEN I TELL YOU THAT NOT ONE BUT MILLIONS OF LIVES ARE AT STAKE?
VERY WELL. AND WHAT WILL *YOU* DO?
CAN OUR CLIENT TRAVEL TOMORROW WITHIN THE CITY, DO YOU THINK? I SHOULD LIKE HER TO MEET SOMEONE.
I DON'T SEE WHY NOT.

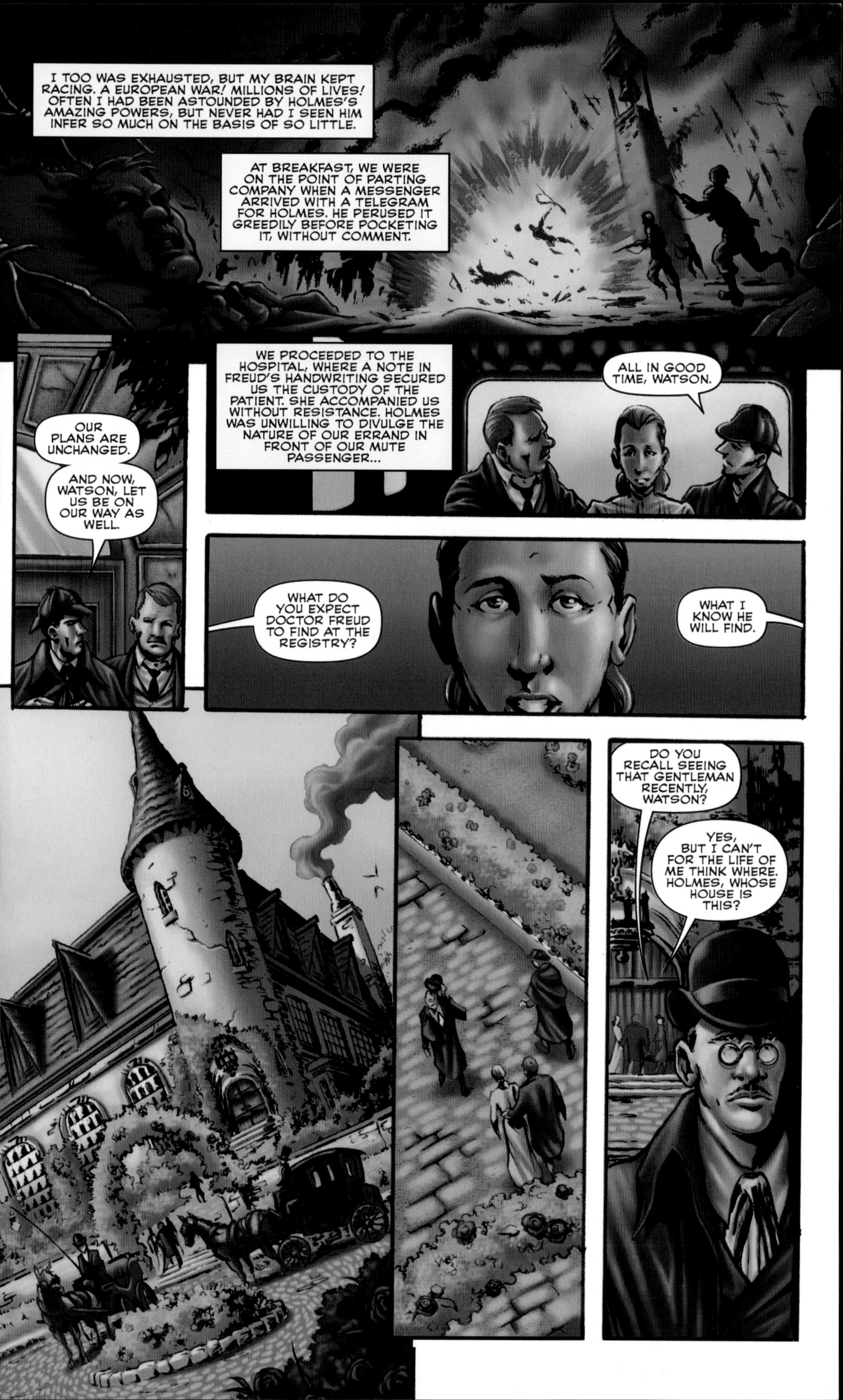
I TOO WAS EXHAUSTED, BUT MY BRAIN KEPT RACING. A EUROPEAN WAR! MILLIONS OF LIVES! OFTEN I HAD BEEN ASTOUNDED BY HOLMES'S AMAZING POWERS, BUT NEVER HAD I SEEN HIM INFER SO MUCH ON THE BASIS OF SO LITTLE.
AT BREAKFAST, WE WERE ON THE POINT OF PARTING COMPANY WHEN A MESSENGER ARRIVED WITH A TELEGRAM FOR HOLMES. HE PERUSED IT GREEDILY BEFORE POCKETING IT, WITHOUT COMMENT.
OUR PLANS ARE UNCHANGED.
AND NOW, WATSON, LET US BE ON OUR WAY AS WELL.
WE PROCEEDED TO THE HOSPITAL, WHERE A NOTE IN FREUD'S HANDWRITING SECURED US THE CUSTODY OF THE PATIENT. SHE ACCOMPANIED US WITHOUT RESISTANCE. HOLMES WAS UNWILLING TO DIVULGE THE NATURE OF OUR ERRAND IN FRONT OF OUR MUTE PASSENGER...
ALL IN GOOD TIME, WATSON.
WHAT DO YOU EXPECT DOCTOR FREUD TO FIND AT THE REGISTRY?
WHAT I KNOW HE WILL FIND.
DO YOU RECALL SEEING THAT GENTLEMAN RECENTLY, WATSON?
YES, BUT I CAN'T FOR THE LIFE OF ME THINK WHERE. HOLMES, WHOSE HOUSE IS THIS?

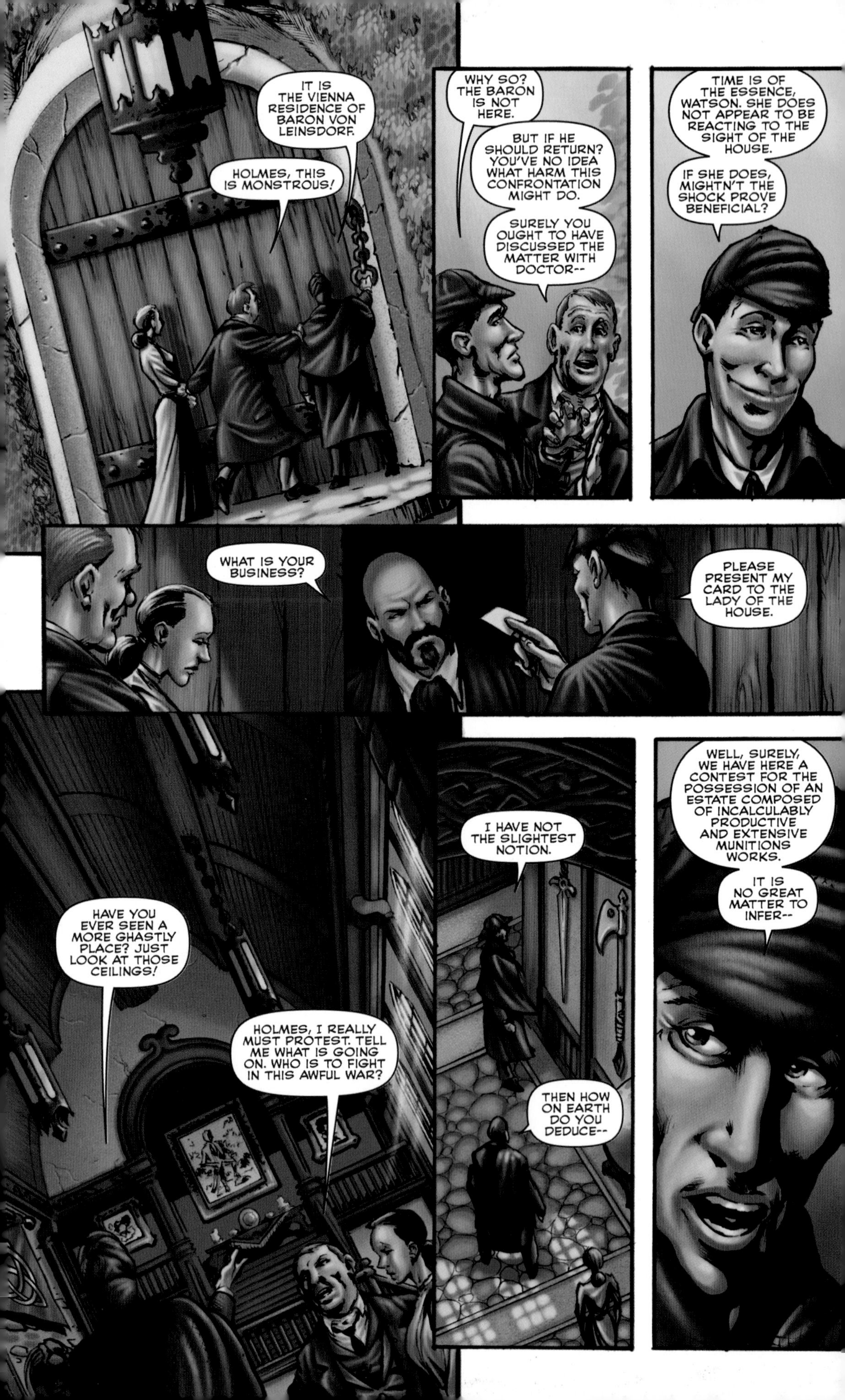
HOLMES, THIS IS MONSTROUS!
IT IS THE VIENNA RESIDENCE OF BARON VON LEINSDORF.
WHY SO? THE BARON IS NOT HERE.
BUT IF HE SHOULD RETURN? YOU'VE NO IDEA WHAT HARM THIS CONFRONTATION MIGHT DO.
SURELY YOU OUGHT TO HAVE DISCUSSED THE MATTER WITH DOCTOR--
TIME IS OF THE ESSENCE, WATSON. SHE DOES NOT APPEAR TO BE REACTING TO THE SIGHT OF THE HOUSE.
IF SHE DOES, MIGHTN'T THE SHOCK PROVE BENEFICIAL?
WHAT IS YOUR BUSINESS?
PLEASE PRESENT MY CARD TO THE LADY OF THE HOUSE.
HAVE YOU EVER SEEN A MORE GHASTLY PLACE? JUST LOOK AT THOSE CEILINGS!
HOLMES, I REALLY MUST PROTEST. TELL ME WHAT IS GOING ON. WHO IS TO FIGHT IN THIS AWFUL WAR?
I HAVE NOT THE SLIGHTEST NOTION.
THEN HOW ON EARTH DO YOU DEDUCE--
WELL, SURELY, WE HAVE HERE A CONTEST FOR THE POSSESSION OF AN ESTATE COMPOSED OF INCALCULABLY PRODUCTIVE AND EXTENSIVE MUNITIONS WORKS.
IT IS NO GREAT MATTER TO INFER--

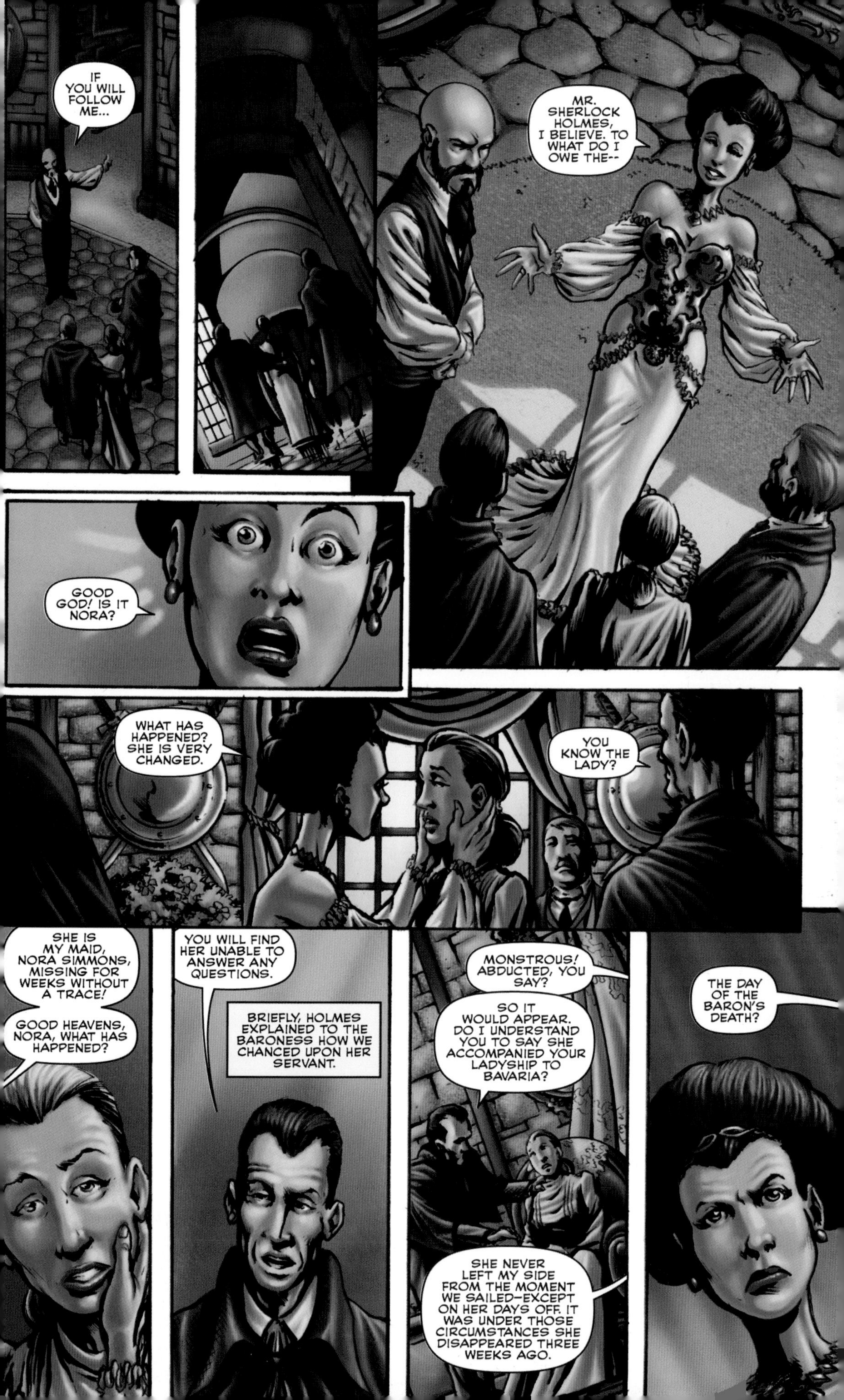
IF YOU WILL FOLLOW ME...
MR. SHERLOCK HOLMES, I BELIEVE. TO WHAT DO I OWE THE--
GOOD GOD! IS IT NORA?
WHAT HAS HAPPENED? SHE IS VERY CHANGED.
YOU KNOW THE LADY?
SHE IS MY MAID, NORA SIMMONS, MISSING FOR WEEKS WITHOUT A TRACE!
GOOD HEAVENS, NORA, WHAT HAS HAPPENED?
YOU WILL FIND HER UNABLE TO ANSWER ANY QUESTIONS.
BRIEFLY, HOLMES EXPLAINED TO THE BARONESS HOW WE CHANCED UPON HER SERVANT.
MONSTROUS! ABDUCTED, YOU SAY?
SO IT WOULD APPEAR. DO I UNDERSTAND YOU TO SAY SHE ACCOMPANIED YOUR LADYSHIP TO BAVARIA?
SHE NEVER LEFT MY SIDE FROM THE MOMENT WE SAILED—EXCEPT ON HER DAYS OFF. IT WAS UNDER THOSE CIRCUMSTANCES SHE DISAPPEARED THREE WEEKS AGO.
THE DAY OF THE BARON'S DEATH?

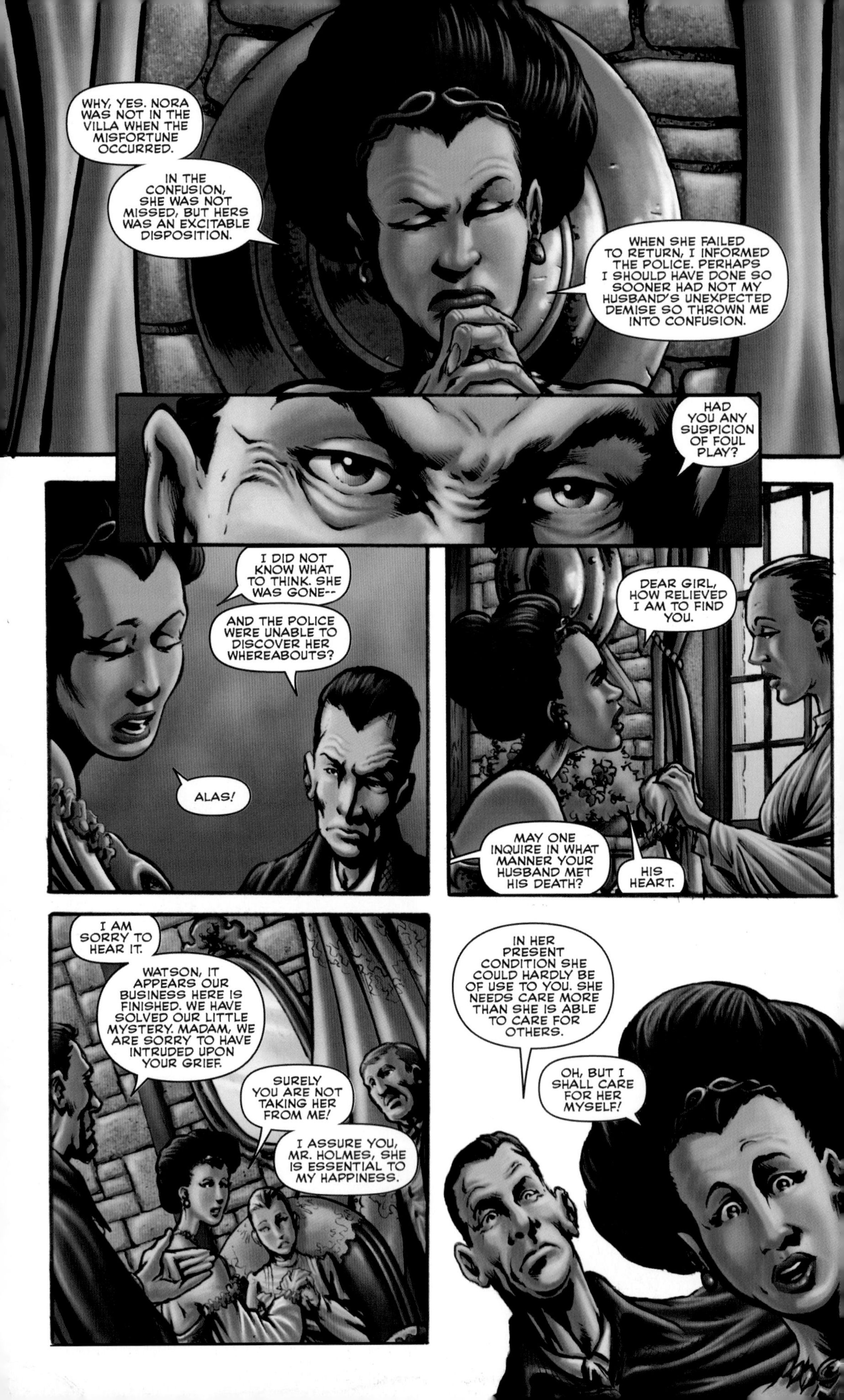
WHY, YES. NORA WAS NOT IN THE VILLA WHEN THE MISFORTUNE OCCURRED.
IN THE CONFUSION, SHE WAS NOT MISSED, BUT HERS WAS AN EXCITABLE DISPOSITION.
WHEN SHE FAILED TO RETURN, I INFORMED THE POLICE. PERHAPS I SHOULD HAVE DONE SO SOONER HAD NOT MY HUSBAND'S UNEXPECTED DEMISE SO THROWN ME INTO CONFUSION.
HAD YOU ANY SUSPICION OF FOUL PLAY?
I DID NOT KNOW WHAT TO THINK. SHE WAS GONE--
AND THE POLICE WERE UNABLE TO DISCOVER HER WHEREABOUTS?
ALAS!
DEAR GIRL, HOW RELIEVED I AM TO FIND YOU.
MAY ONE INQUIRE IN WHAT MANNER YOUR HUSBAND MET HIS DEATH?
HIS HEART.
I AM SORRY TO HEAR IT.
WATSON, IT APPEARS OUR BUSINESS HERE IS FINISHED. WE HAVE SOLVED OUR LITTLE MYSTERY. MADAM, WE ARE SORRY TO HAVE INTRUDED UPON YOUR GRIEF.
SURELY YOU ARE NOT TAKING HER FROM ME!
I ASSURE YOU, MR. HOLMES, SHE IS ESSENTIAL TO MY HAPPINESS.
IN HER PRESENT CONDITION SHE COULD HARDLY BE OF USE TO YOU. SHE NEEDS CARE MORE THAN SHE IS ABLE TO CARE FOR OTHERS.
OH, BUT I SHALL CARE FOR HER MYSELF!

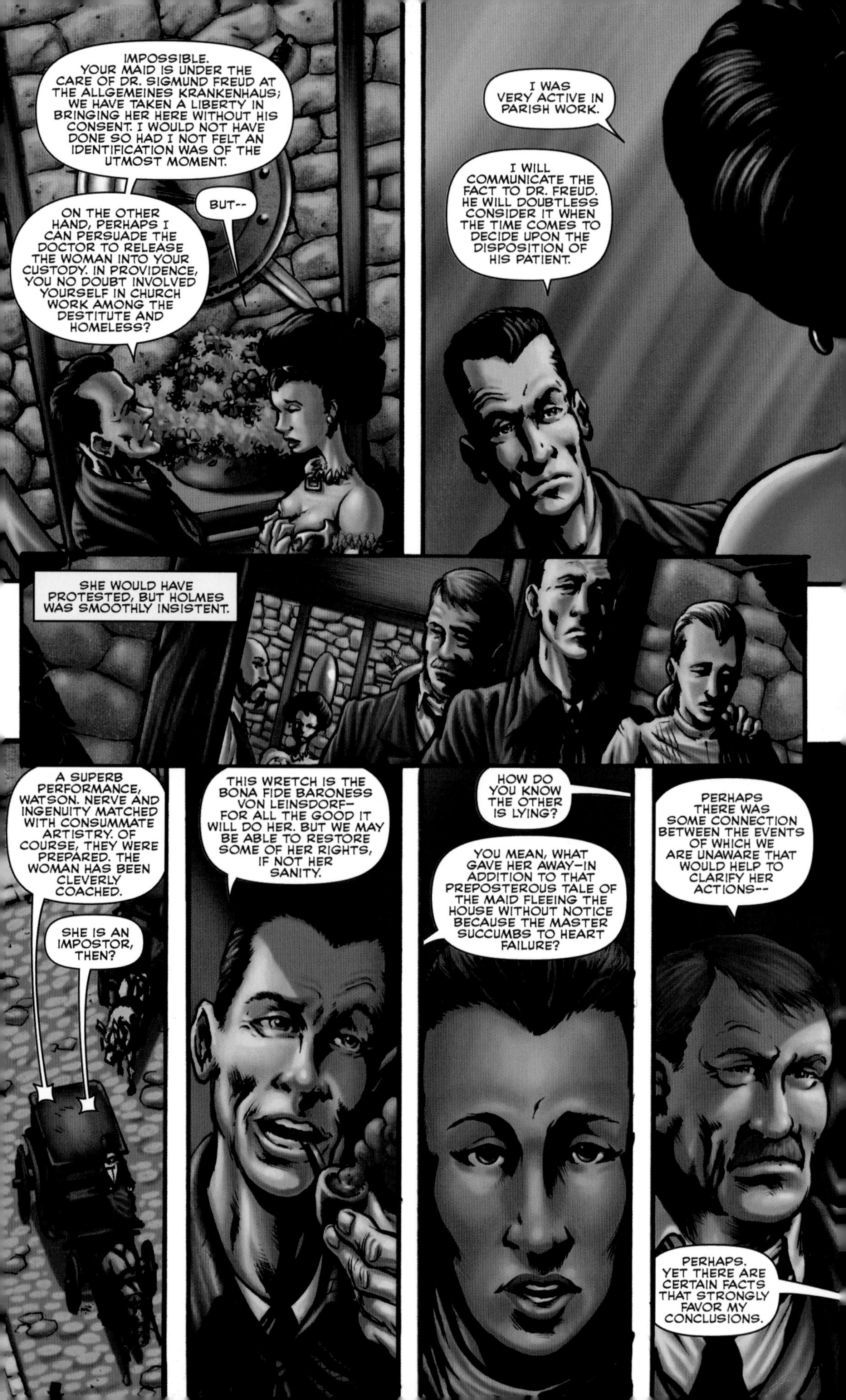
IMPOSSIBLE. YOUR MAID IS UNDER THE CARE OF DR. SIGMUND FREUD AT THE ALLGEMEINES KRANKENHAUS; WE HAVE TAKEN A LIBERTY IN BRINGING HER HERE WITHOUT HIS CONSENT. I WOULD NOT HAVE DONE SO HAD I NOT FELT AN IDENTIFICATION WAS OF THE UTMOST MOMENT.
BUT--
ON THE OTHER HAND, PERHAPS I CAN PERSUADE THE DOCTOR TO RELEASE THE WOMAN INTO YOUR CUSTODY. IN PROVIDENCE, YOU NO DOUBT INVOLVED YOURSELF IN CHURCH WORK AMONG THE DESTITUTE AND HOMELESS?
I WAS VERY ACTIVE IN PARISH WORK.
I WILL COMMUNICATE THE FACT TO DR. FREUD. HE WILL DOUBTLESS CONSIDER IT WHEN THE TIME COMES TO DECIDE UPON THE DISPOSITION OF HIS PATIENT.
SHE WOULD HAVE PROTESTED, BUT HOLMES WAS SMOOTHLY INSISTENT.
A SUPERB PERFORMANCE, WATSON. NERVE AND INGENUITY MATCHED WITH CONSUMMATE ARTISTRY. OF COURSE, THEY WERE PREPARED. THE WOMAN HAS BEEN CLEVERLY COACHED.
SHE IS AN IMPOSTOR, THEN?
THIS WRETCH IS THE BONA FIDE BARONESS VON LEINSDORF—FOR ALL THE GOOD IT WILL DO HER. BUT WE MAY BE ABLE TO RESTORE SOME OF HER RIGHTS, IF NOT HER SANITY.
HOW DO YOU KNOW THE OTHER IS LYING?
YOU MEAN, WHAT GAVE HER AWAY—IN ADDITION TO THAT PREPOSTEROUS TALE OF THE MAID FLEEING THE HOUSE WITHOUT NOTICE BECAUSE THE MASTER SUCCUMBS TO HEART FAILURE?
PERHAPS THERE WAS SOME CONNECTION BETWEEN THE EVENTS OF WHICH WE ARE UNAWARE THAT WOULD HELP TO CLARIFY HER ACTIONS--
PERHAPS. YET THERE ARE CERTAIN FACTS THAT STRONGLY FAVOR MY CONCLUSIONS.

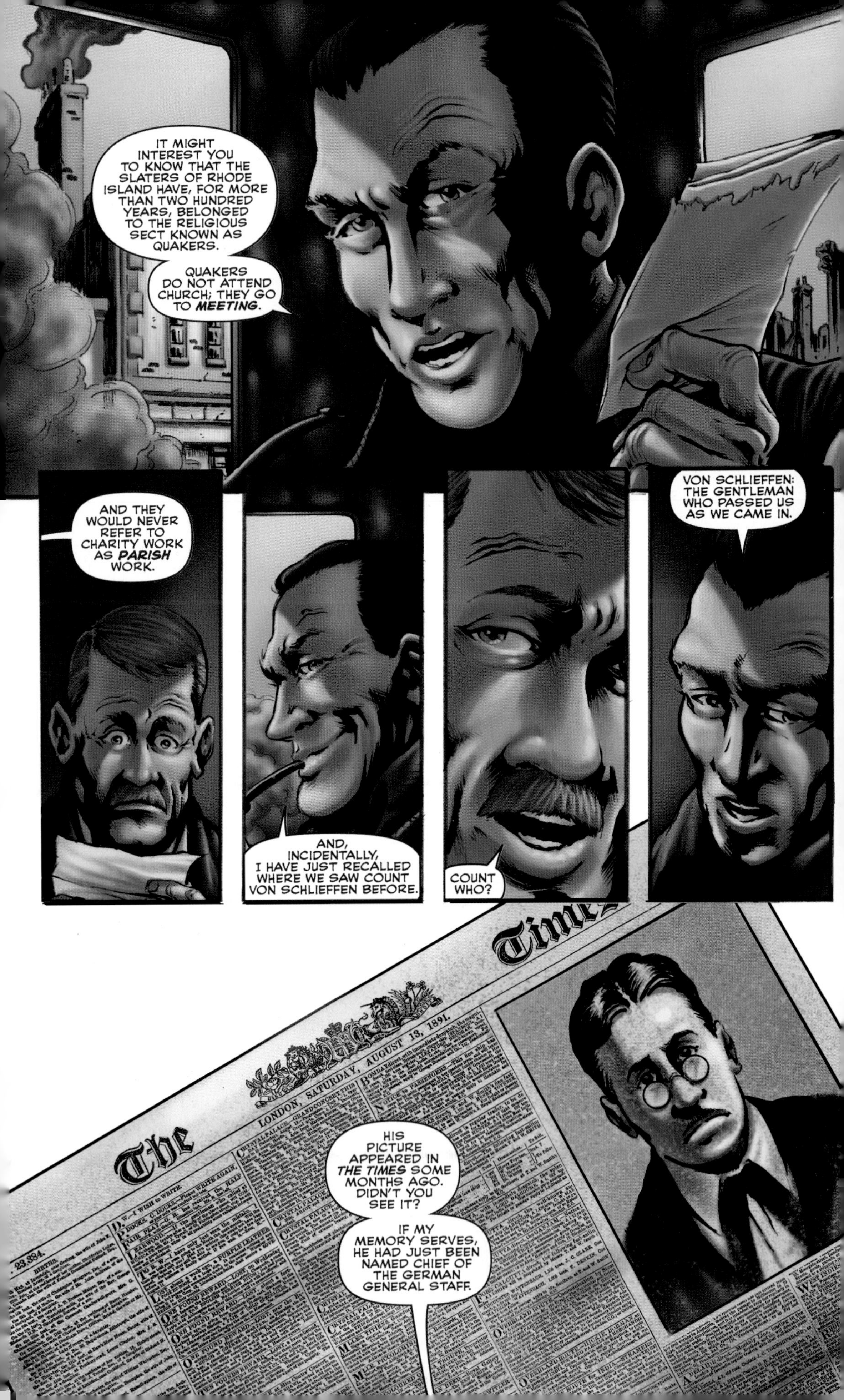
IT MIGHT INTEREST YOU TO KNOW THAT THE SLATERS OF RHODE ISLAND HAVE, FOR MORE THAN TWO HUNDRED YEARS, BELONGED TO THE RELIGIOUS SECT KNOWN AS QUAKERS.
QUAKERS DO NOT ATTEND CHURCH; THEY GO TO *MEETING*.
AND THEY WOULD NEVER REFER TO CHARITY WORK AS *PARISH* WORK.
AND, INCIDENTALLY, I HAVE JUST RECALLED WHERE WE SAW COUNT VON SCHLIEFFEN BEFORE.
COUNT WHO?
VON SCHLIEFFEN: THE GENTLEMAN WHO PASSED US AS WE CAME IN.
LONDON, SATURDAY, AUGUST 13, 1891.
HIS PICTURE APPEARED IN *THE TIMES* SOME MONTHS AGO. DIDN'T YOU SEE IT?
IF MY MEMORY SERVES, HE HAD JUST BEEN NAMED CHIEF OF THE GERMAN GENERAL STAFF.

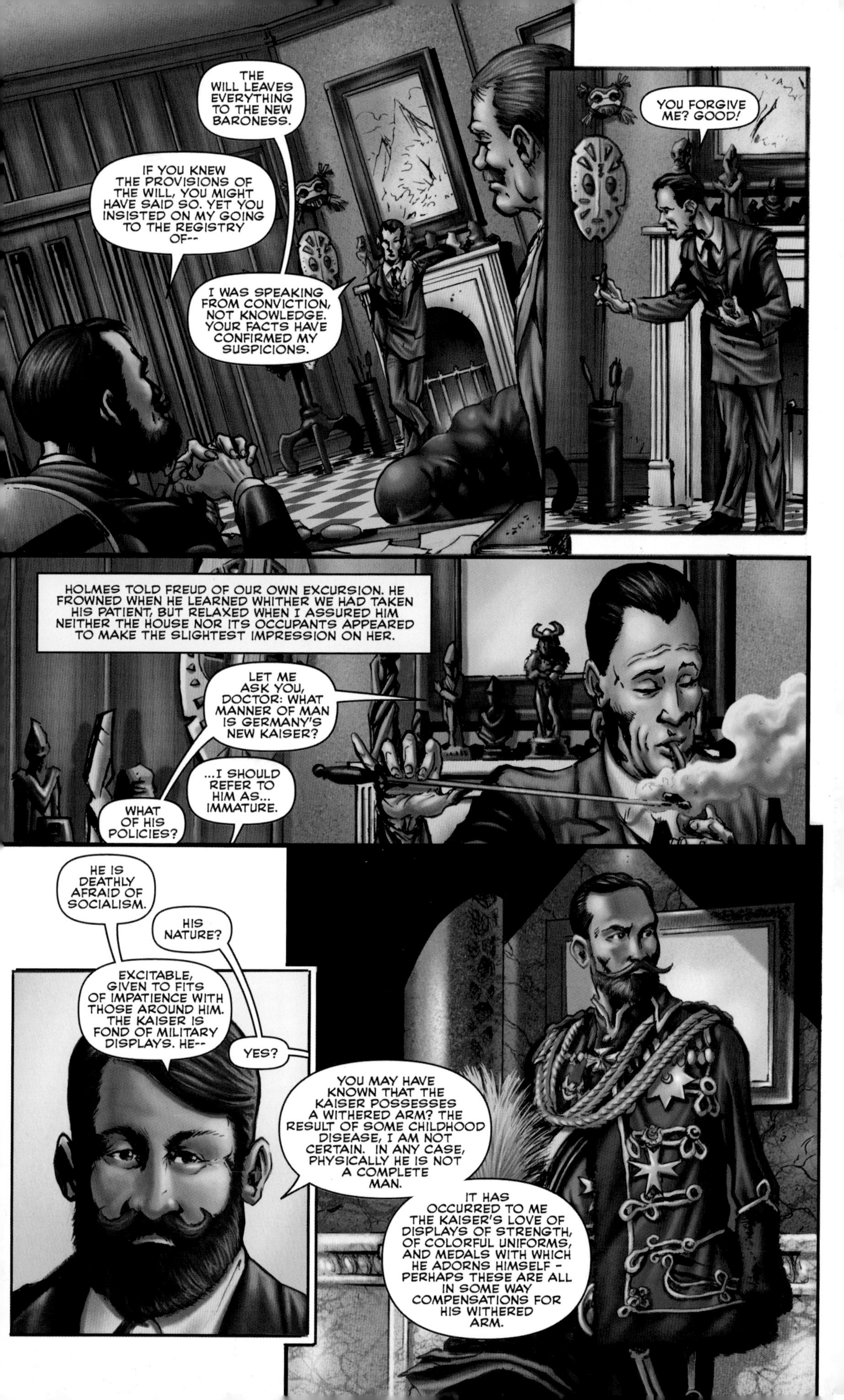
THE WILL LEAVES EVERYTHING TO THE NEW BARONESS.
IF YOU KNEW THE PROVISIONS OF THE WILL, YOU MIGHT HAVE SAID SO. YET YOU INSISTED ON MY GOING TO THE REGISTRY OF--
I WAS SPEAKING FROM CONVICTION, NOT KNOWLEDGE. YOUR FACTS HAVE CONFIRMED MY SUSPICIONS.
YOU FORGIVE ME? GOOD!
HOLMES TOLD FREUD OF OUR OWN EXCURSION. HE FROWNED WHEN HE LEARNED WHITHER WE HAD TAKEN HIS PATIENT, BUT RELAXED WHEN I ASSURED HIM NEITHER THE HOUSE NOR ITS OCCUPANTS APPEARED TO MAKE THE SLIGHTEST IMPRESSION ON HER.
LET ME ASK YOU, DOCTOR: WHAT MANNER OF MAN IS GERMANY'S NEW KAISER?
...I SHOULD REFER TO HIM AS... IMMATURE.
WHAT OF HIS POLICIES?
HE IS DEATHLY AFRAID OF SOCIALISM.
HIS NATURE?
EXCITABLE, GIVEN TO FITS OF IMPATIENCE WITH THOSE AROUND HIM. THE KAISER IS FOND OF MILITARY DISPLAYS. HE--
YES?
YOU MAY HAVE KNOWN THAT THE KAISER POSSESSES A WITHERED ARM? THE RESULT OF SOME CHILDHOOD DISEASE, I AM NOT CERTAIN. IN ANY CASE, PHYSICALLY HE IS NOT A COMPLETE MAN.
IT HAS OCCURRED TO ME THE KAISER'S LOVE OF DISPLAYS OF STRENGTH, OF COLORFUL UNIFORMS, AND MEDALS WITH WHICH HE ADORNS HIMSELF - PERHAPS THESE ARE ALL IN SOME WAY COMPENSATIONS FOR HIS WITHERED ARM.

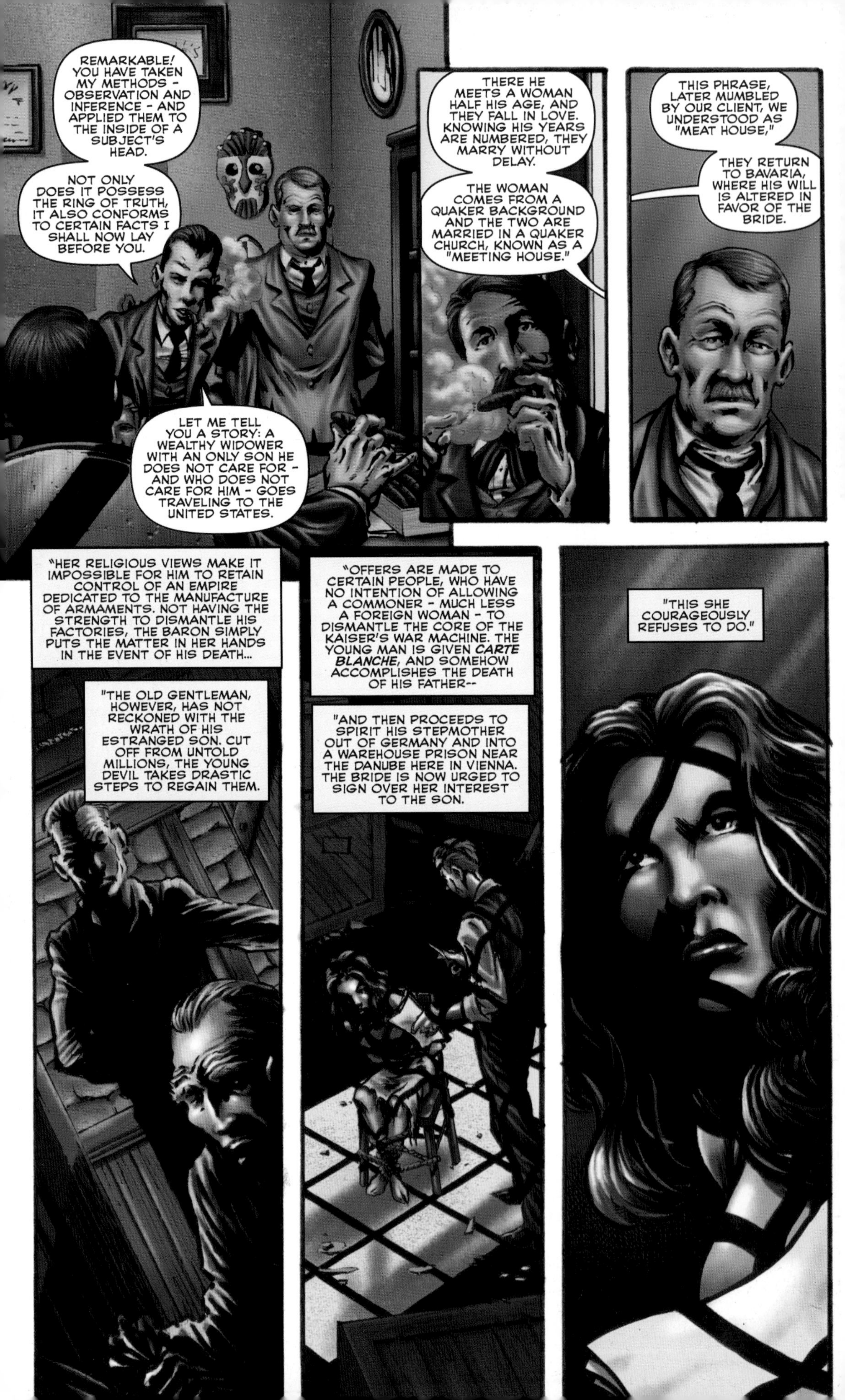
REMARKABLE! YOU HAVE TAKEN MY METHODS - OBSERVATION AND INFERENCE - AND APPLIED THEM TO THE INSIDE OF A SUBJECT'S HEAD.
NOT ONLY DOES IT POSSESS THE RING OF TRUTH, IT ALSO CONFORMS TO CERTAIN FACTS I SHALL NOW LAY BEFORE YOU.
LET ME TELL YOU A STORY: A WEALTHY WIDOWER WITH AN ONLY SON HE DOES NOT CARE FOR - AND WHO DOES NOT CARE FOR HIM - GOES TRAVELING TO THE UNITED STATES.
THERE HE MEETS A WOMAN HALF HIS AGE, AND THEY FALL IN LOVE. KNOWING HIS YEARS ARE NUMBERED, THEY MARRY WITHOUT DELAY.
THE WOMAN COMES FROM A QUAKER BACKGROUND AND THE TWO ARE MARRIED IN A QUAKER CHURCH, KNOWN AS A "MEETING HOUSE."
THIS PHRASE, LATER MUMBLED BY OUR CLIENT, WE UNDERSTOOD AS "MEAT HOUSE,"
THEY RETURN TO BAVARIA, WHERE HIS WILL IS ALTERED IN FAVOR OF THE BRIDE.
"HER RELIGIOUS VIEWS MAKE IT IMPOSSIBLE FOR HIM TO RETAIN CONTROL OF AN EMPIRE DEDICATED TO THE MANUFACTURE OF ARMAMENTS. NOT HAVING THE STRENGTH TO DISMANTLE HIS FACTORIES, THE BARON SIMPLY PUTS THE MATTER IN HER HANDS IN THE EVENT OF HIS DEATH...
"THE OLD GENTLEMAN, HOWEVER, HAS NOT RECKONED WITH THE WRATH OF HIS ESTRANGED SON. CUT OFF FROM UNTOLD MILLIONS, THE YOUNG DEVIL TAKES DRASTIC STEPS TO REGAIN THEM.
"OFFERS ARE MADE TO CERTAIN PEOPLE, WHO HAVE NO INTENTION OF ALLOWING A COMMONER - MUCH LESS A FOREIGN WOMAN - TO DISMANTLE THE CORE OF THE KAISER'S WAR MACHINE. THE YOUNG MAN IS GIVEN *CARTE BLANCHE*, AND SOMEHOW ACCOMPLISHES THE DEATH OF HIS FATHER--
"AND THEN PROCEEDS TO SPIRIT HIS STEPMOTHER OUT OF GERMANY AND INTO A WAREHOUSE PRISON NEAR THE DANUBE HERE IN VIENNA. THE BRIDE IS NOW URGED TO SIGN OVER HER INTEREST TO THE SON.
"THIS SHE COURAGEOUSLY REFUSES TO DO."

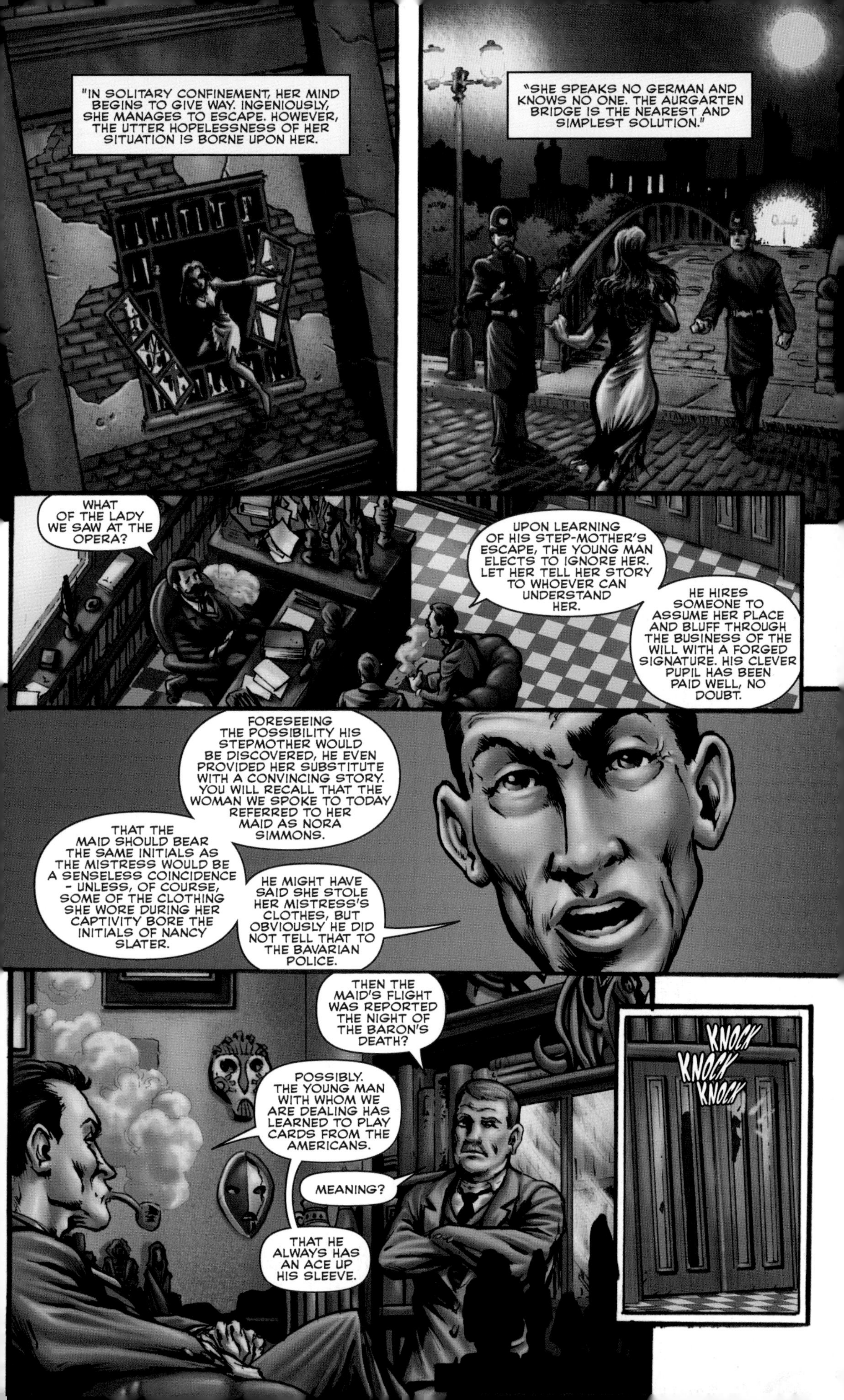
"IN SOLITARY CONFINEMENT, HER MIND BEGINS TO GIVE WAY. INGENIOUSLY, SHE MANAGES TO ESCAPE. HOWEVER, THE UTTER HOPELESSNESS OF HER SITUATION IS BORNE UPON HER.
"SHE SPEAKS NO GERMAN AND KNOWS NO ONE. THE AURGARTEN BRIDGE IS THE NEAREST AND SIMPLEST SOLUTION."
WHAT OF THE LADY WE SAW AT THE OPERA?
UPON LEARNING OF HIS STEP-MOTHER'S ESCAPE, THE YOUNG MAN ELECTS TO IGNORE HER. LET HER TELL HER STORY TO WHOEVER CAN UNDERSTAND HER.
HE HIRES SOMEONE TO ASSUME HER PLACE AND BLUFF THROUGH THE BUSINESS OF THE WILL WITH A FORGED SIGNATURE. HIS CLEVER PUPIL HAS BEEN PAID WELL, NO DOUBT.
FORESEEING THE POSSIBILITY HIS STEPMOTHER WOULD BE DISCOVERED, HE EVEN PROVIDED HER SUBSTITUTE WITH A CONVINCING STORY. YOU WILL RECALL THAT THE WOMAN WE SPOKE TO TODAY REFERRED TO HER MAID AS NORA SIMMONS.
THAT THE MAID SHOULD BEAR THE SAME INITIALS AS THE MISTRESS WOULD BE A SENSELESS COINCIDENCE - UNLESS, OF COURSE, SOME OF THE CLOTHING SHE WORE DURING HER CAPTIVITY BORE THE INITIALS OF NANCY SLATER.
HE MIGHT HAVE SAID SHE STOLE HER MISTRESS'S CLOTHES, BUT OBVIOUSLY HE DID NOT TELL THAT TO THE BAVARIAN POLICE.
THEN THE MAID'S FLIGHT WAS REPORTED THE NIGHT OF THE BARON'S DEATH?
POSSIBLY. THE YOUNG MAN WITH WHOM WE ARE DEALING HAS LEARNED TO PLAY CARDS FROM THE AMERICANS.
MEANING?
THAT HE ALWAYS HAS AN ACE UP HIS SLEEVE.
KNOCK
KNOCK
KNOCK

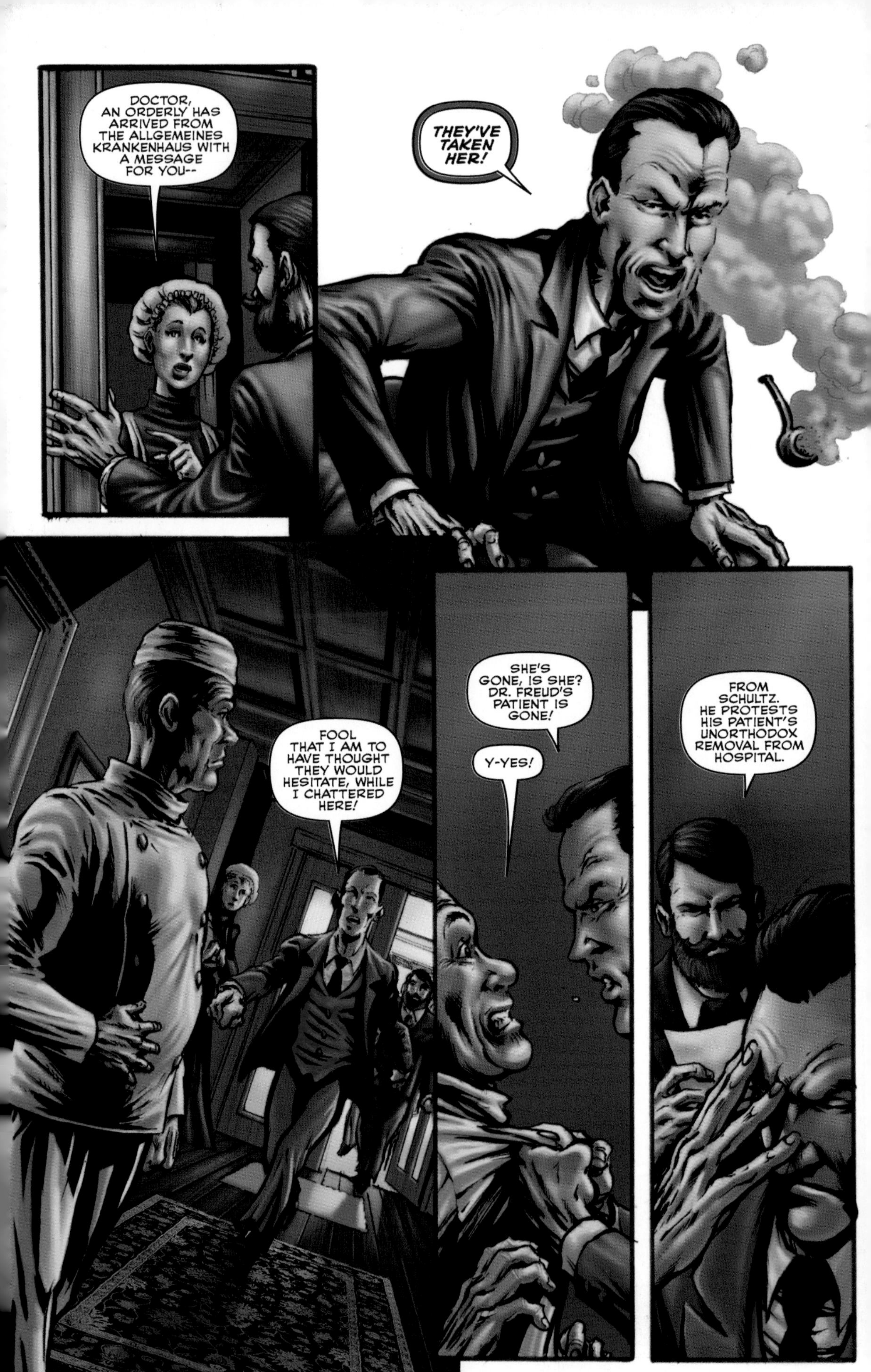
DOCTOR, AN ORDERLY HAS ARRIVED FROM THE ALLGEMEINES KRANKENHAUS WITH A MESSAGE FOR YOU--
THEY'VE TAKEN HER!
FOOL THAT I AM TO HAVE THOUGHT THEY WOULD HESITATE, WHILE I CHATTERED HERE!
SHE'S GONE, IS SHE? DR. FREUD'S PATIENT IS GONE!
Y-YES!
FROM SCHULTZ. HE PROTESTS HIS PATIENT'S UNORTHODOX REMOVAL FROM HOSPITAL.

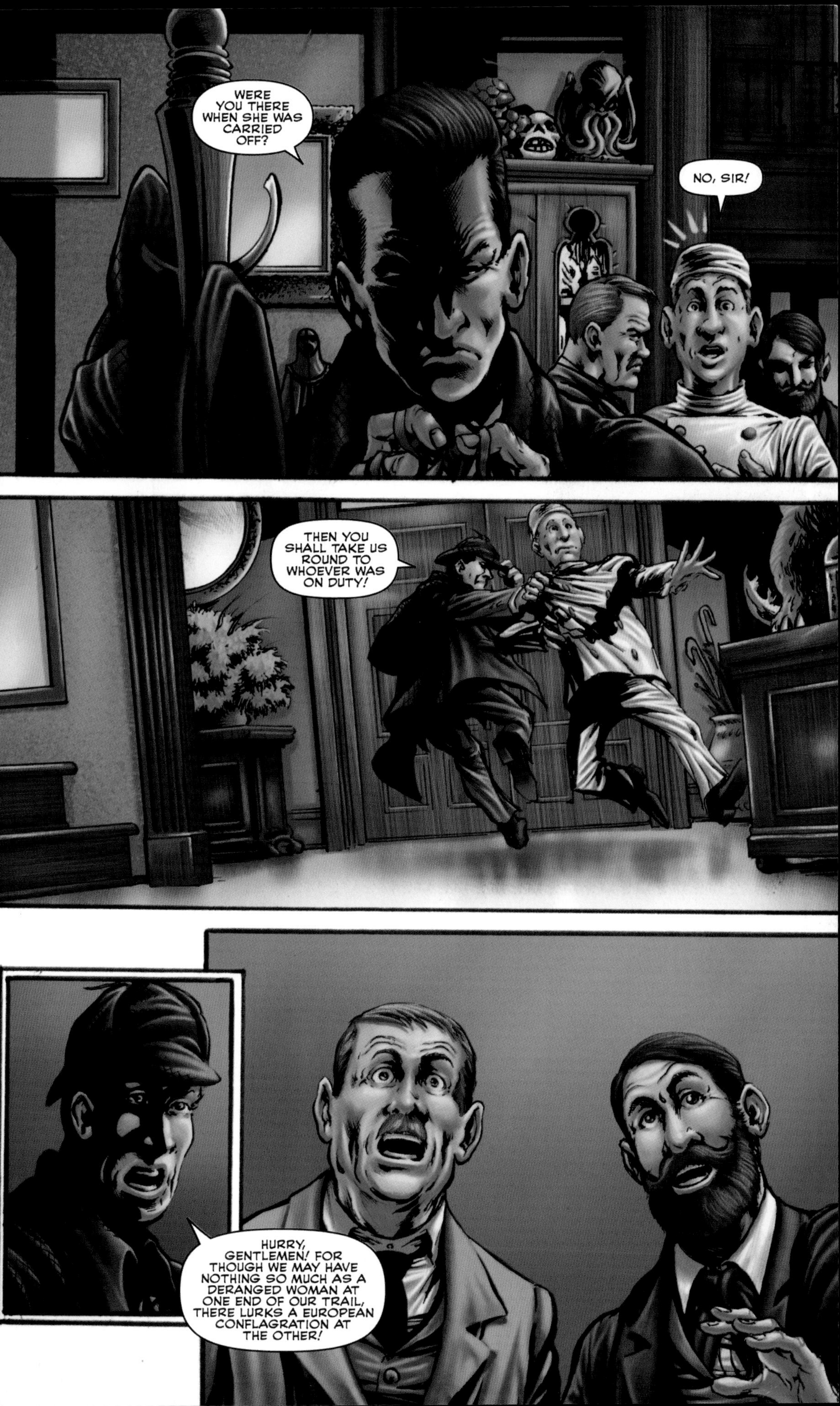
WERE YOU THERE WHEN SHE WAS CARRIED OFF?
NO, SIR!
THEN YOU SHALL TAKE US ROUND TO WHOEVER WAS ON DUTY!
HURRY, GENTLEMEN! FOR THOUGH WE MAY HAVE NOTHING SO MUCH AS A DERANGED WOMAN AT ONE END OF OUR TRAIL, THERE LURKS A EUROPEAN CONFLAGRATION AT THE OTHER!

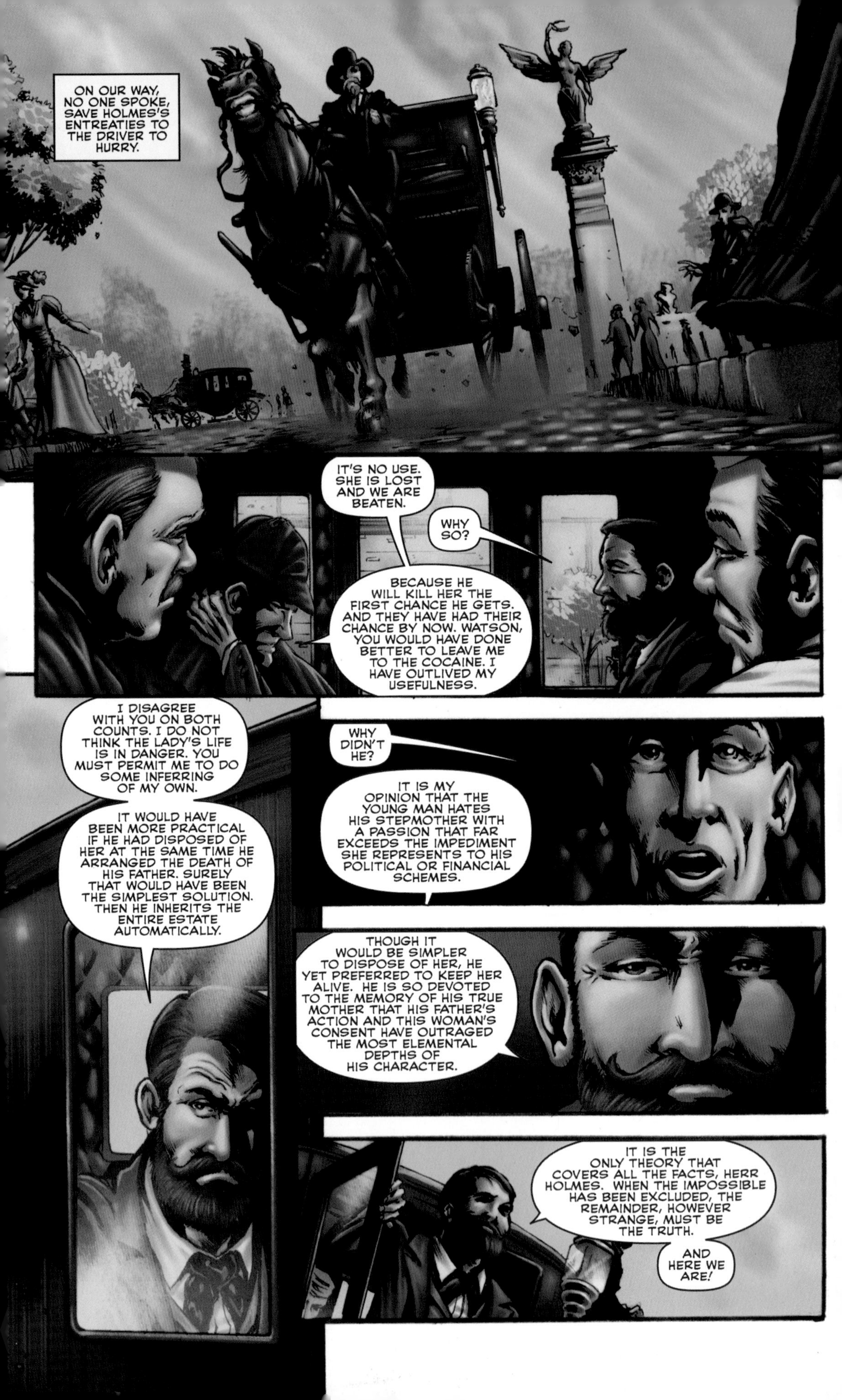
ON OUR WAY, NO ONE SPOKE, SAVE HOLMES'S ENTREATIES TO THE DRIVER TO HURRY.
IT'S NO USE. SHE IS LOST AND WE ARE BEATEN.
WHY SO?
BECAUSE HE WILL KILL HER THE FIRST CHANCE HE GETS. AND THEY HAVE HAD THEIR CHANCE BY NOW. WATSON, YOU WOULD HAVE DONE BETTER TO LEAVE ME TO THE COCAINE. I HAVE OUTLIVED MY USEFULNESS.
I DISAGREE WITH YOU ON BOTH COUNTS. I DO NOT THINK THE LADY'S LIFE IS IN DANGER. YOU MUST PERMIT ME TO DO SOME INFERRING OF MY OWN.
IT WOULD HAVE BEEN MORE PRACTICAL IF HE HAD DISPOSED OF HER AT THE SAME TIME HE ARRANGED THE DEATH OF HIS FATHER. SURELY THAT WOULD HAVE BEEN THE SIMPLEST SOLUTION. THEN HE INHERITS THE ENTIRE ESTATE AUTOMATICALLY.
WHY DIDN'T HE?
IT IS MY OPINION THAT THE YOUNG MAN HATES HIS STEPMOTHER WITH A PASSION THAT FAR EXCEEDS THE IMPEDIMENT SHE REPRESENTS TO HIS POLITICAL OR FINANCIAL SCHEMES.
THOUGH IT WOULD BE SIMPLER TO DISPOSE OF HER, HE YET PREFERRED TO KEEP HER ALIVE. HE IS SO DEVOTED TO THE MEMORY OF HIS TRUE MOTHER THAT HIS FATHER'S ACTION AND THIS WOMAN'S CONSENT HAVE OUTRAGED THE MOST ELEMENTAL DEPTHS OF HIS CHARACTER.
IT IS THE ONLY THEORY THAT COVERS ALL THE FACTS, HERR HOLMES. WHEN THE IMPOSSIBLE HAS BEEN EXCLUDED, THE REMAINDER, HOWEVER STRANGE, MUST BE THE TRUTH.
AND HERE WE ARE!

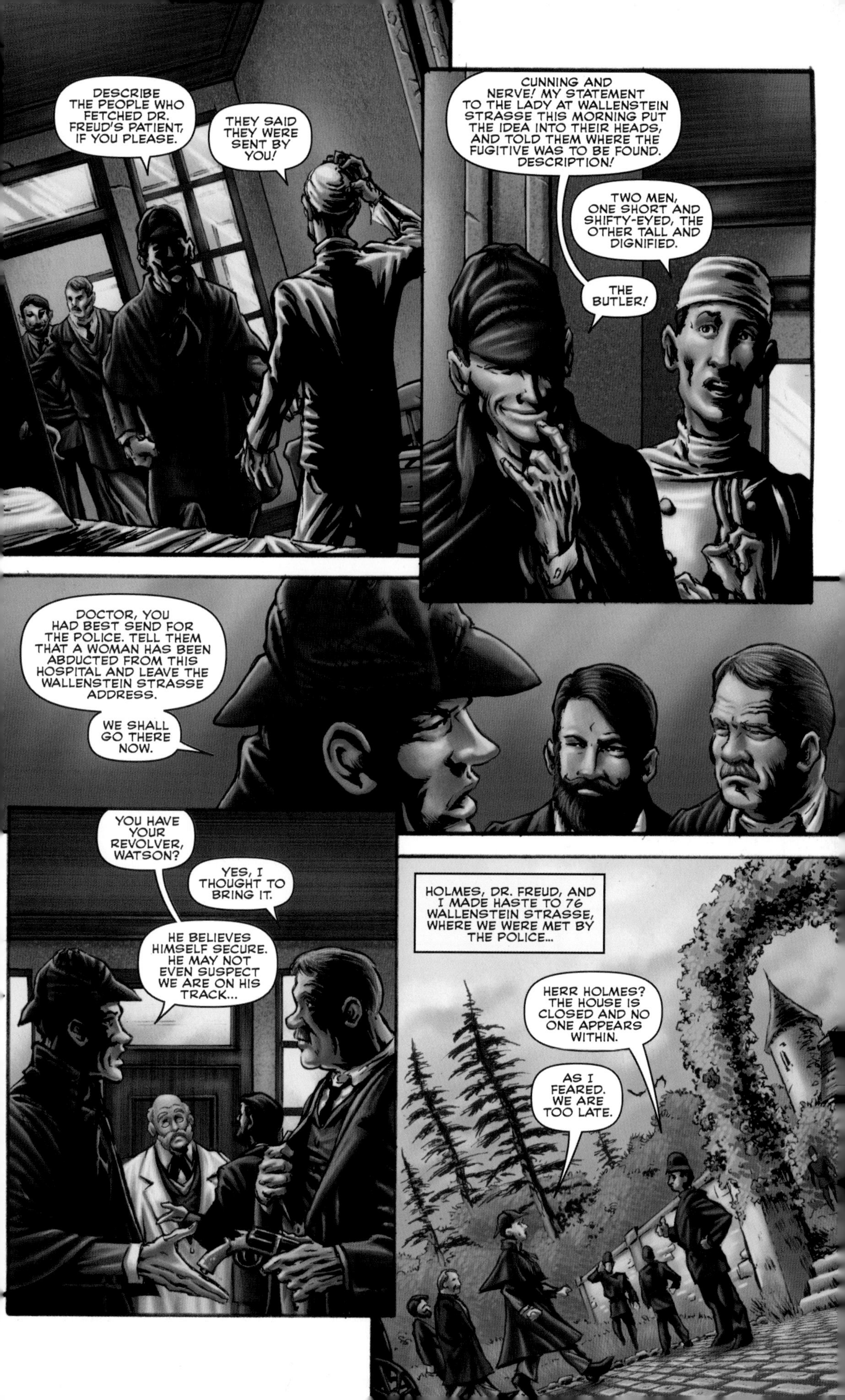
DESCRIBE THE PEOPLE WHO FETCHED DR. FREUD'S PATIENT, IF YOU PLEASE.
THEY SAID THEY WERE SENT BY YOU!
CUNNING AND NERVE! MY STATEMENT TO THE LADY AT WALLENSTEIN STRASSE THIS MORNING PUT THE IDEA INTO THEIR HEADS, AND TOLD THEM WHERE THE FUGITIVE WAS TO BE FOUND. DESCRIPTION!
TWO MEN, ONE SHORT AND SHIFTY-EYED, THE OTHER TALL AND DIGNIFIED.
THE BUTLER!
DOCTOR, YOU HAD BEST SEND FOR THE POLICE. TELL THEM THAT A WOMAN HAS BEEN ABDUCTED FROM THIS HOSPITAL AND LEAVE THE WALLENSTEIN STRASSE ADDRESS.
WE SHALL GO THERE NOW.
YOU HAVE YOUR REVOLVER, WATSON?
YES, I THOUGHT TO BRING IT.
HE BELIEVES HIMSELF SECURE. HE MAY NOT EVEN SUSPECT WE ARE ON HIS TRACK...
HOLMES, DR. FREUD, AND I MADE HASTE TO 76 WALLENSTEIN STRASSE, WHERE WE WERE MET BY THE POLICE...
HERR HOLMES? THE HOUSE IS CLOSED AND NO ONE APPEARS WITHIN.
AS I FEARED. WE ARE TOO LATE.

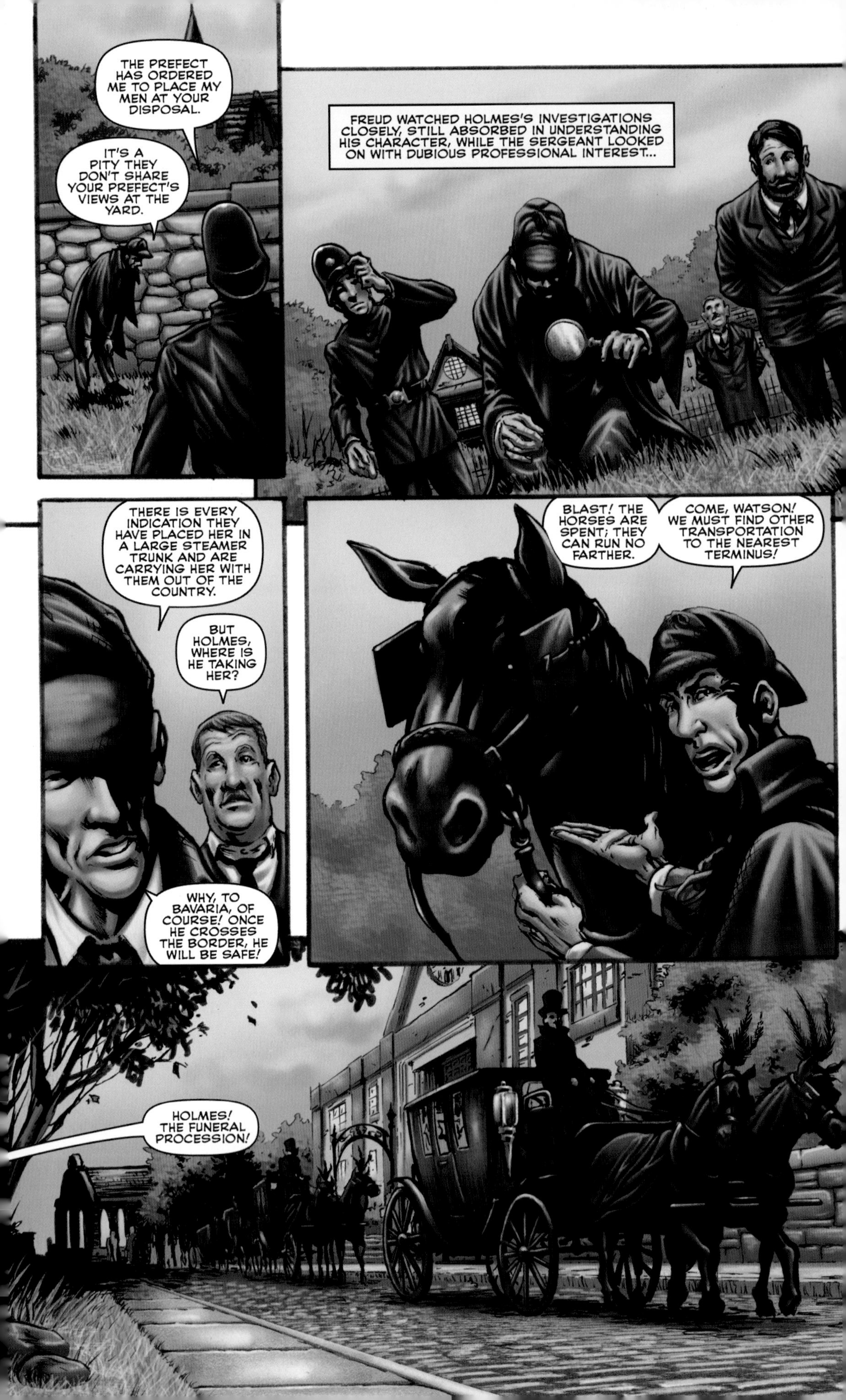
THE PREFECT HAS ORDERED ME TO PLACE MY MEN AT YOUR DISPOSAL.
IT'S A PITY THEY DON'T SHARE YOUR PREFECT'S VIEWS AT THE YARD.
FREUD WATCHED HOLMES'S INVESTIGATIONS CLOSELY, STILL ABSORBED IN UNDERSTANDING HIS CHARACTER, WHILE THE SERGEANT LOOKED ON WITH DUBIOUS PROFESSIONAL INTEREST...
THERE IS EVERY INDICATION THEY HAVE PLACED HER IN A LARGE STEAMER TRUNK AND ARE CARRYING HER WITH THEM OUT OF THE COUNTRY.
BUT HOLMES, WHERE IS HE TAKING HER?
WHY, TO BAVARIA, OF COURSE! ONCE HE CROSSES THE BORDER, HE WILL BE SAFE!
BLAST! THE HORSES ARE SPENT; THEY CAN RUN NO FARTHER.
COME, WATSON! WE MUST FIND OTHER TRANSPORTATION TO THE NEAREST TERMINUS!
HOLMES! THE FUNERAL PROCESSION!

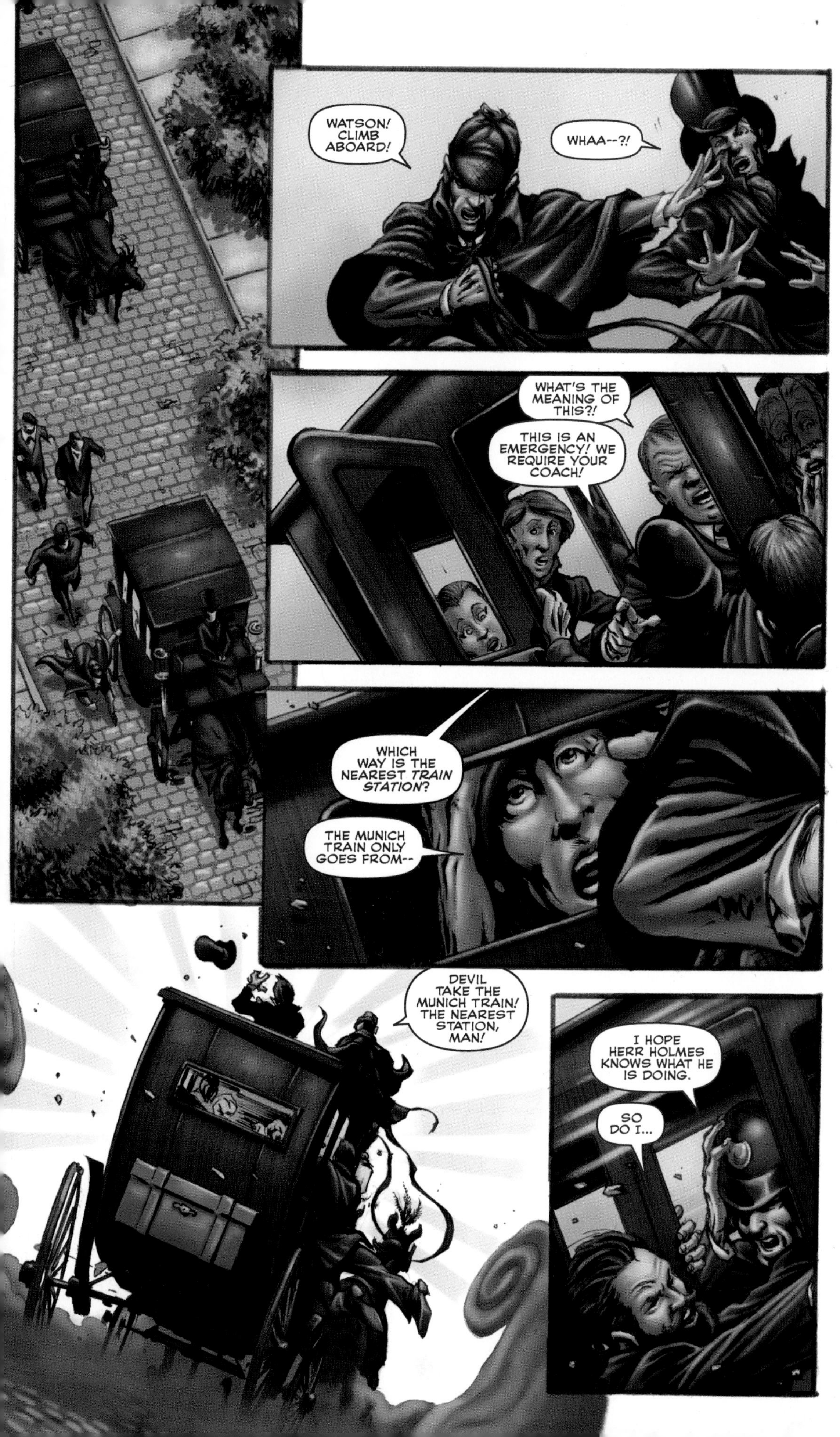
WATSON! CLIMB ABOARD!
WHAA--?!
WHAT'S THE MEANING OF THIS?!
THIS IS AN EMERGENCY! WE REQUIRE YOUR COACH!
WHICH WAY IS THE NEAREST *TRAIN STATION*?
THE MUNICH TRAIN ONLY GOES FROM--
DEVIL TAKE THE MUNICH TRAIN! THE NEAREST STATION, MAN!
I HOPE HERR HOLMES KNOWS WHAT HE IS DOING.
SO DO I...

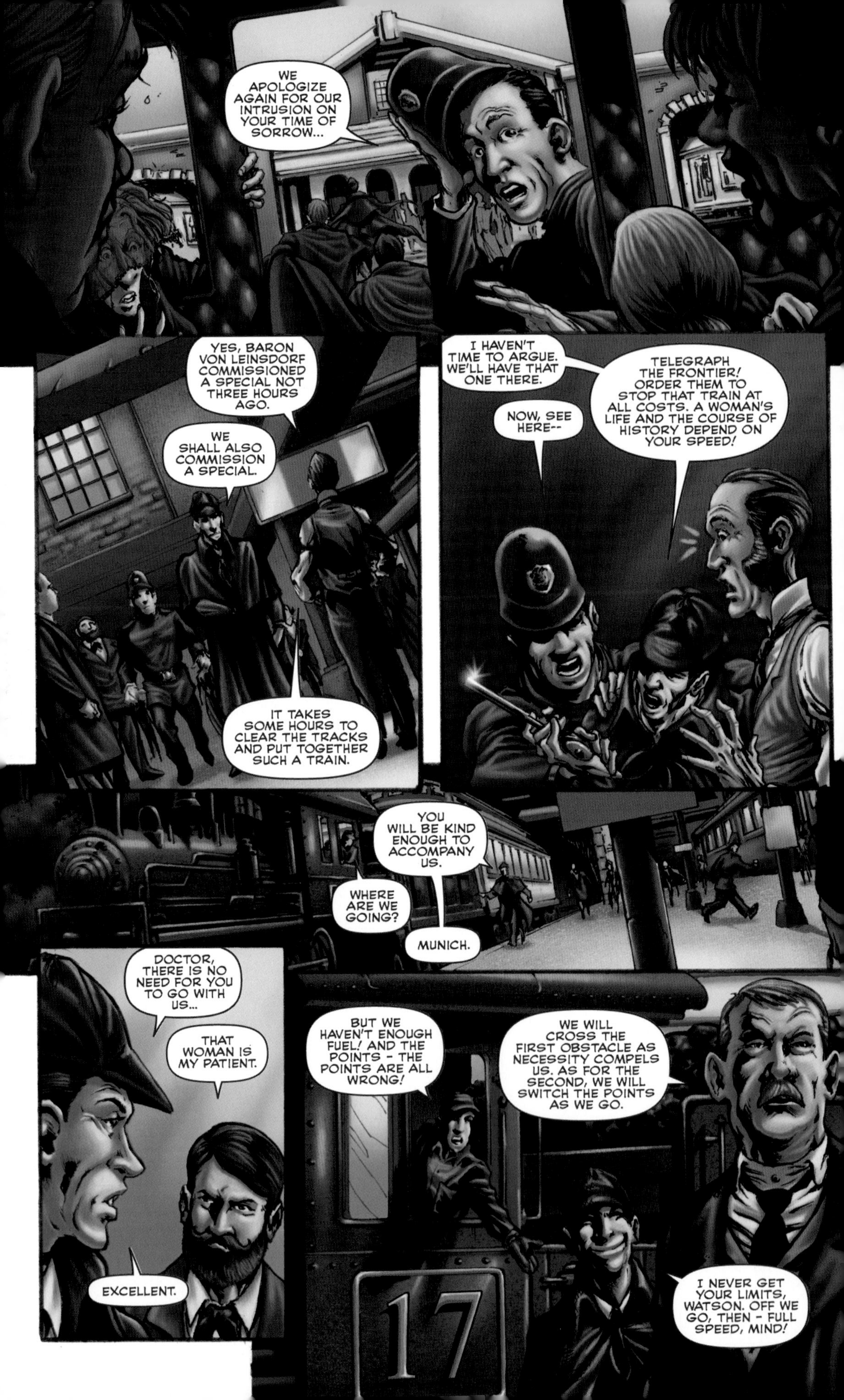
WE APOLOGIZE AGAIN FOR OUR INTRUSION ON YOUR TIME OF SORROW...
YES, BARON VON LEINSDORF COMMISSIONED A SPECIAL NOT THREE HOURS AGO.
WE SHALL ALSO COMMISSION A SPECIAL.
IT TAKES SOME HOURS TO CLEAR THE TRACKS AND PUT TOGETHER SUCH A TRAIN.
I HAVEN'T TIME TO ARGUE. WE'LL HAVE THAT ONE THERE.
NOW, SEE HERE--
TELEGRAPH THE FRONTIER! ORDER THEM TO STOP THAT TRAIN AT ALL COSTS. A WOMAN'S LIFE AND THE COURSE OF HISTORY DEPEND ON YOUR SPEED!
YOU WILL BE KIND ENOUGH TO ACCOMPANY US.
WHERE ARE WE GOING?
MUNICH.
DOCTOR, THERE IS NO NEED FOR YOU TO GO WITH US...
THAT WOMAN IS MY PATIENT.
EXCELLENT.
BUT WE HAVEN'T ENOUGH FUEL! AND THE POINTS - THE POINTS ARE ALL WRONG!
WE WILL CROSS THE FIRST OBSTACLE AS NECESSITY COMPELS US. AS FOR THE SECOND, WE WILL SWITCH THE POINTS AS WE GO.
I NEVER GET YOUR LIMITS, WATSON. OFF WE GO, THEN - FULL SPEED, MIND!
17

ART BY
KELLEY JONES

COLORS BY
JAY FOTOS

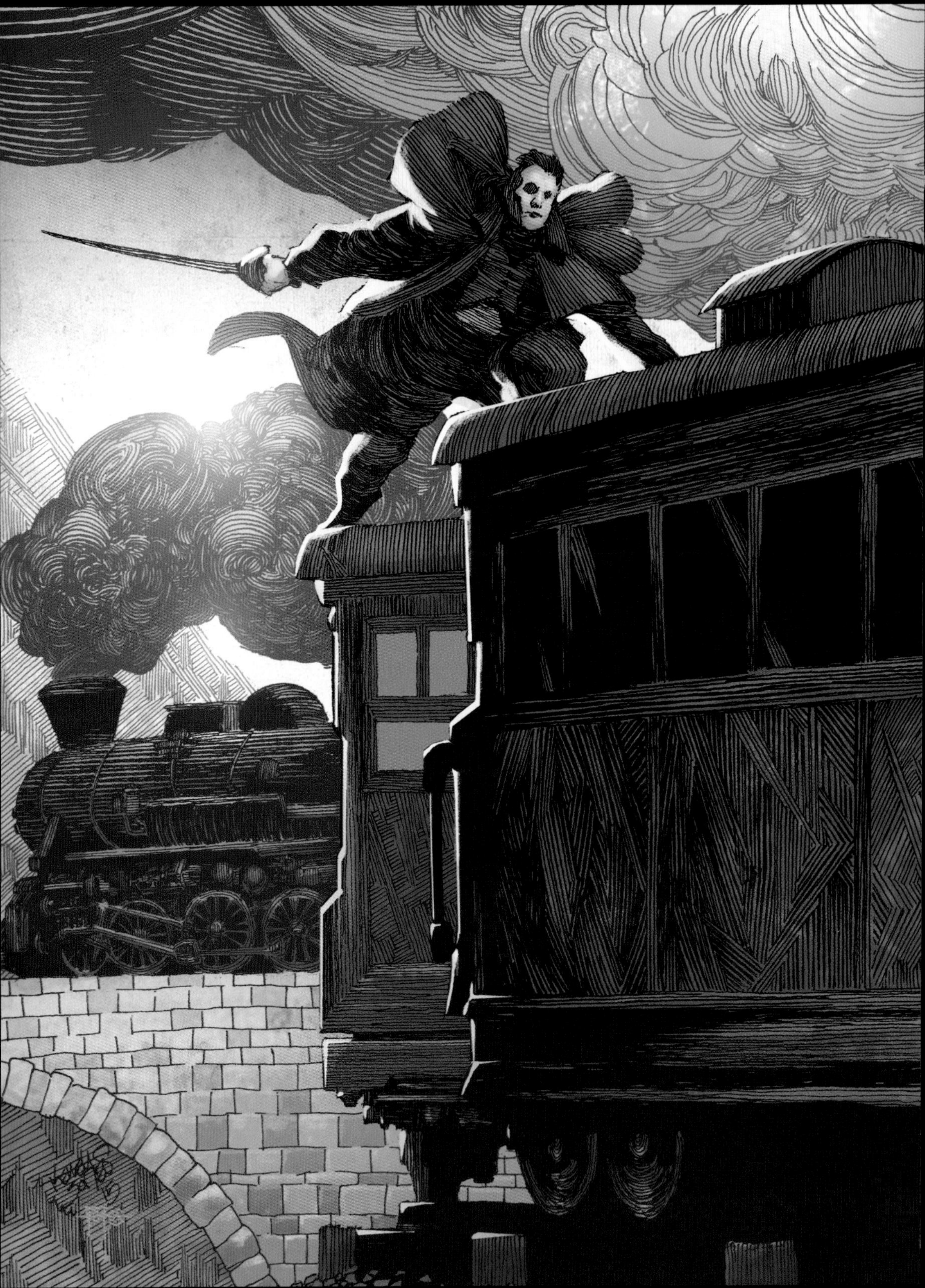

CHAPTER FIVE

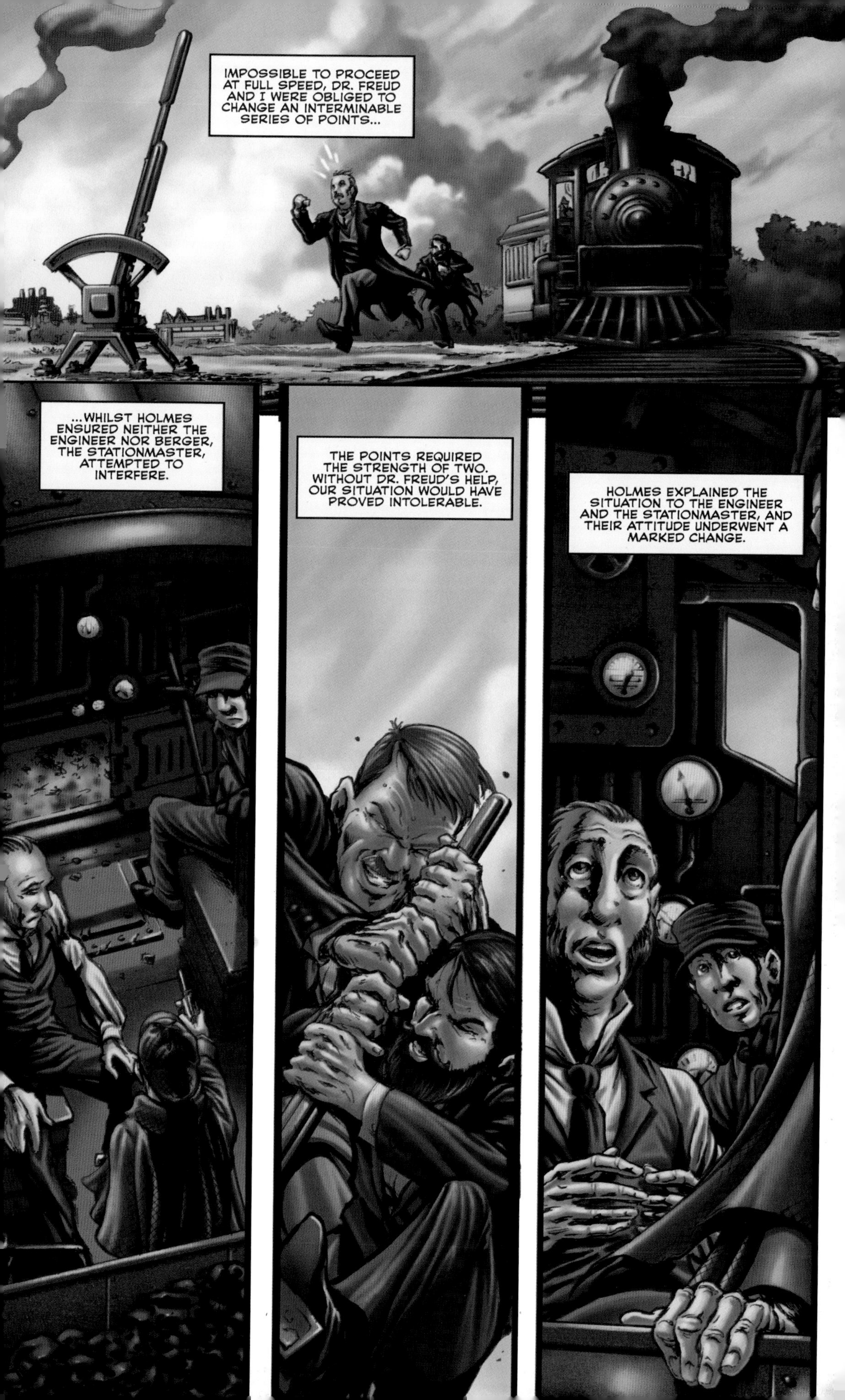
IMPOSSIBLE TO PROCEED AT FULL SPEED, DR. FREUD AND I WERE OBLIGED TO CHANGE AN INTERMINABLE SERIES OF POINTS...
...WHILST HOLMES ENSURED NEITHER THE ENGINEER NOR BERGER, THE STATIONMASTER, ATTEMPTED TO INTERFERE.
THE POINTS REQUIRED THE STRENGTH OF TWO. WITHOUT DR. FREUD'S HELP, OUR SITUATION WOULD HAVE PROVED INTOLERABLE.
HOLMES EXPLAINED THE SITUATION TO THE ENGINEER AND THE STATIONMASTER, AND THEIR ATTITUDE UNDERWENT A MARKED CHANGE.

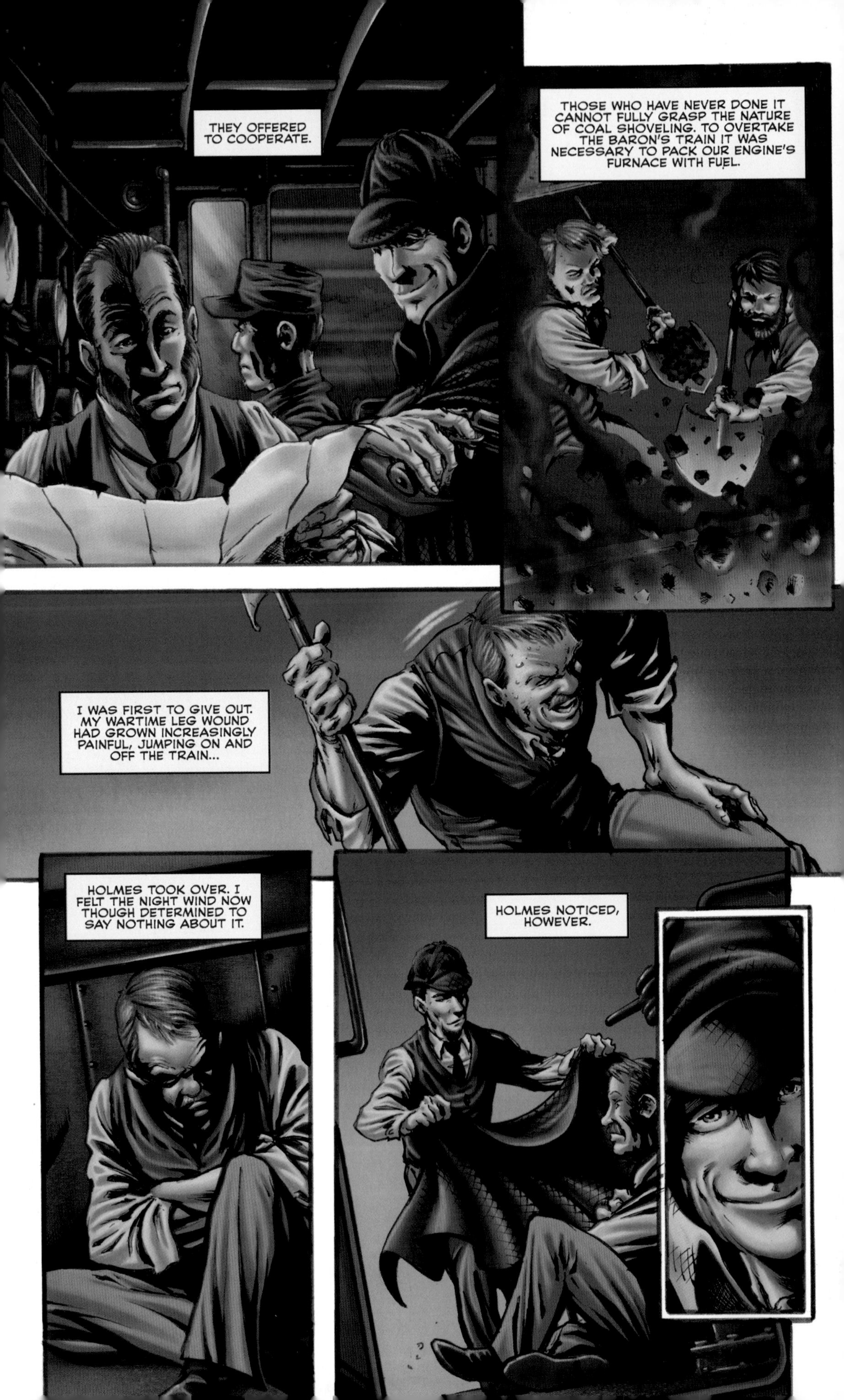
THEY OFFERED TO COOPERATE.
THOSE WHO HAVE NEVER DONE IT CANNOT FULLY GRASP THE NATURE OF COAL SHOVELING. TO OVERTAKE THE BARON'S TRAIN IT WAS NECESSARY TO PACK OUR ENGINE'S FURNACE WITH FUEL.
I WAS FIRST TO GIVE OUT. MY WARTIME LEG WOUND HAD GROWN INCREASINGLY PAINFUL, JUMPING ON AND OFF THE TRAIN...
HOLMES TOOK OVER. I FELT THE NIGHT WIND NOW THOUGH DETERMINED TO SAY NOTHING ABOUT IT.
HOLMES NOTICED, HOWEVER.

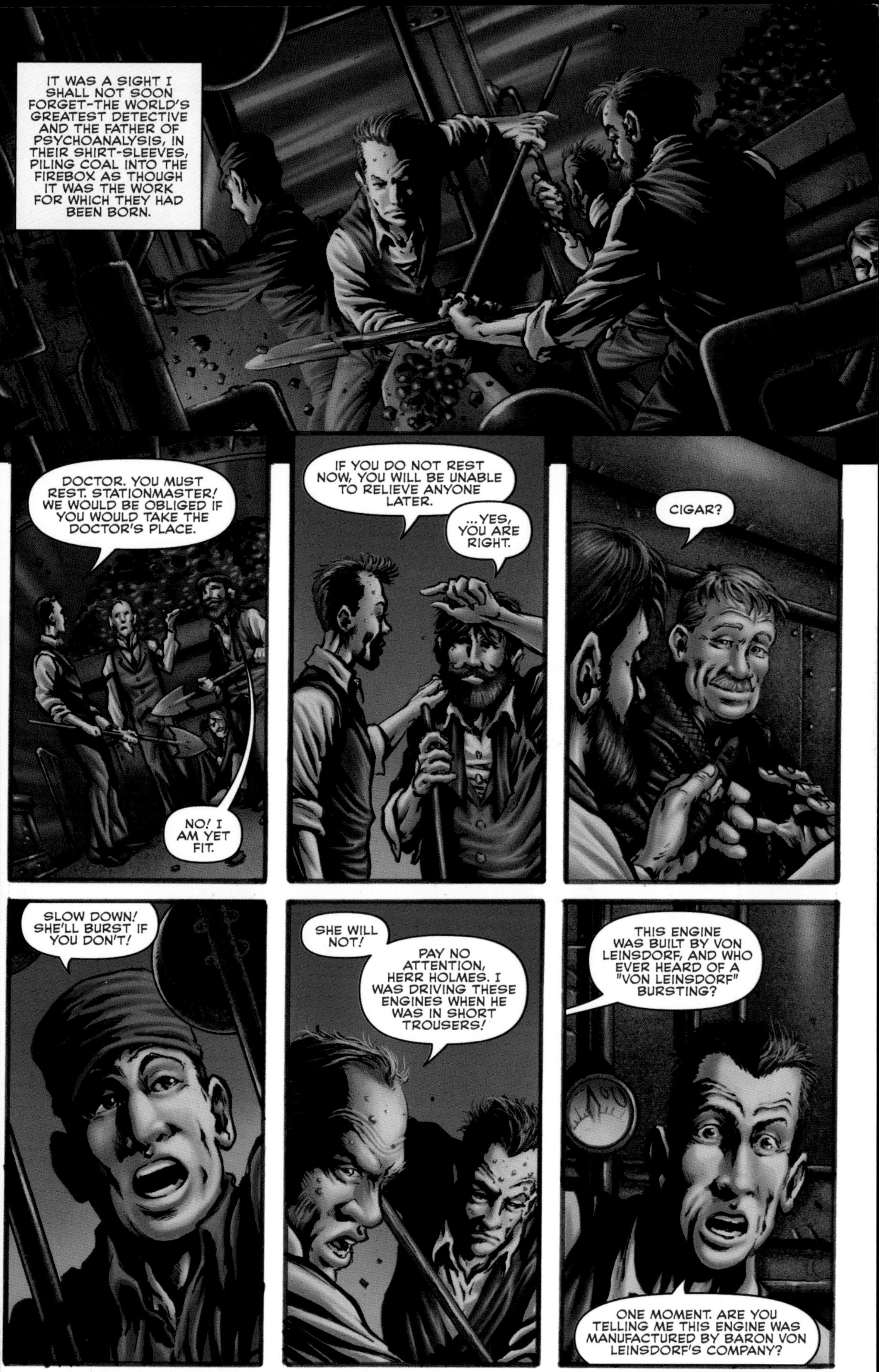
IT WAS A SIGHT I SHALL NOT SOON FORGET–THE WORLD'S GREATEST DETECTIVE AND THE FATHER OF PSYCHOANALYSIS, IN THEIR SHIRT-SLEEVES, PILING COAL INTO THE FIREBOX AS THOUGH IT WAS THE WORK FOR WHICH THEY HAD BEEN BORN.
DOCTOR. YOU MUST REST. STATIONMASTER! WE WOULD BE OBLIGED IF YOU WOULD TAKE THE DOCTOR'S PLACE.
NO! I AM YET FIT.
IF YOU DO NOT REST NOW, YOU WILL BE UNABLE TO RELIEVE ANYONE LATER.
...YES, YOU ARE RIGHT.
CIGAR?
SLOW DOWN! SHE'LL BURST IF YOU DON'T!
SHE WILL NOT!
PAY NO ATTENTION, HERR HOLMES. I WAS DRIVING THESE ENGINES WHEN HE WAS IN SHORT TROUSERS!
THIS ENGINE WAS BUILT BY VON LEINSDORF, AND WHO EVER HEARD OF A "VON LEINSDORF" BURSTING?
ONE MOMENT. ARE YOU TELLING ME THIS ENGINE WAS MANUFACTURED BY BARON VON LEINSDORF'S COMPANY?

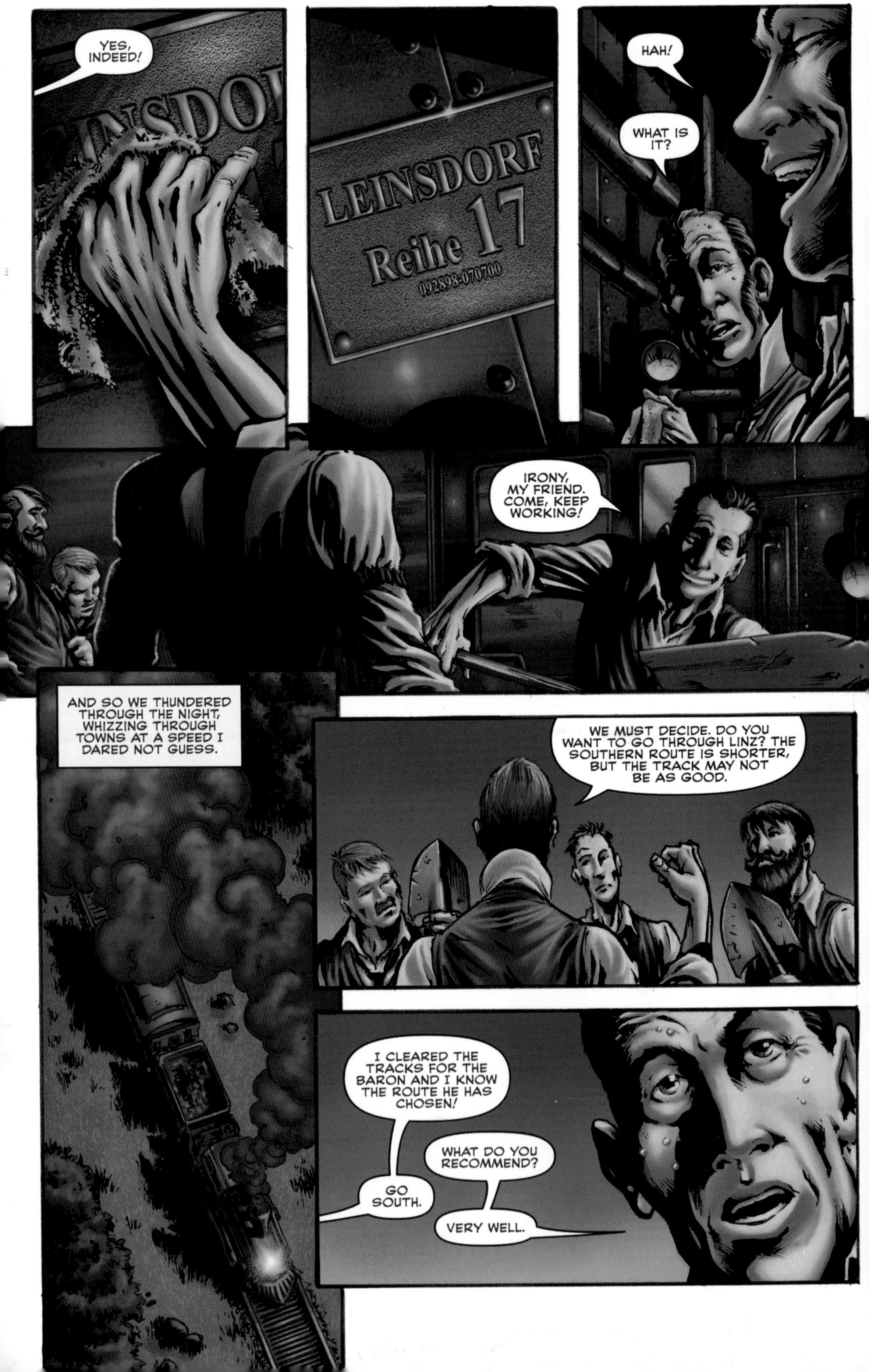
YES, INDEED!
LEINSDORF
Reihe 17
092898-070700
HAH!
WHAT IS IT?
IRONY, MY FRIEND. COME, KEEP WORKING!
AND SO WE THUNDERED THROUGH THE NIGHT, WHIZZING THROUGH TOWNS AT A SPEED I DARED NOT GUESS.
WE MUST DECIDE. DO YOU WANT TO GO THROUGH LINZ? THE SOUTHERN ROUTE IS SHORTER, BUT THE TRACK MAY NOT BE AS GOOD.
I CLEARED THE TRACKS FOR THE BARON AND I KNOW THE ROUTE HE HAS CHOSEN!
WHAT DO YOU RECOMMEND?
GO SOUTH.
VERY WELL.

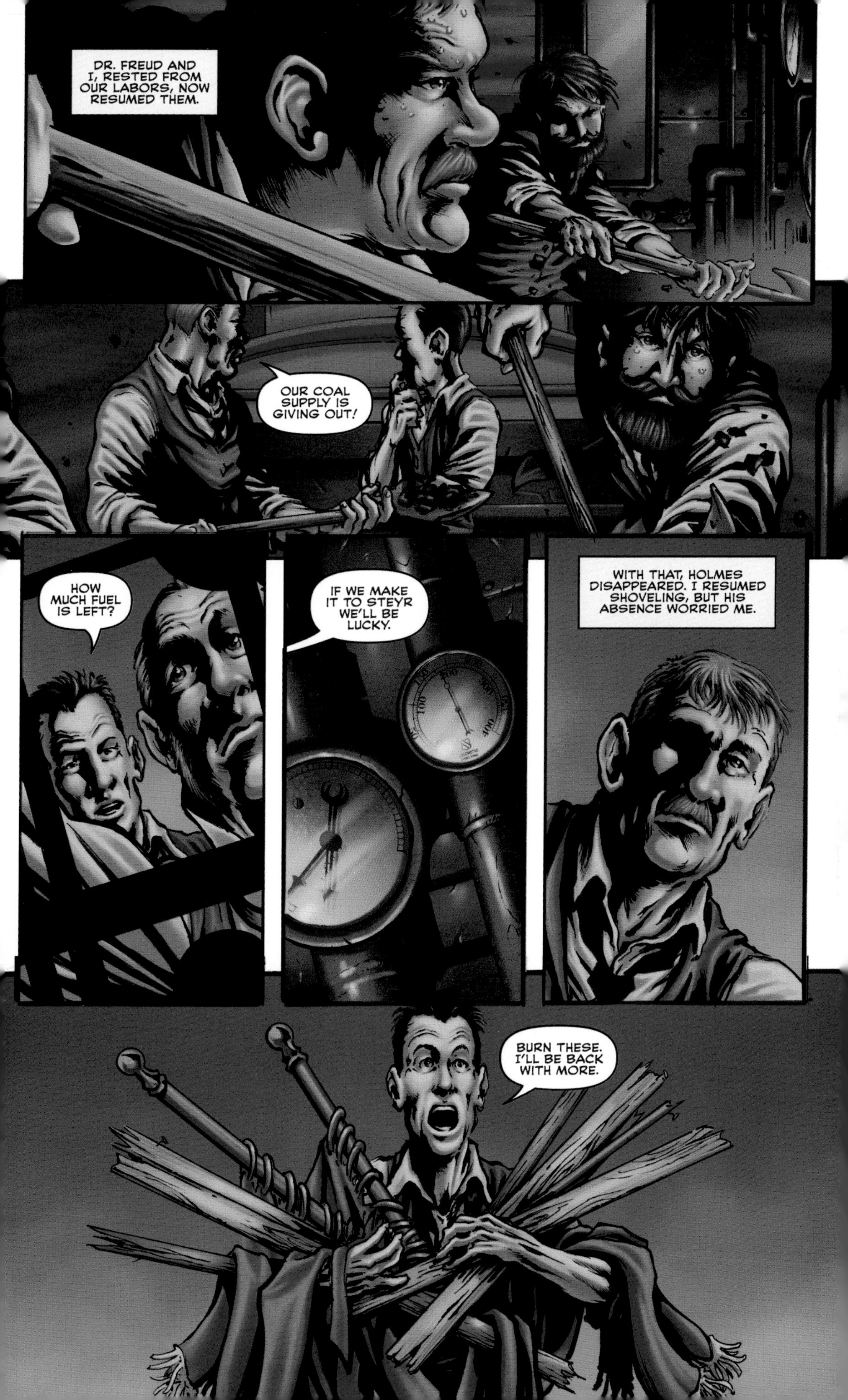
DR. FREUD AND I, RESTED FROM OUR LABORS, NOW RESUMED THEM.
OUR COAL SUPPLY IS GIVING OUT!
HOW MUCH FUEL IS LEFT?
IF WE MAKE IT TO STEYR WE'LL BE LUCKY.
WITH THAT, HOLMES DISAPPEARED. I RESUMED SHOVELING, BUT HIS ABSENCE WORRIED ME.
BURN THESE. I'LL BE BACK WITH MORE.

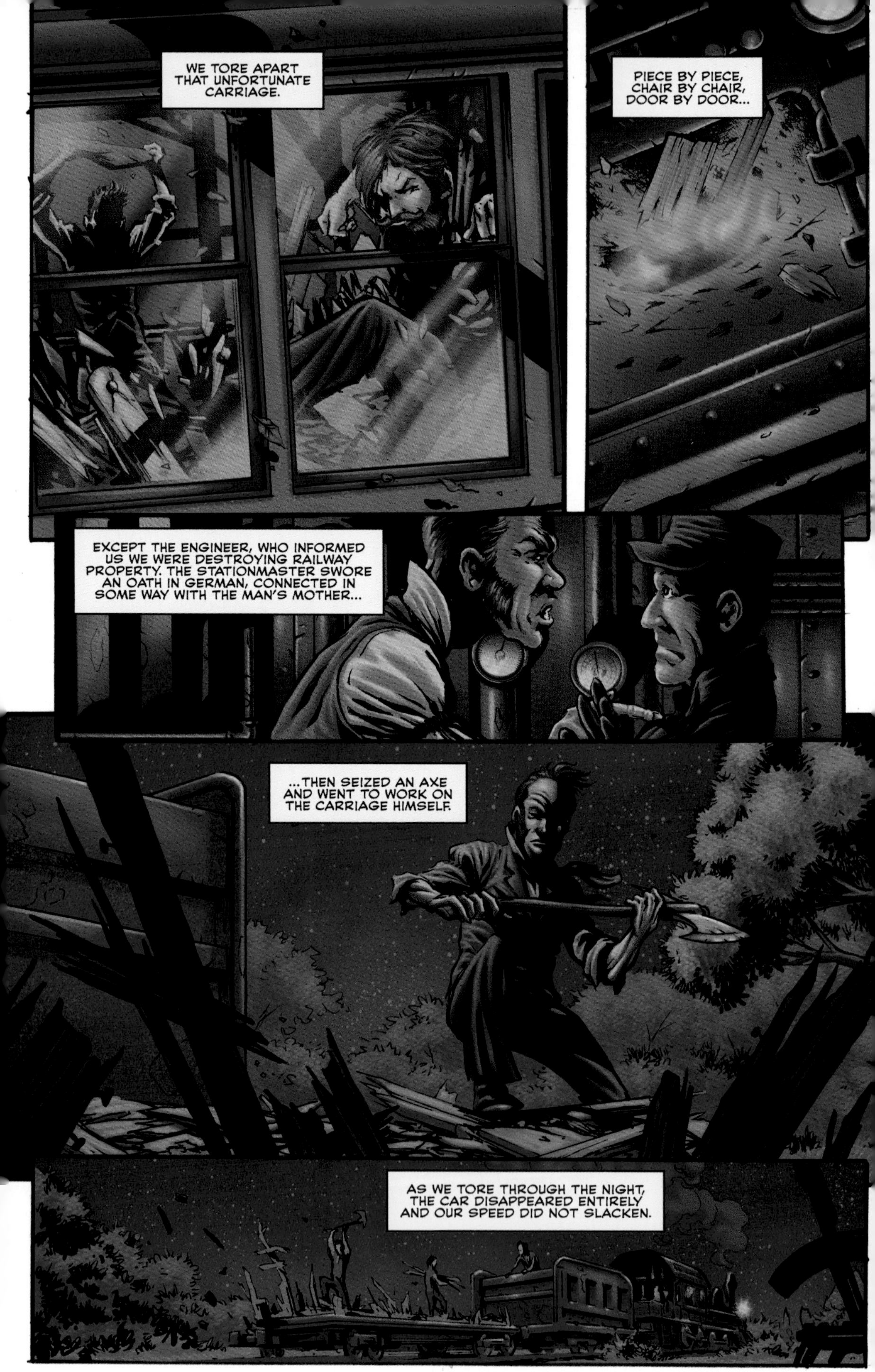
WE TORE APART THAT UNFORTUNATE CARRIAGE.
PIECE BY PIECE, CHAIR BY CHAIR, DOOR BY DOOR...
EXCEPT THE ENGINEER, WHO INFORMED US WE WERE DESTROYING RAILWAY PROPERTY. THE STATIONMASTER SWORE AN OATH IN GERMAN, CONNECTED IN SOME WAY WITH THE MAN'S MOTHER...
...THEN SEIZED AN AXE AND WENT TO WORK ON THE CARRIAGE HIMSELF.
AS WE TORE THROUGH THE NIGHT, THE CAR DISAPPEARED ENTIRELY AND OUR SPEED DID NOT SLACKEN.

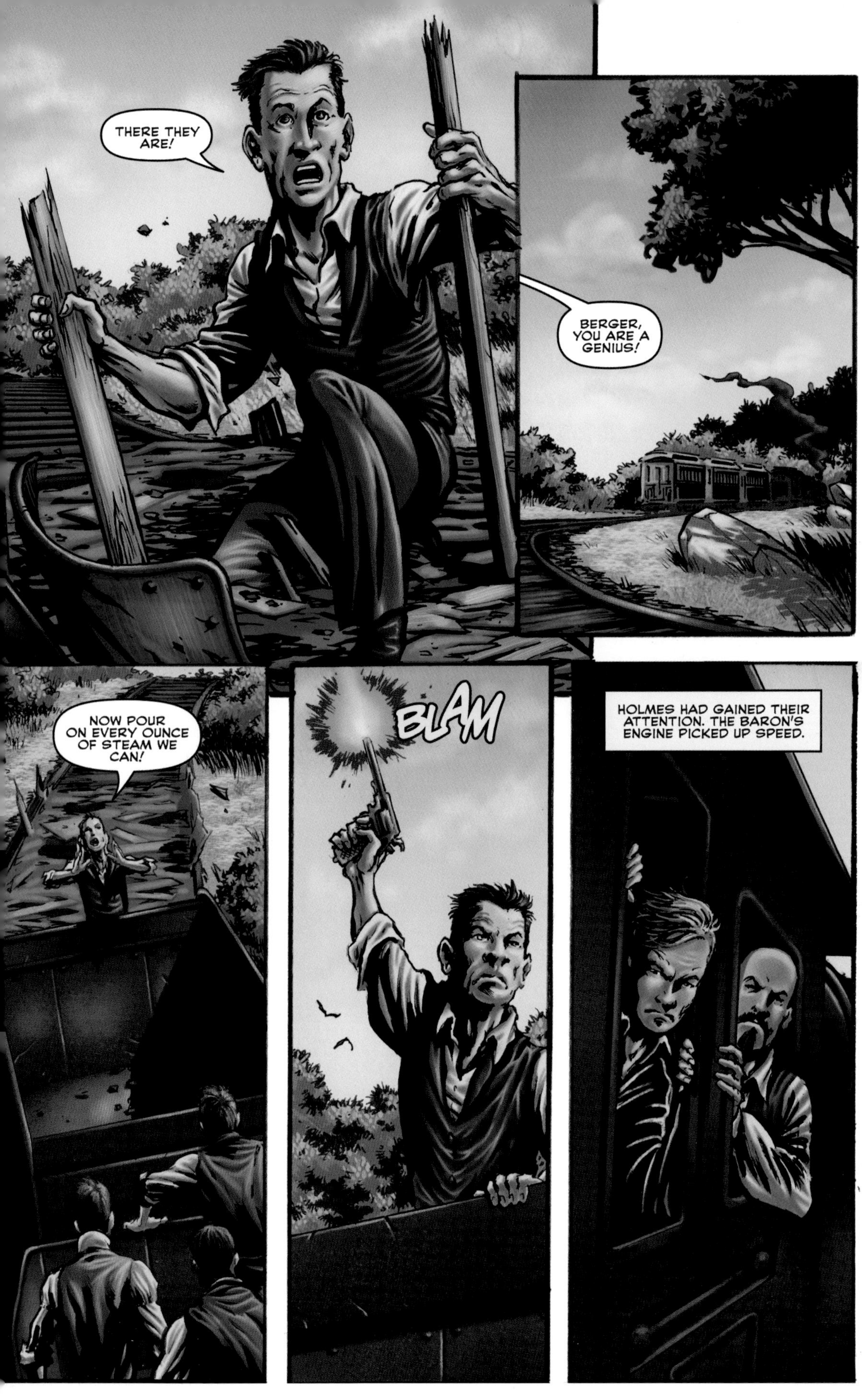
THERE THEY ARE!
BERGER, YOU ARE A GENIUS!
NOW POUR ON EVERY OUNCE OF STEAM WE CAN!
BLAM
HOLMES HAD GAINED THEIR ATTENTION. THE BARON'S ENGINE PICKED UP SPEED.

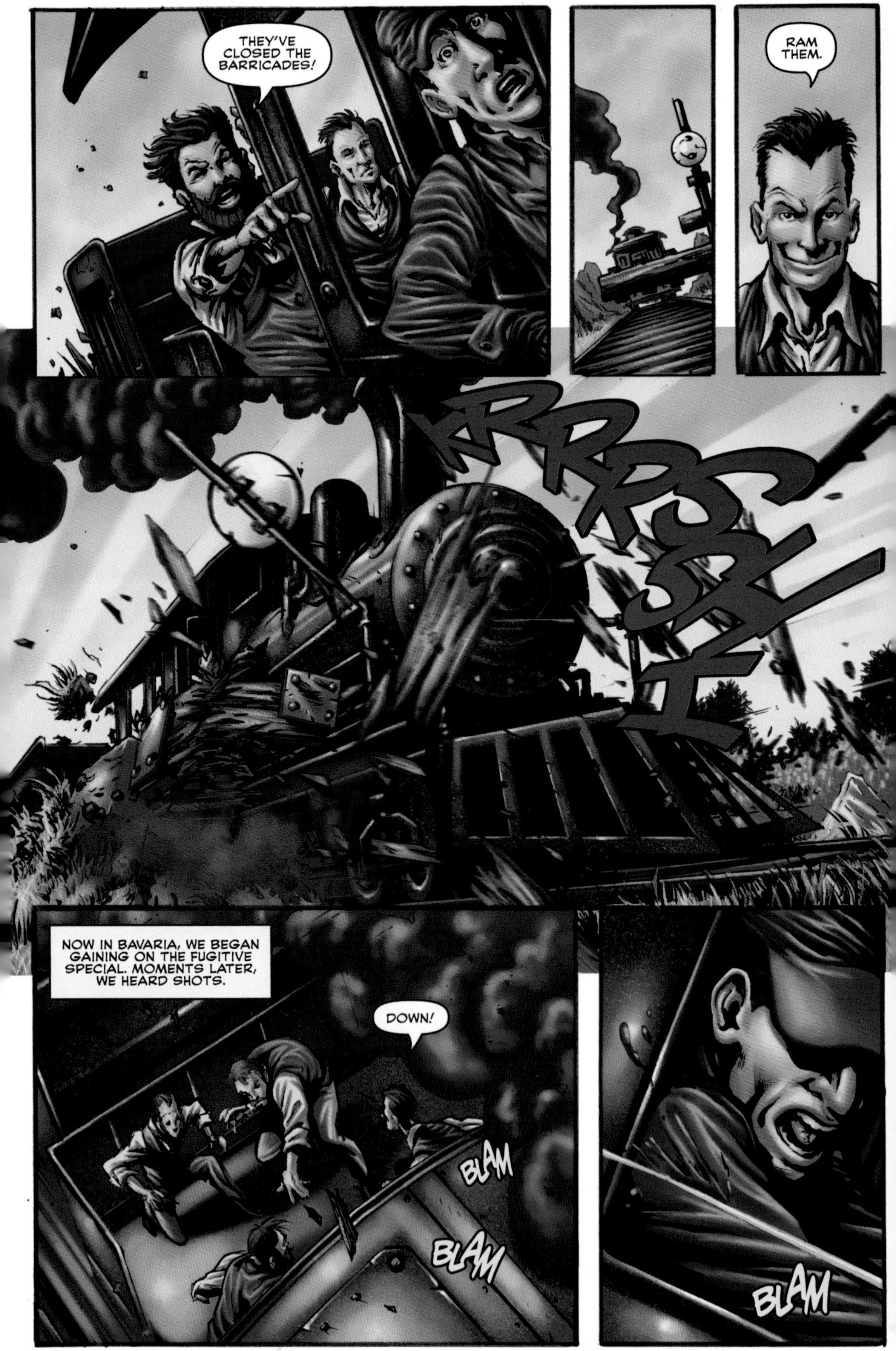
THEY'VE CLOSED THE BARRICADES!
RAM THEM.
NOW IN BAVARIA, WE BEGAN GAINING ON THE FUGITIVE SPECIAL. MOMENTS LATER, WE HEARD SHOTS.
DOWN!
BLAM
BLAM
BLAM

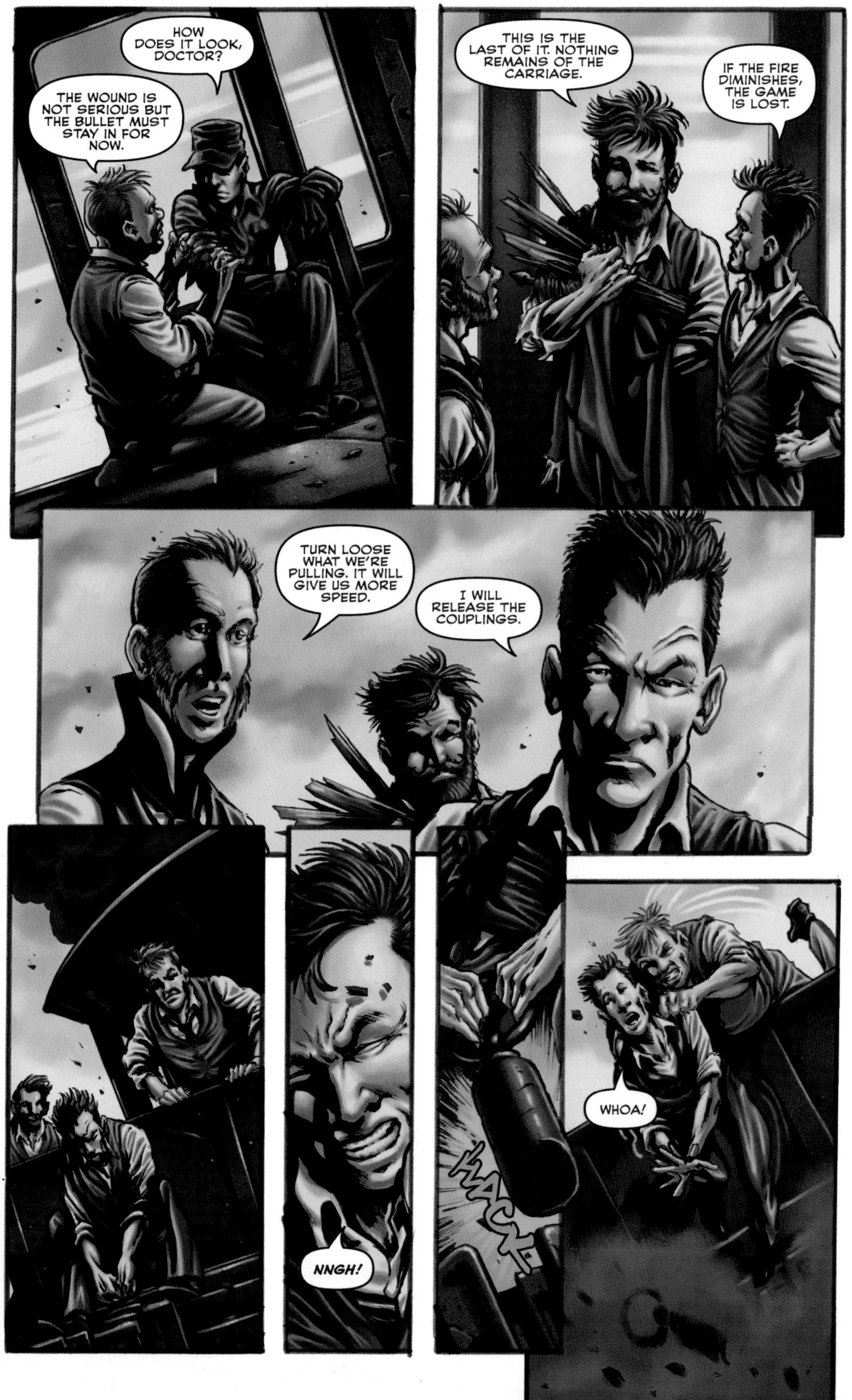
HOW DOES IT LOOK, DOCTOR?
THE WOUND IS NOT SERIOUS BUT THE BULLET MUST STAY IN FOR NOW.
THIS IS THE LAST OF IT. NOTHING REMAINS OF THE CARRIAGE.
IF THE FIRE DIMINISHES, THE GAME IS LOST.
TURN LOOSE WHAT WE'RE PULLING. IT WILL GIVE US MORE SPEED.
I WILL RELEASE THE COUPLINGS.
NNGH!
HACK!
WHOA!

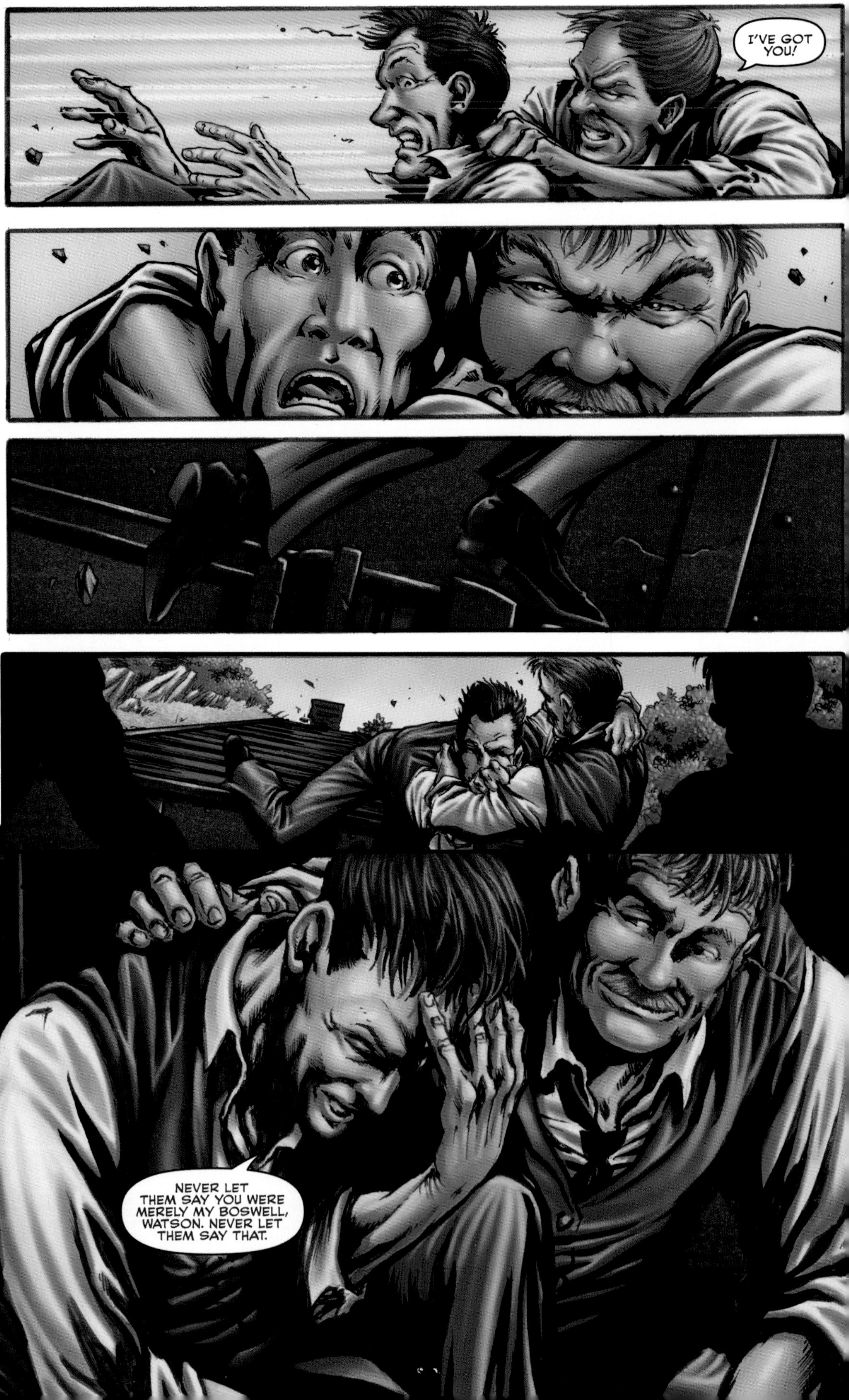
I'VE GOT YOU!
NEVER LET THEM SAY YOU WERE MERELY MY BOSWELL, WATSON. NEVER LET THEM SAY THAT.

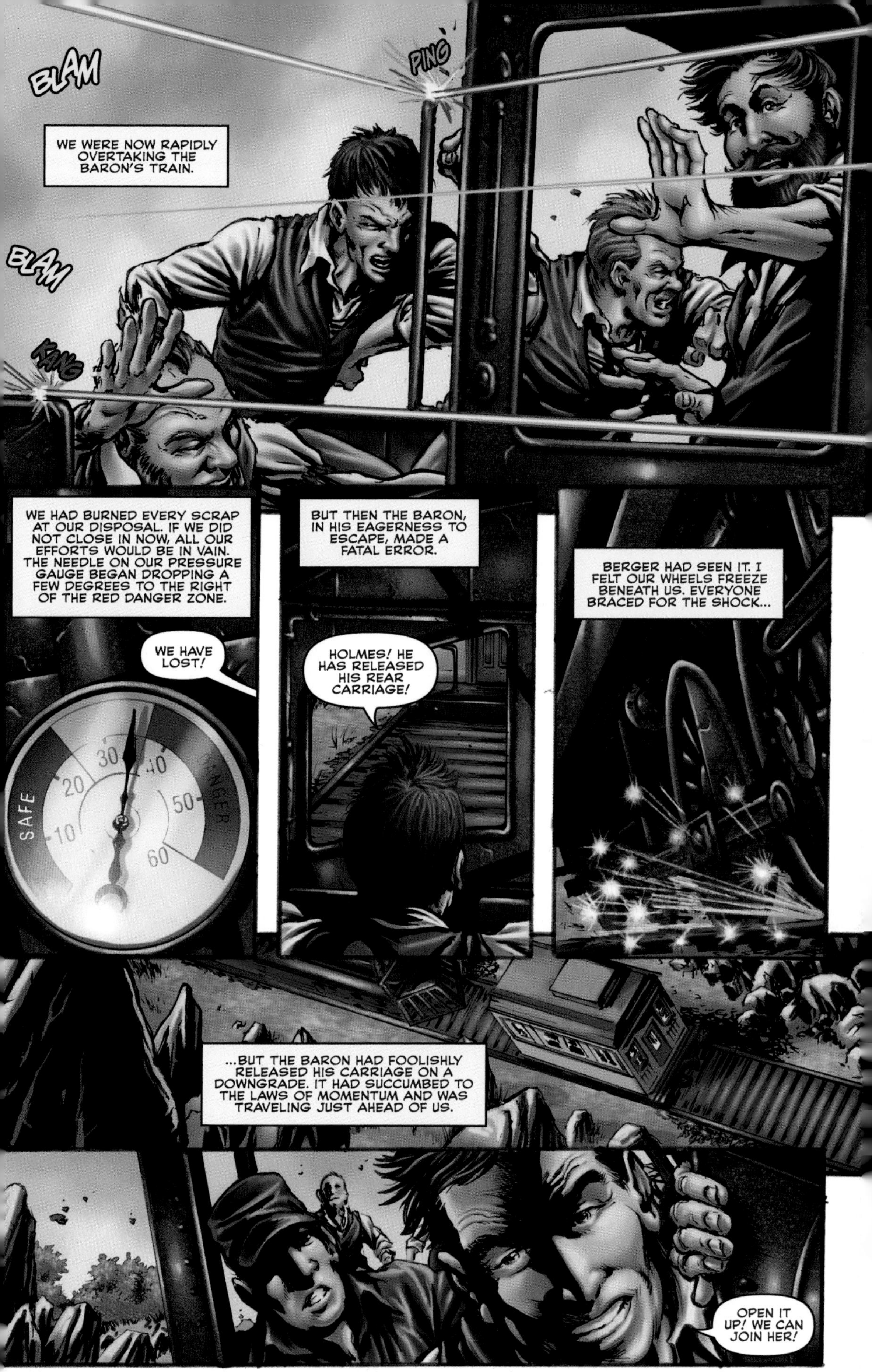
BLAM
PING
WE WERE NOW RAPIDLY OVERTAKING THE BARON'S TRAIN.
BLAM
KANG
WE HAD BURNED EVERY SCRAP AT OUR DISPOSAL. IF WE DID NOT CLOSE IN NOW, ALL OUR EFFORTS WOULD BE IN VAIN. THE NEEDLE ON OUR PRESSURE GAUGE BEGAN DROPPING A FEW DEGREES TO THE RIGHT OF THE RED DANGER ZONE.
WE HAVE LOST!
SAFE
10
20
30
40
50
60
DANGER
BUT THEN THE BARON, IN HIS EAGERNESS TO ESCAPE, MADE A FATAL ERROR.
HOLMES! HE HAS RELEASED HIS REAR CARRIAGE!
BERGER HAD SEEN IT. I FELT OUR WHEELS FREEZE BENEATH US. EVERYONE BRACED FOR THE SHOCK...
...BUT THE BARON HAD FOOLISHLY RELEASED HIS CARRIAGE ON A DOWNGRADE. IT HAD SUCCUMBED TO THE LAWS OF MOMENTUM AND WAS TRAVELING JUST AHEAD OF US.
OPEN IT UP! WE CAN JOIN HER!

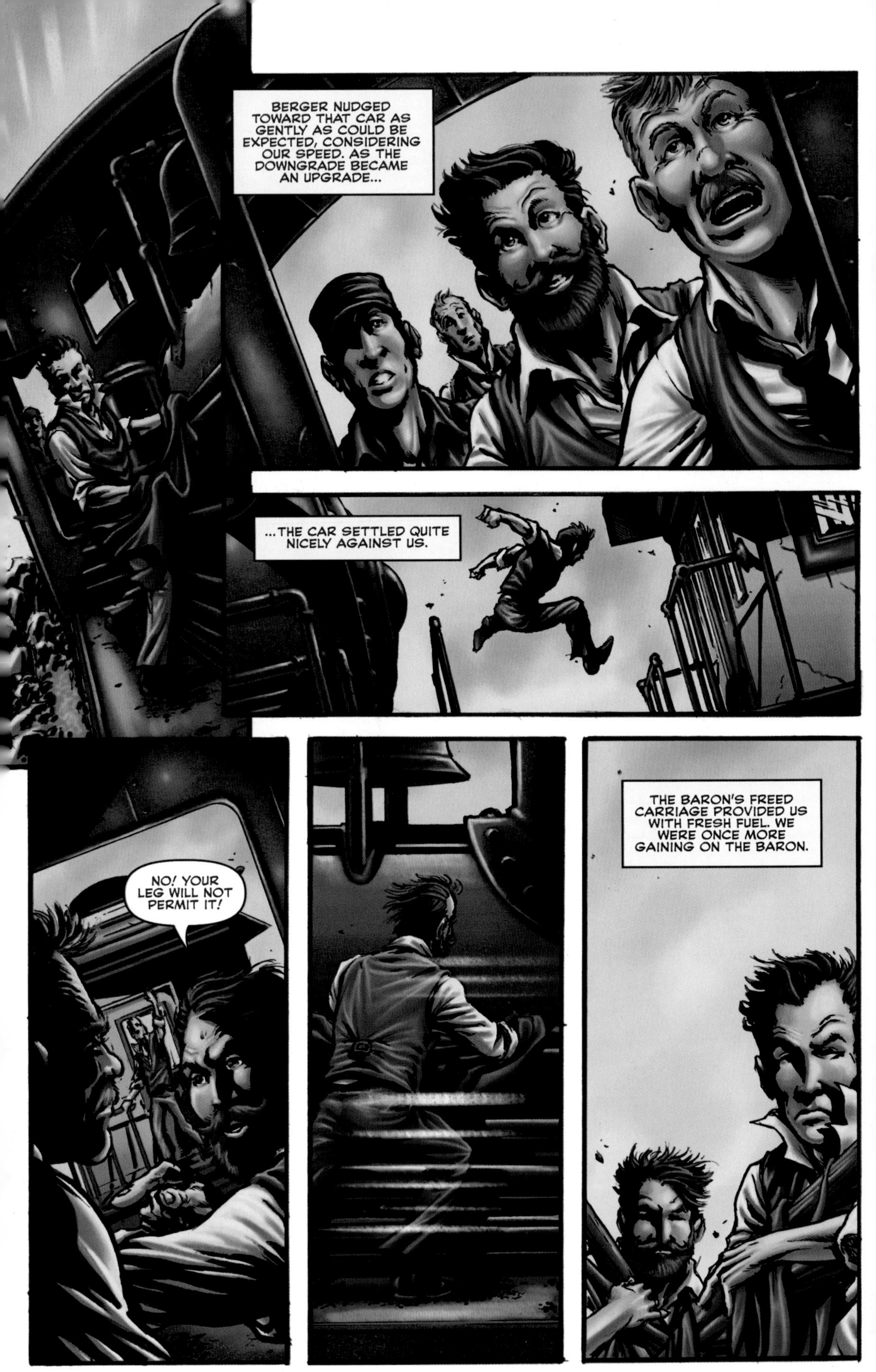
BERGER NUDGED TOWARD THAT CAR AS GENTLY AS COULD BE EXPECTED, CONSIDERING OUR SPEED. AS THE DOWNGRADE BECAME AN UPGRADE...
...THE CAR SETTLED QUITE NICELY AGAINST US.
NO! YOUR LEG WILL NOT PERMIT IT!
THE BARON'S FREED CARRIAGE PROVIDED US WITH FRESH FUEL. WE WERE ONCE MORE GAINING ON THE BARON.

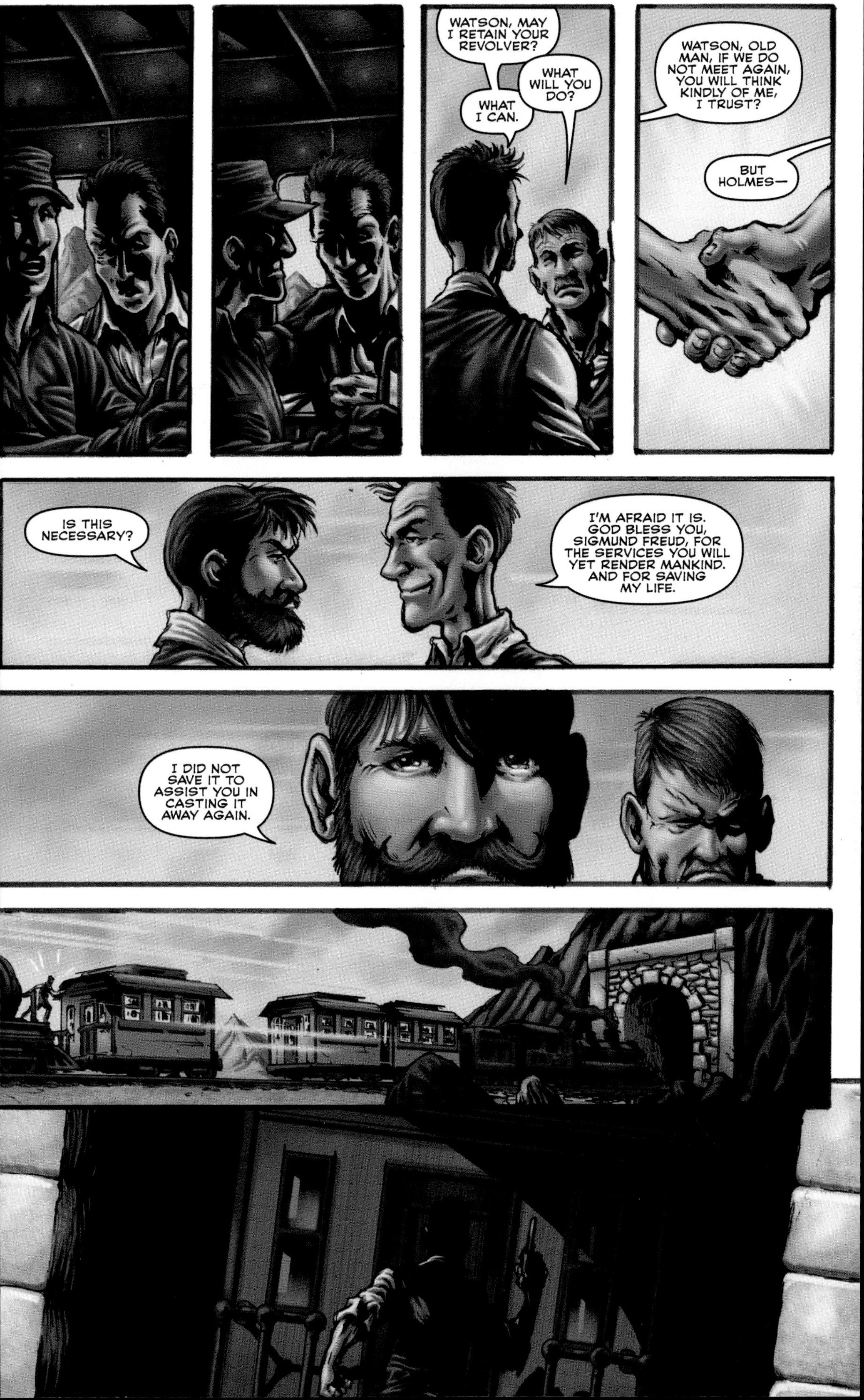
WATSON, MAY I RETAIN YOUR REVOLVER?
WHAT WILL YOU DO?
WHAT I CAN.
WATSON, OLD MAN, IF WE DO NOT MEET AGAIN, YOU WILL THINK KINDLY OF ME, I TRUST?
BUT HOLMES—
IS THIS NECESSARY?
I'M AFRAID IT IS. GOD BLESS YOU, SIGMUND FREUD, FOR THE SERVICES YOU WILL YET RENDER MANKIND. AND FOR SAVING MY LIFE.
I DID NOT SAVE IT TO ASSIST YOU IN CASTING IT AWAY AGAIN.

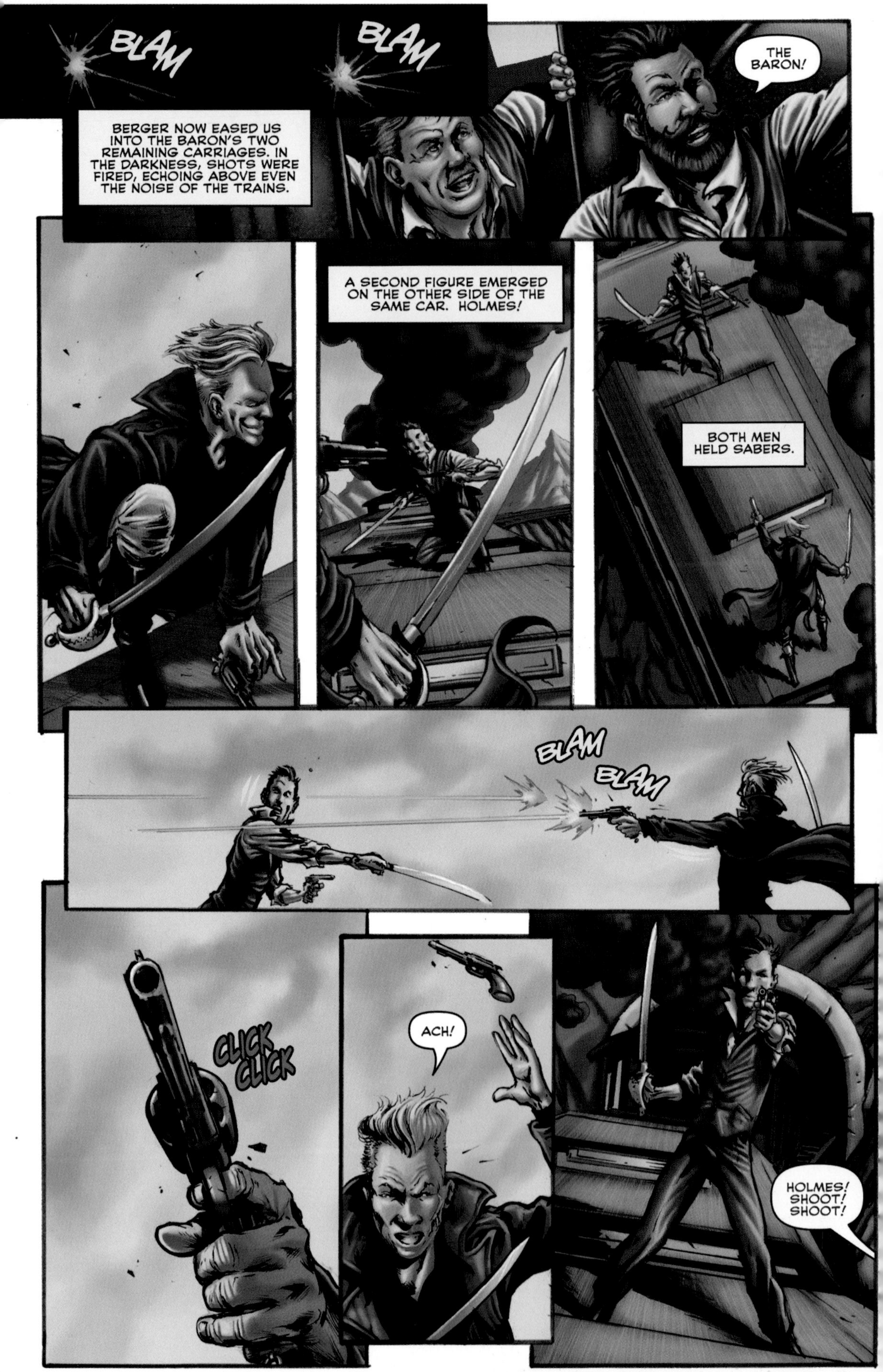
BLAM
BLAM
BERGER NOW EASED US INTO THE BARON'S TWO REMAINING CARRIAGES. IN THE DARKNESS, SHOTS WERE FIRED, ECHOING ABOVE EVEN THE NOISE OF THE TRAINS.
THE BARON!
A SECOND FIGURE EMERGED ON THE OTHER SIDE OF THE SAME CAR. HOLMES!
BOTH MEN HELD SABERS.
BLAM
BLAM
CLICK
CLICK
ACH!
HOLMES! SHOOT! SHOOT!

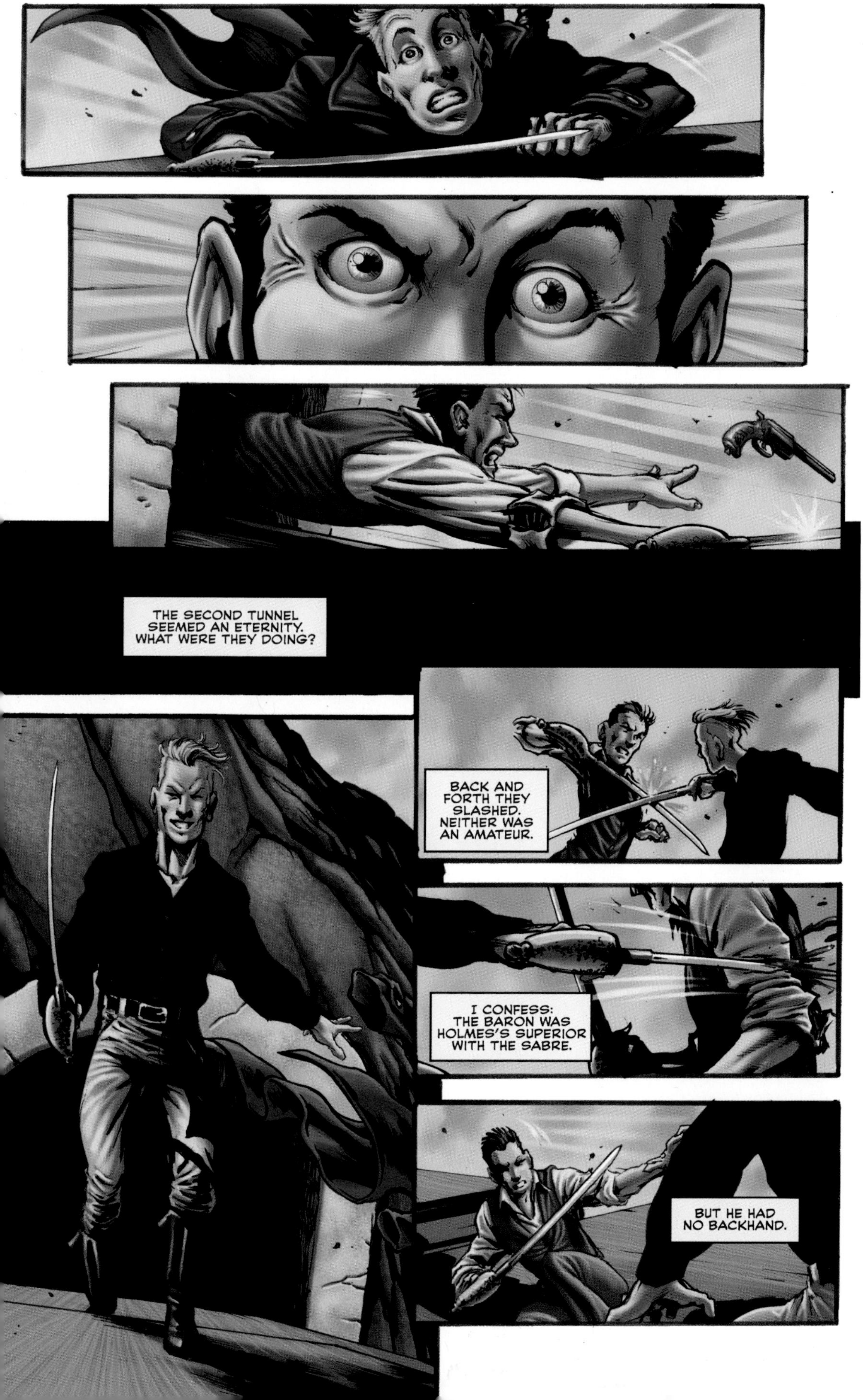
THE SECOND TUNNEL SEEMED AN ETERNITY. WHAT WERE THEY DOING?
BACK AND FORTH THEY SLASHED. NEITHER WAS AN AMATEUR.
I CONFESS: THE BARON WAS HOLMES'S SUPERIOR WITH THE SABRE.
BUT HE HAD NO BACKHAND.

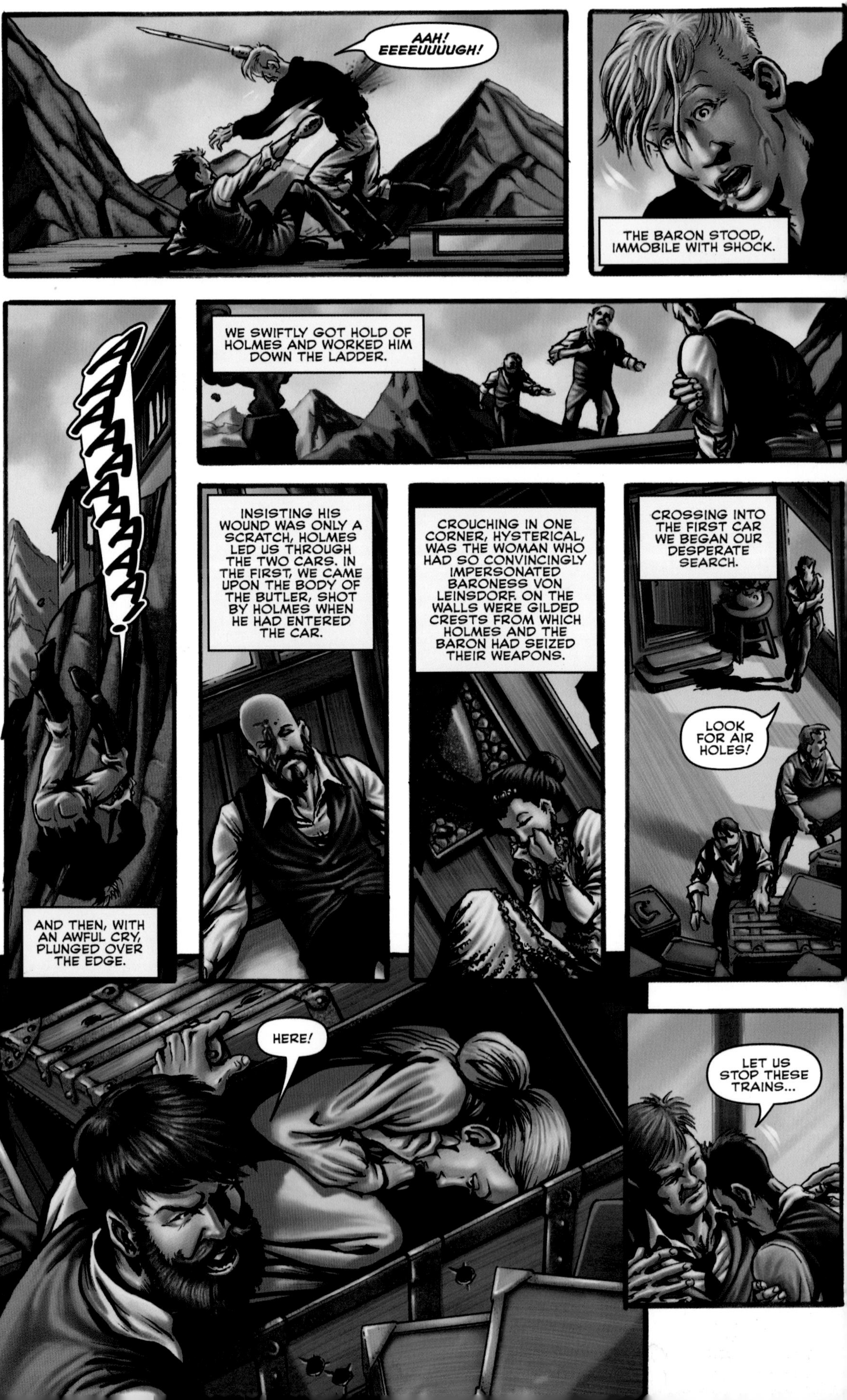
AAH! EEEEUUUUGH!
THE BARON STOOD, IMMOBILE WITH SHOCK.
WE SWIFTLY GOT HOLD OF HOLMES AND WORKED HIM DOWN THE LADDER.
AND THEN, WITH AN AWFUL CRY, PLUNGED OVER THE EDGE.
INSISTING HIS WOUND WAS ONLY A SCRATCH, HOLMES LED US THROUGH THE TWO CARS. IN THE FIRST, WE CAME UPON THE BODY OF THE BUTLER, SHOT BY HOLMES WHEN HE HAD ENTERED THE CAR.
CROUCHING IN ONE CORNER, HYSTERICAL, WAS THE WOMAN WHO HAD SO CONVINCINGLY IMPERSONATED BARONESS VON LEINSDORF. ON THE WALLS WERE GILDED CRESTS FROM WHICH HOLMES AND THE BARON HAD SEIZED THEIR WEAPONS.
CROSSING INTO THE FIRST CAR WE BEGAN OUR DESPERATE SEARCH.
LOOK FOR AIR HOLES!
HERE!
LET US STOP THESE TRAINS...

WE HAVE NOT REALLY PREVENTED A WAR. BUT PERHAPS WE HAVE POSTPONED IT.

IF THE KAISER WANTS TO GO TO WAR WITH RUSSIA, HE WILL FIND THE MEANS. AND THEN, HERR DOCTOR, YOU AND I MAY FIND OURSELVES ON OPPOSING SIDES.

THEN PERHAPS ALL OF OUR LABORS HAVE AVAILED NOTHING.

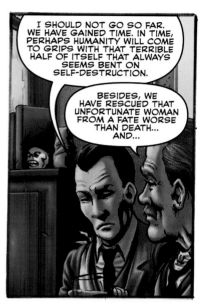

I SHOULD NOT GO SO FAR. WE HAVE GAINED TIME. IN TIME, PERHAPS HUMANITY WILL COME TO GRIPS WITH THAT TERRIBLE HALF OF ITSELF THAT ALWAYS SEEMS BENT ON SELF-DESTRUCTION.

BESIDES, WE HAVE RESCUED THAT UNFORTUNATE WOMAN FROM A FATE WORSE THAN DEATH... AND...

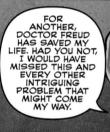

FOR ANOTHER, DOCTOR FREUD HAS SAVED MY LIFE. HAD YOU NOT, I WOULD HAVE MISSED THIS AND EVERY OTHER INTRIGUING PROBLEM THAT MIGHT COME MY WAY.

AND HAD YOU, WATSON, NOT CONTRIVED TO GET ME HERE, DOCTOR FREUD WOULD HAVE NEVER HAD THE OPPORTUNITY TO SAVE A DOOMED ADDICT. TO WATSON, THERE WILL BE A LIFETIME TO REPAY MY DEBT. BUT HOW CAN I REPAY YOU, HERR DOCTOR?

LET ME THINK ABOUT IT.

THE BARON WAS DEAD. OUR BAGS WERE PACKED, THE CASE WAS CLOSED. THE IMPERSONATOR OF BARONESS VON LEINSDORF PROVED TO BE AN AMERICAN ACTRESS SEDUCED BY THE YOUNG BARON. MISS MARLOWE WAS RELEASED AFTER SWEARING NEVER TO REVEAL THE EVENTS IN WHICH SHE HAD TAKEN PART. PLEDGING NEVER TO RETURN TO AUSTRIA OR GERMANY.

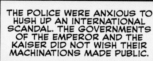

THE POLICE WERE ANXIOUS TO HUSH UP AN INTERNATIONAL SCANDAL. THE GOVERNMENTS OF THE EMPEROR AND THE KAISER DID NOT WISH THEIR MACHINATIONS MADE PUBLIC.

LATER I LEARNED IT WAS NOT THE OLD EMPEROR WHO ENTERED INTO THE CABAL WITH THE BARON, BUT HIS SCHEMING NEPHEW, ARCHDUKE FRANZ FERDINAND, WHO RECEIVED HIS TERRIBLE MUNITIONS AFTER GERMANY PRESENTED THEM TO AUSTRIA FOLLOWING HIS ASSASSINATION IN SARAJEVO. THE ENSUING WAR COST THE KAISER HIS THRONE.

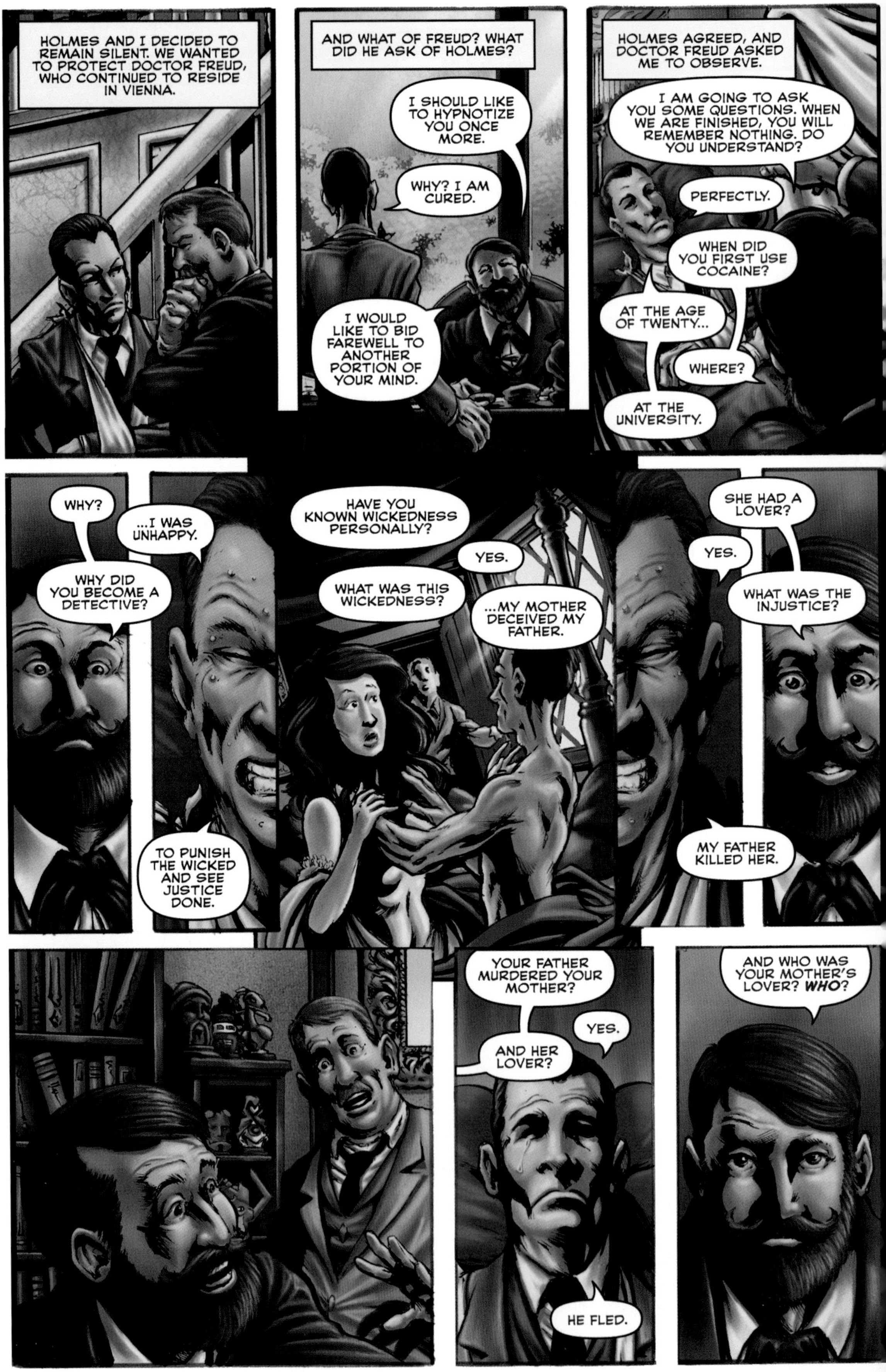
HOLMES AND I DECIDED TO REMAIN SILENT. WE WANTED TO PROTECT DOCTOR FREUD, WHO CONTINUED TO RESIDE IN VIENNA.
AND WHAT OF FREUD? WHAT DID HE ASK OF HOLMES?
I SHOULD LIKE TO HYPNOTIZE YOU ONCE MORE.
WHY? I AM CURED.
I WOULD LIKE TO BID FAREWELL TO ANOTHER PORTION OF YOUR MIND.
HOLMES AGREED, AND DOCTOR FREUD ASKED ME TO OBSERVE.
I AM GOING TO ASK YOU SOME QUESTIONS. WHEN WE ARE FINISHED, YOU WILL REMEMBER NOTHING. DO YOU UNDERSTAND?
PERFECTLY.
WHEN DID YOU FIRST USE COCAINE?
AT THE AGE OF TWENTY...
WHERE?
AT THE UNIVERSITY.
WHY?
...I WAS UNHAPPY.
WHY DID YOU BECOME A DETECTIVE?
TO PUNISH THE WICKED AND SEE JUSTICE DONE.
HAVE YOU KNOWN WICKEDNESS PERSONALLY?
YES.
WHAT WAS THIS WICKEDNESS?
...MY MOTHER DECEIVED MY FATHER.
SHE HAD A LOVER?
YES.
WHAT WAS THE INJUSTICE?
MY FATHER KILLED HER.
YOUR FATHER MURDERED YOUR MOTHER?
YES.
AND HER LOVER?
HE FLED.
AND WHO WAS YOUR MOTHER'S LOVER? *WHO*?

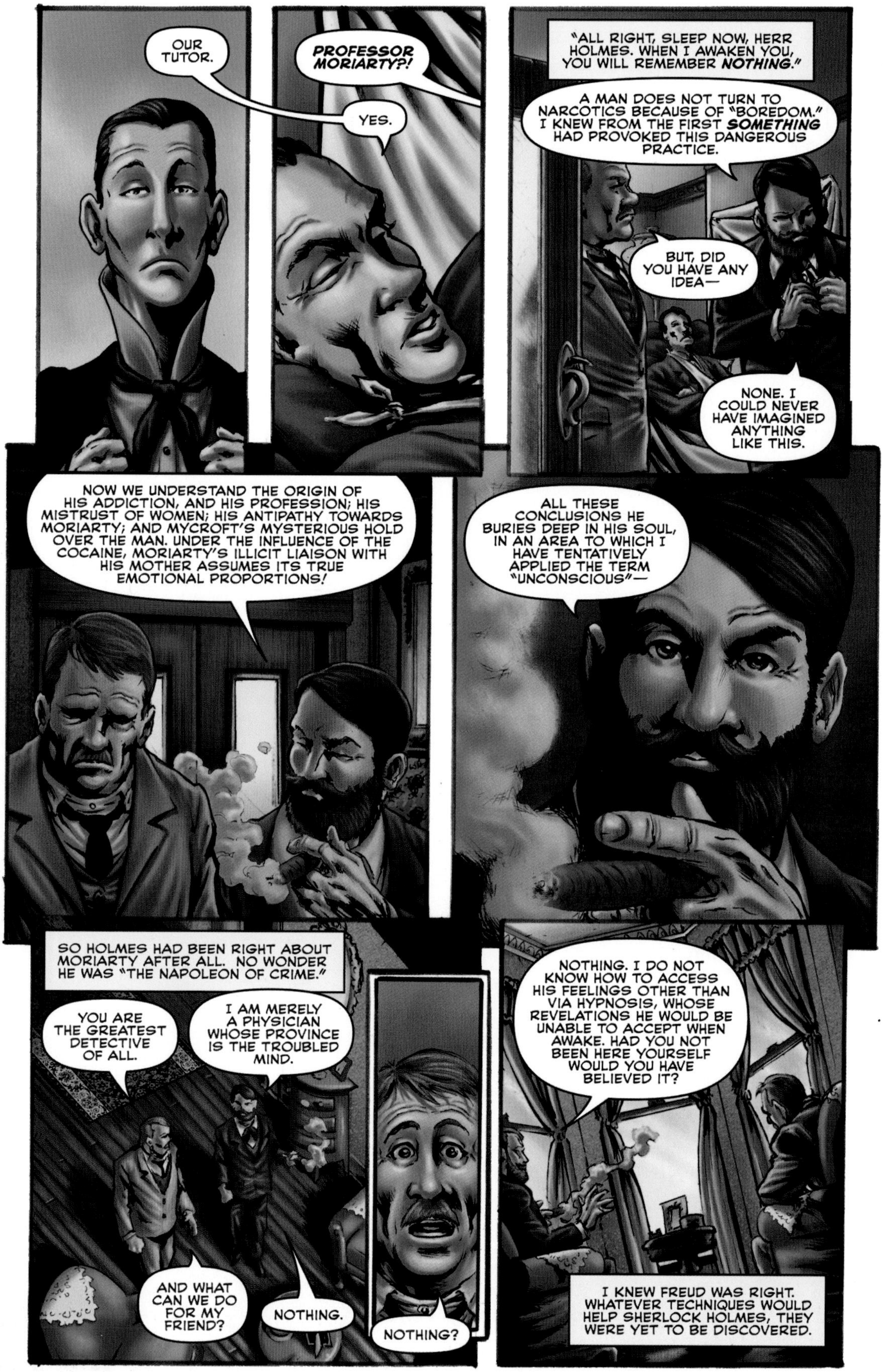
OUR TUTOR.
PROFESSOR MORIARTY?!
YES.
"ALL RIGHT, SLEEP NOW, HERR HOLMES. WHEN I AWAKEN YOU, YOU WILL REMEMBER NOTHING."
A MAN DOES NOT TURN TO NARCOTICS BECAUSE OF "BOREDOM." I KNEW FROM THE FIRST SOMETHING HAD PROVOKED THIS DANGEROUS PRACTICE.
BUT, DID YOU HAVE ANY IDEA—
NONE. I COULD NEVER HAVE IMAGINED ANYTHING LIKE THIS.
NOW WE UNDERSTAND THE ORIGIN OF HIS ADDICTION, AND HIS PROFESSION; HIS MISTRUST OF WOMEN; HIS ANTIPATHY TOWARDS MORIARTY; AND MYCROFT'S MYSTERIOUS HOLD OVER THE MAN. UNDER THE INFLUENCE OF THE COCAINE, MORIARTY'S ILLICIT LIAISON WITH HIS MOTHER ASSUMES ITS TRUE EMOTIONAL PROPORTIONS!
ALL THESE CONCLUSIONS HE BURIES DEEP IN HIS SOUL, IN AN AREA TO WHICH I HAVE TENTATIVELY APPLIED THE TERM "UNCONSCIOUS"—
SO HOLMES HAD BEEN RIGHT ABOUT MORIARTY AFTER ALL. NO WONDER HE WAS "THE NAPOLEON OF CRIME."
YOU ARE THE GREATEST DETECTIVE OF ALL.
I AM MERELY A PHYSICIAN WHOSE PROVINCE IS THE TROUBLED MIND.
AND WHAT CAN WE DO FOR MY FRIEND?
NOTHING.
NOTHING?
NOTHING. I DO NOT KNOW HOW TO ACCESS HIS FEELINGS OTHER THAN VIA HYPNOSIS, WHOSE REVELATIONS HE WOULD BE UNABLE TO ACCEPT WHEN AWAKE. HAD YOU NOT BEEN HERE YOURSELF WOULD YOU HAVE BELIEVED IT?
I KNEW FREUD WAS RIGHT. WHATEVER TECHNIQUES WOULD HELP SHERLOCK HOLMES, THEY WERE YET TO BE DISCOVERED.

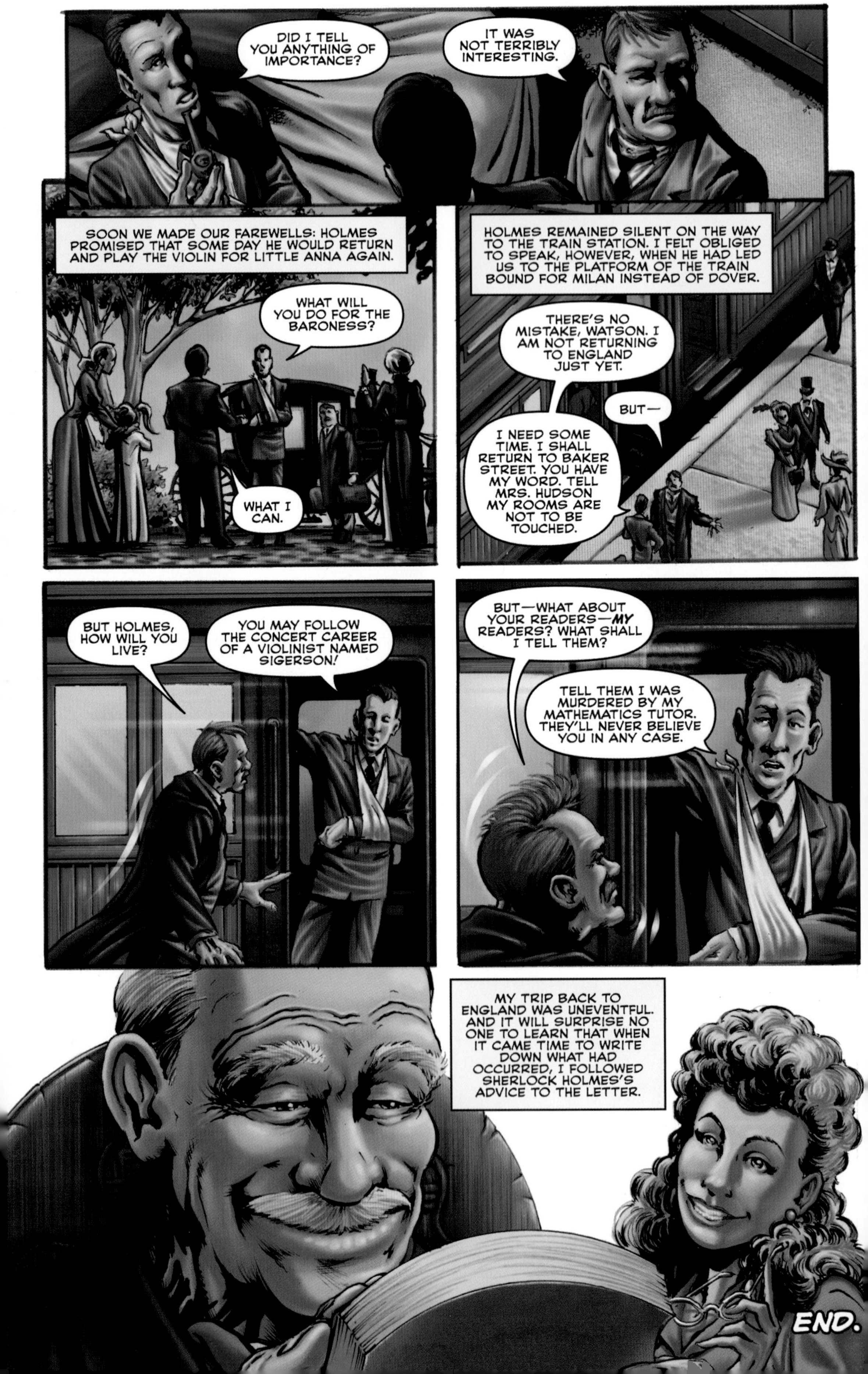
DID I TELL YOU ANYTHING OF IMPORTANCE?
IT WAS NOT TERRIBLY INTERESTING.
SOON WE MADE OUR FAREWELLS: HOLMES PROMISED THAT SOME DAY HE WOULD RETURN AND PLAY THE VIOLIN FOR LITTLE ANNA AGAIN.
WHAT WILL YOU DO FOR THE BARONESS?
WHAT I CAN.
HOLMES REMAINED SILENT ON THE WAY TO THE TRAIN STATION. I FELT OBLIGED TO SPEAK, HOWEVER, WHEN HE HAD LED US TO THE PLATFORM OF THE TRAIN BOUND FOR MILAN INSTEAD OF DOVER.
THERE'S NO MISTAKE, WATSON. I AM NOT RETURNING TO ENGLAND JUST YET.
BUT—
I NEED SOME TIME. I SHALL RETURN TO BAKER STREET. YOU HAVE MY WORD. TELL MRS. HUDSON MY ROOMS ARE NOT TO BE TOUCHED.
BUT HOLMES, HOW WILL YOU LIVE?
YOU MAY FOLLOW THE CONCERT CAREER OF A VIOLINIST NAMED SIGERSON!
BUT—WHAT ABOUT YOUR READERS—*MY* READERS? WHAT SHALL I TELL THEM?
TELL THEM I WAS MURDERED BY MY MATHEMATICS TUTOR. THEY'LL NEVER BELIEVE YOU IN ANY CASE.
MY TRIP BACK TO ENGLAND WAS UNEVENTFUL. AND IT WILL SURPRISE NO ONE TO LEARN THAT WHEN IT CAME TIME TO WRITE DOWN WHAT HAD OCCURRED, I FOLLOWED SHERLOCK HOLMES'S ADVICE TO THE LETTER.
END.

ART BY
RON JOSEPH

COLORS BY
JORDI ESCUIN

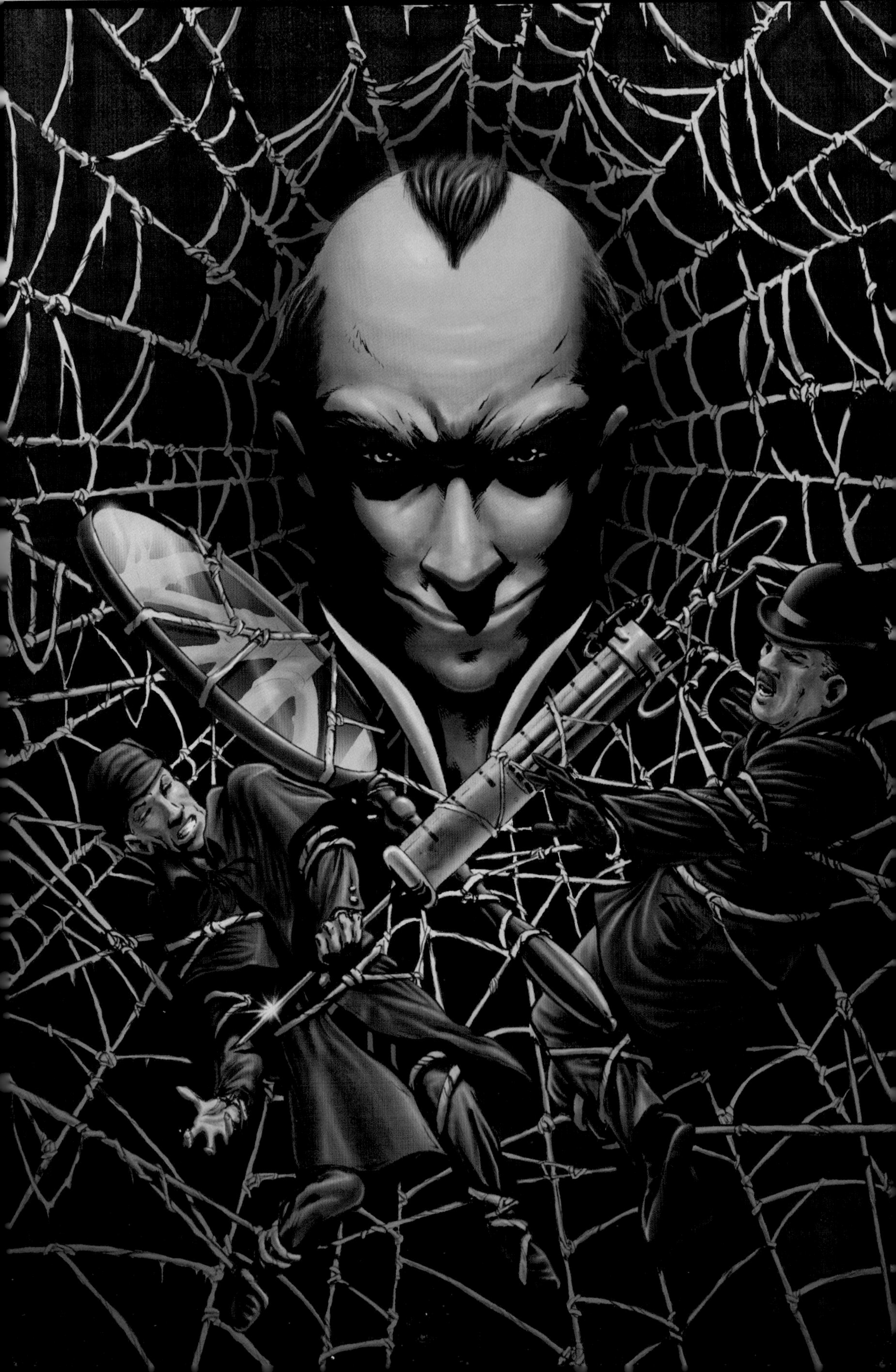

ART BY
JUAN CARLOS RUIZ BURGOS

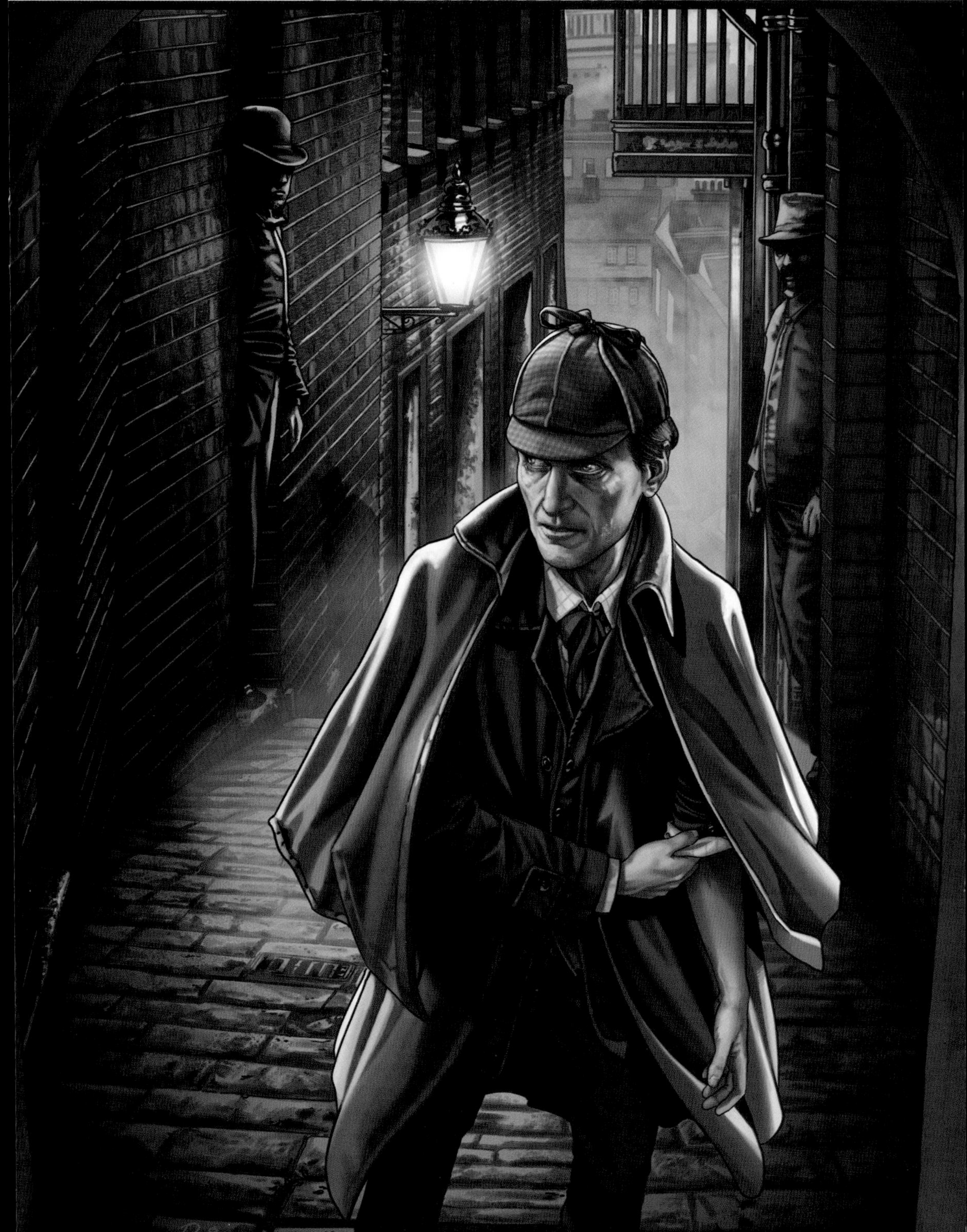

ART BY
JUAN CARLOS RUIZ BURGOS

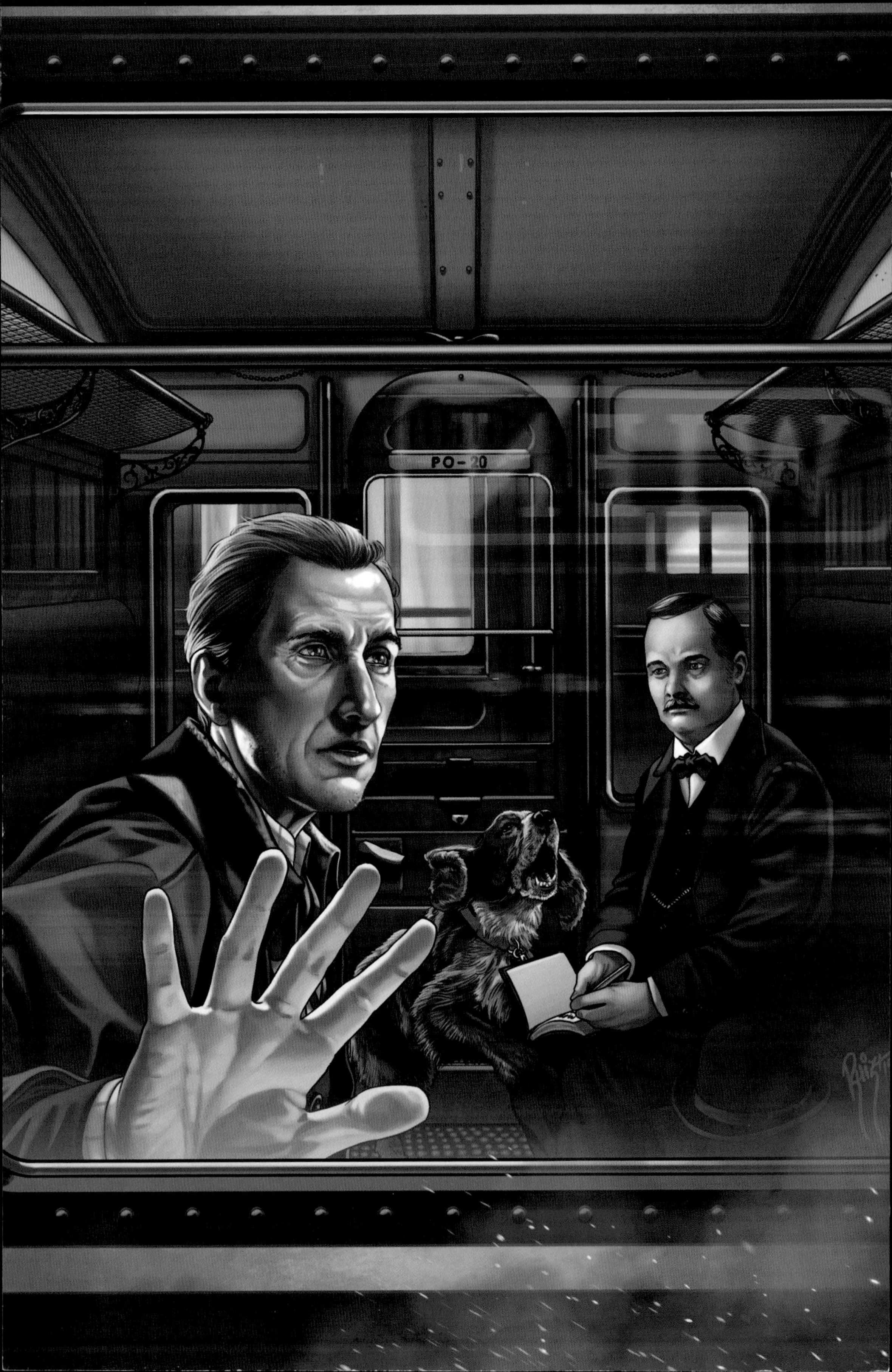
PO-20

ART BY
JUAN CARLOS RUIZ BURGOS

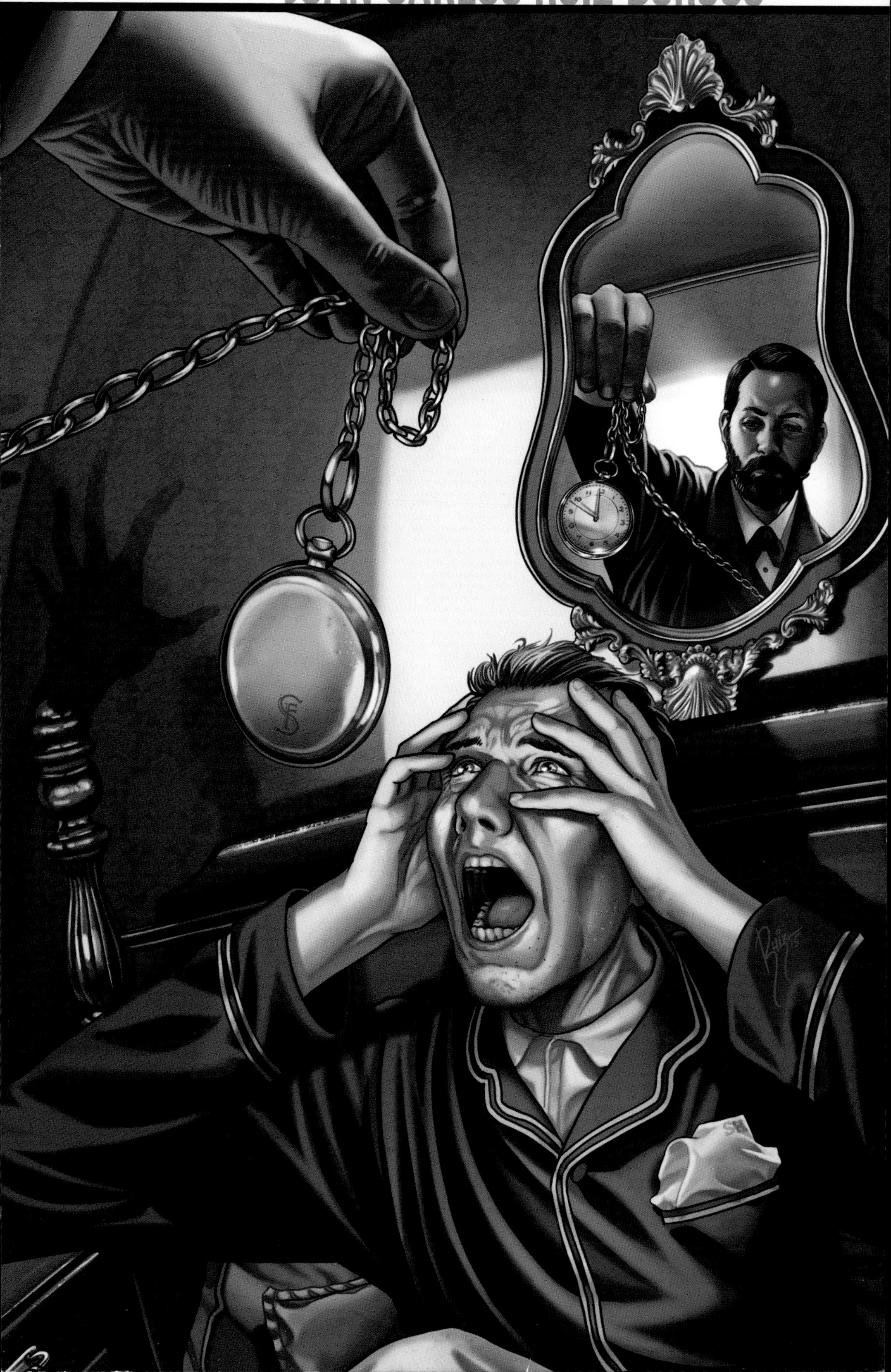

ART BY
JUAN CARLOS RUIZ BURGOS

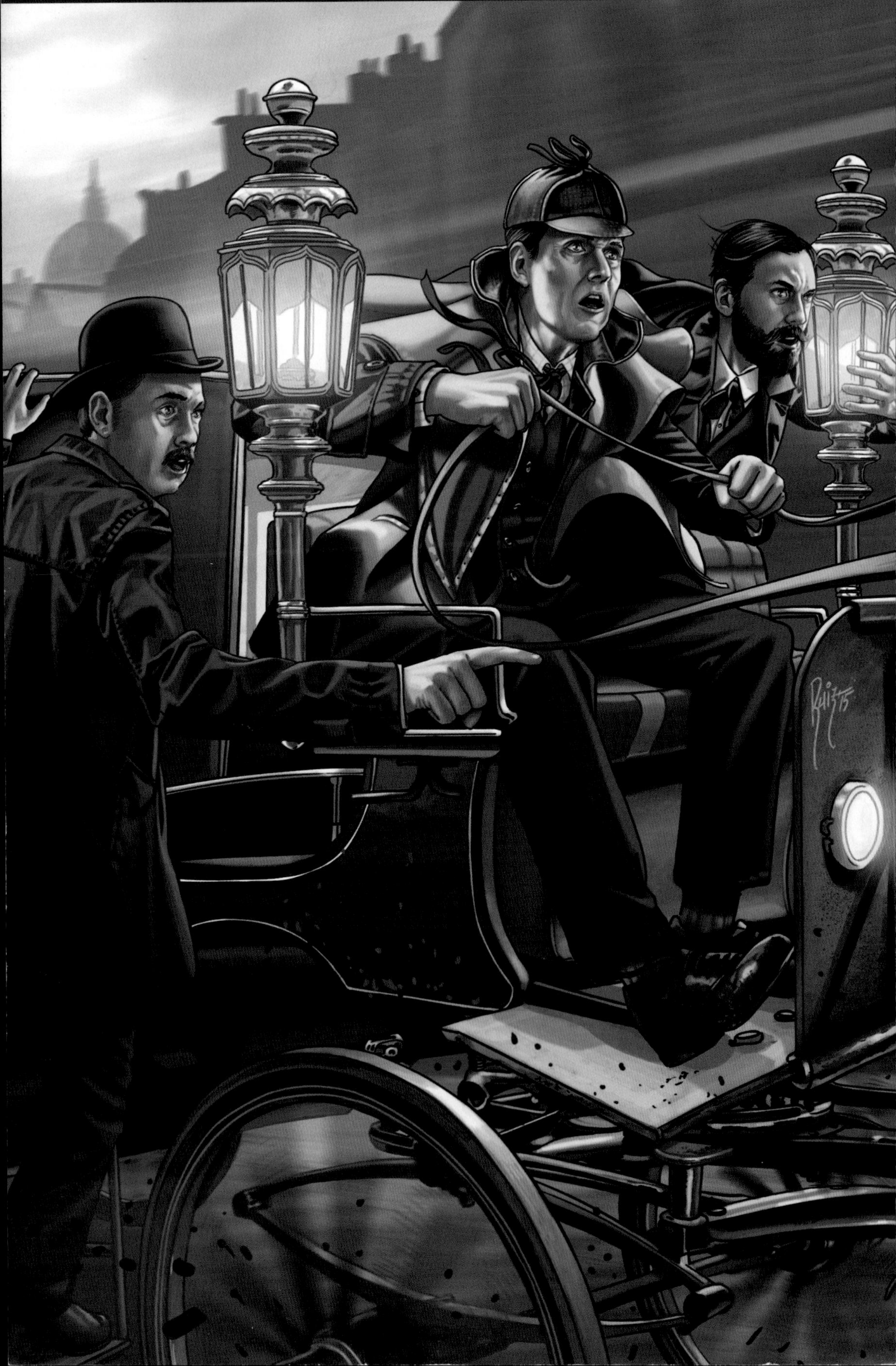
Ruiz 15

ART BY
JUAN CARLOS RUIZ BURGOS

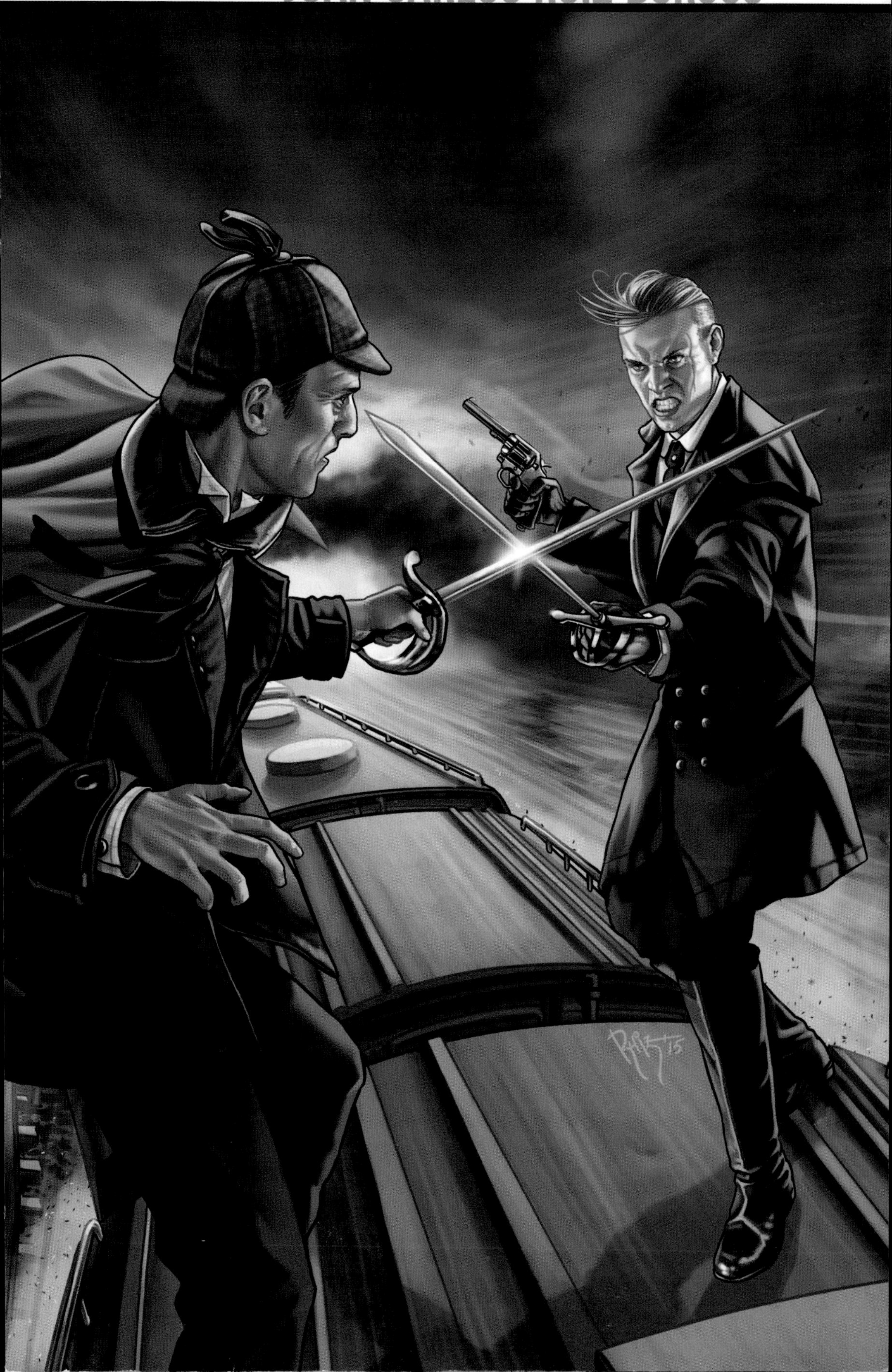

A

Sherlock Holmes

COLLECTION

AS MASTERFUL AS ITS NAMESAKE

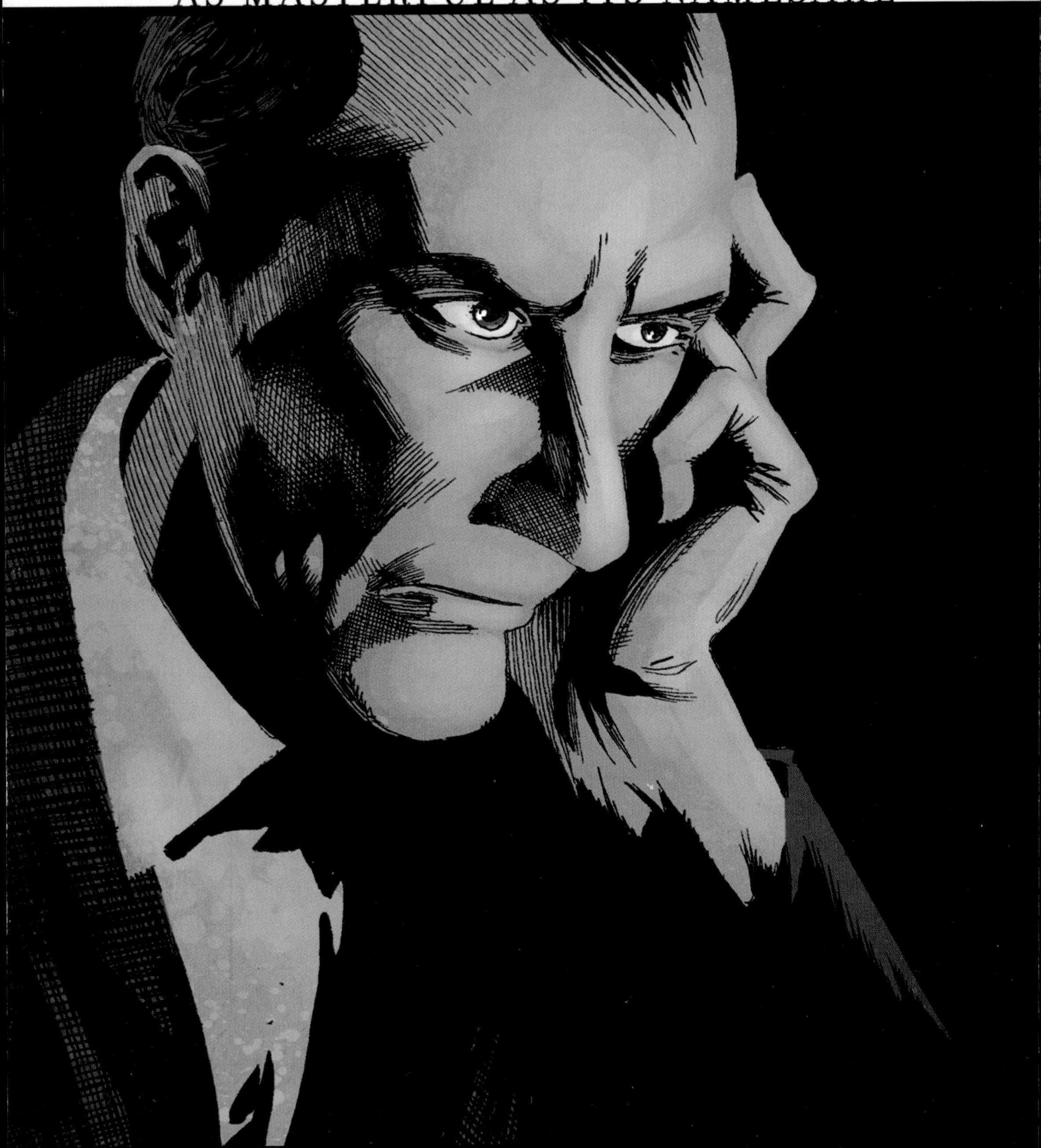

THE GREATEST CASES OF SHERLOCK HOLMES
WITH ILLUSTRATIONS BY KELLEY JONES